Additiona 

God Chose a Woman First: Disco

through the Voices of Biblical Women

"This powerful book is filled with spiritual truths and insight for women in the 21st century. Laura inspires the reader to be empowered by the same God that sanctioned the inclusion of the women from the Bible stories she references. 'Resilient confidence' is ours through the pages of this book as it leads us through the study of biblical women, their stories, and God's purposes for them—and God's purposes for women today."

—**Deborah Aarts**, career and life coach
and ladies ministry leader

"*God Chose a Woman First* is a fresh, interesting, and enlightening look at biblical women whose lives were not much different from ours today. Through storytelling and biblical accounts, Laura reminds us how much we actually have in common with those who lived thousands of years ago. This uplifting read reminds us that our great God not only loves women, God values them. Get a cup of coffee and settle in a comfy chair as you follow the journey of women God chose to be first. You might just see a little of yourself in the stories."

—**Susan Campbell, MEd**, speaker, author of *A Wild & Wonderful Life*,
and founder of More Than You Imagine Ministries

"Laura has a sharp mind combined with a deep love for Christ and the Scriptures. That combination is reflected in *God Chose a Woman First*. She has used rigorous scholarship and a gentle heart to give new hearing to the often-overlooked stories of biblical women, whose lives inform our walk with Christ."

—**Rev. Larry Coulter**, Senior Pastor, The Lakeway Church

"It's been said, and too-often rightly so, women tend to put everyone else first. Even an objective glance at the lot of women throughout the centuries, in a world where patriarchy has shaped so much of culture, reveals that females are often sent to the back of the line and treated as second-class citizens, at best.

"How heartening, then, to learn that God often chose women to *be first* and to *go first*—not because there weren't qualified men nearby, but because God wanted it that way. In *God Chose a Woman First,* author Laura Savage-Rains pulls back the heavy curtains that have long obscured the stories of biblical women to show that they are not recipients of the leftovers of God's grace and purposes. This thoroughly researched and beautifully written book reminds me that my voice (and yours), raised for God and empowered by the Spirit, matters. It gives me courage to say, *'Yes,'* the next time God turns my way and says, 'You go first,' because I know God is for and goes with me."

—**Dr. Jodi Detrick**, author of *The Jesus-Hearted Woman: 10 Qualities for Enduring & Endearing Influence*

"From the rich experience of her own calling to ministry, Dr. Savage-Rains has provided an inspiring book based on 13 women in the Bible whom God called—not because a male follower was not available, but because the woman was strong and gifted and willing to serve. The unique feature of the book is the story-teller's narrative of what may have happened in each case."

—**Rev. Dr. Russell Dilday**, former president, Southwestern Baptist Theological Seminary (1978-1994)

"I believe that this book is not only very informative, but is very practical in how it can be applied to life. This book is needed!"

—**Alice Draving, PhD**, Bible teacher and retired psychologist

"As a woman in college, I think the book is very relatable and unique. By comparing our daily lives and tribulations with those of the women in biblical settings, one can gain a better understanding of our roles as women and how we can serve and contribute to the kingdom of God in a greater way."

—**Rebecca Keathley**, student, family and child studies major, Louisiana Tech University

"Through careful research and vivid retelling, Laura Savage-Rains has written a powerful testimony to the place of biblical women in the purposes of God. She clears the ground around each one, exposing what can be learned from their encounters with God. Especially useful are Laura's practical encouragements to resilient confidence in a culture of victim-mentality. A book to inspire the faith and rejoice the heart of both men and women."

—**Rev. Deacon Gill Kimber**, Warden, College of St Philip the Deacon, Diocese of Exeter, Church of England

"Laura Savage-Rains shows us that God gave high priority to women as His vessels of ministry in her new book *God Chose a Woman First*. It provides a unique look at the cultures and lives of several women of the Bible, and allows readers to see these women as people who faced many of the same concerns we face today, yet had great influence and power as they served the God who created, loved, and called them. Laura's style is easy to read, interesting, and challenging, and will no doubt provide a fresh understanding of God's work through and with women, not only in the past, but in the present as well. I recommend that every Bible student add *God Chose a Woman First* to their theological library. It is a resource Bible students will return to again and again."

—**Andrea J. Mullins, DMin**, speaker, author, Bible teacher, and retired Christian publisher

"*God Chose a Woman First* is an incredible display of women's influence on our world and culture about which most people have never heard. Some of the stories and women highlighted I never knew existed in the Bible. I enjoyed the organization of the book: the narrative stories of the women, the biblical explanations, and the cultural contexts. This book had me reading till the early hours of the morning. I particularly loved how I was learning so much about women, normal ladies, who made amazing impacts because God chose them. I can't remember any teaching in my churches that focused specifically on how God chose women. This book creates a deeper understanding and gives a broader perspective for how women effected many significant events in the Bible. I think it is important for women—and men—to read and know these stories."

—**Rachel Nager, Esq.**, housing justice attorney

"This is a truth and fact: Women have been leaders in every facet of life since the beginning of time. Laura's book illuminates that leadership in the very province in which women's gifts, knowledge, wisdom, abilities, and expertise are, to this day, all too routinely, doctrinally, and functionally, regarded as secondary, at best—the faith story of Christians. Read this book, discover your history, and find and use your voice as a leader in your community of faith and beyond."

—**Cathleen Parsley, J.D.**, former administrative law judge and Texas agency head

"Laura is able to place herself in the life of each biblical woman and write from her perspective while remaining true to the Scriptures. She brings to the reader's heart things unique to women, such as the value of older/younger relationships. The compelling narrative connects historical world events to the biblical accounts and makes the women's stories come alive. These stories encourage women to reach upward and outward to fulfill God's greatest potential for their lives."

—**Barbara Tittle**, Bible study teacher

"Dr. Laura Savage-Rains' book is filled with stories of God's call upon the lives of women in the Bible. This volume fills a niche that has been missing in other literary works about biblical women. The author provides both an insightful and scholarly look at the history and culture of the times these women lived and also provides profound reflections to consider for personal and group Bible study. This unique and important book will bless many women and give them the courage they need to realize they are equal with men in God's eyes and in God's gifting. I highly recommend this book!"

—**Rev. Brenda Griffin Warren**,
Christian Church (Disciples of Christ) pastor,
blogger at www.saintsbridge.org

God Chose a Woman First

Discover the Keys to Resilient Confidence through the Voices of Biblical Women

Be Brave!
Heb. 10:35-36
—Laura Savage-Rains

Laura Savage-Rains

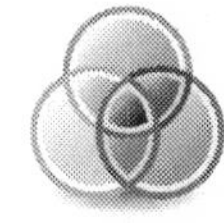

Three Circle Press

God Chose a Woman First:
Discover the Keys to Resilient Confidence through the Voices of Biblical Women.

Published by Three Circle Press, 114 World of Tennis Sq., Lakeway, Texas 78738

Printed in the United States of America
First Printing 2019

Book design by Three Circle Press
Cover design by Jane Wilson
Cover illustration: Detail from *The Empty Tomb* by He Qi. Copyright 2000. Used by permission. Visit HeQiArt.com
Author photos: Kristina Barry Photography, Austin, TX

ISBN: (paperback) 978-1-7333166-1-3

Library of Congress Control Number: 2019910304

For

Angela,

who graciously named me her "Now Mom,"

and her three daughters,

Celeste, Tallis, and Brynn,

the ones who call me "Grammy"

and

for my husband,

Mark Savage-Rains,

who is my source of unconditional love and

deep, secure joy

through our shared life in Christ

TABLE OF CONTENTS

NOTES ON ABBREVIATIONS AND SPECIAL NAMES

BCE

BCE is an abbreviation for Before Common Era or Before Christian Era, which is the designation of the time before Christ's life on earth and corresponds to the times otherwise dated BC, known traditionally as Before Christ.

CE

CE is an abbreviation for Common Era or Christian Era, which is the designation of the times otherwise dated AD, for *Anno Domini*, which is Medieval Latin for "in the Year of the Lord."

CEB

I have purposely used a newer English translation of the Bible known as the *Common English Bible*, published in 2011, for the majority of Scripture quotations. It is abbreviated CEB throughout the text.

LORD

Throughout the book, you may see the word LORD in all caps. This is taken directly from the pages of the Scriptures and it is a designation of the name for God, which appears in various translations as Yahweh, YHWH, Jehovah, G-d, or Adonai.

MSG

The Message

NIV

New International Version of the Bible

NRSV

New Revised Standard Version of the Bible

"Happy is she who believed
that the Lord would fulfill the promises
he made to her."

Luke 1:45 (CEB)

INTRODUCTION

Seeing Yourself in Scripture

What do you do when you are feeling called to a task much bigger than you? How do you respond when you sense God is asking you to fulfill a mission beyond your reach or to pursue a particular vocation, and yet others around you are discouraging you from such a pursuit—*because* you're a woman? How can you know if God would want you in that role? Where can you turn for empowering confidence?

What if you had access to a guide or a document that provided step-by-step instructions for living confidently and boldly into your calling? Wouldn't it be great if you could sit and visit with women who had done incredible things for God's kingdom? That would be a treasure indeed.

Well, I have good news! You do have such a document and you do have access to the personal stories of such women! Such a treasure is your Bible. It is my hope that this book will serve as a treasure map to the keys to resilient confidence found in the stories of biblical women, which will unlock your own pursuit of God's unique purpose for you.

This book's purpose is to empower you with biblical truth about how much God values women's voices, abilities, and bodies. As our world spirals with continued consequences of women being treated as "less-than," role models of *real* women are needed who have exhibited faithfulness, wisdom, courage, and leadership against the odds. The Bible offers many such stories, yet even biblical women's voices are often silenced by the lack of teaching and preaching on the women in Scripture.

You can discover the keys to resilient confidence through the voices of each of the 13 women presented in this book. **Each of these women was *chosen by God*—instead of a man—to be the *first person* in Scripture to experience God in a new way, to express a new truth about God, or to proclaim a new message from God.** This book will help women renew their confidence in their equal status with men as God's image-bearers capable of following God's call. These choices on God's part indicate the infinite and loving value, trust, and confidence God has had in women since the beginning when they were created in the image of God—along with men—and given the same responsibilities as men (see Gen. 1:26-28).

This book will help you see these biblical women's stories come to life in the context of world history and other ancient women's accomplishments. These stories will also inspire men readers with a deeper appreciation of the women they know. Since women are still the majority among churchgoers worldwide (Pew Research Center 2016), they deserve to hear the biblical stories to which they can relate most readily. These are the stories of their foremothers.

In Scripture, we see that God chose women's voices throughout biblical history to prophesy God's messages, to lead God's people, to teach God's truth, and to announce God's activity in the world. God chose to work through women's physical bodies to continue to bring new human life into the world—even to birth our Savior— demonstrating that the entire childbirth process is ordained worthy of God's purposes and calling. If these truths alone were embraced by all people today, women would enjoy the respect they deserve as God's image-bearers and God's instruments of grace and mercy. There would be no sexual harassment or mistreatment of women, and no dismissal of women's ideas and callings just because of their gender. Unfortunately, the fallen world we live in functions in a way God never intended.

I am grateful that God has preserved for us the biblical stories of many women who have endured the sinful condition of people and lived in ways that exemplify the power and purposes of a loving, forgiving God. The "sheroes" from the Hebrew Scriptures we will study in this book include

- Eve
- Hagar
- Miriam
- Deborah
- Hannah, and
- Huldah.

The "sheroes" from the New Testament include

- Elizabeth
- Mary of Nazareth

- Anna
- The Samaritan Woman at the Well
- Martha of Bethany
- Mary Magdalene, and
- Lydia.

I want this book to help you see these biblical women in a fresh way and to hear their voices in clearer tones. I want you to see yourself in Scripture. These stories have power. These stories have built nations. These stories have shaped church history. These stories are still changing lives! *These biblical women's stories can teach you the keys to resilient confidence.*

Which Stories are Shaping Girls and Women Today?

Do you remember your favorite stories from your childhood or youth? Did you spend time daydreaming that you were the main character in those stories? Did those stories ever come true for you? The stories we love the most are the ones in which we can envision ourselves. Whether or not those stories come true in real life, stories influence your thinking about your place in the world and affect your sense of self-confidence in some way, positively or negatively.

Consider the damsel-in-distress and princess stories little girls have heard for centuries and today's newer depictions of girls and women as make-believe superheroes. I'm concerned that girls and women today may know the names and stories of fictional and fantasy characters more than they know the life-equipping truths taught by the stories of these powerful, historical, biblical women. *This is why it is vital that these biblical women's voices are heard in our churches today.*

The Potential Impact of These Stories

The Bible has shaped my life since I gave my life to Christ at the age of seven (See the Appendix). Because I was taught by a woman committed to helping youth discover how to read the Bible for themselves, I learned to love the study of God's Word as a young teen. As a seminary student, I learned to use trustworthy sources to enhance my study of God's Word. When I worked as a writer and trainer for a Christian women's organization, I began to sense the longing of women in my audiences to see themselves in Scripture, so I began my deep dive into the stories of biblical women. As a graduate student in a women's studies program, I developed a keen awareness of the blatant omission of women's stories in much of the historical research we have all been exposed to in our schooling. As a university instructor in a former Communist country, I saw firsthand the lingering effects of misguided beliefs about women's bodies and value.

Today, as a speaker, author, trainer, and Bible teacher, I have committed myself to helping my audiences learn the truths of God taught through the stories of often-overlooked biblical women—the stories God inspired and ensured were preserved "for teaching, for reproof, for correction, and for training in righteousness, so that everyone who belongs to God may be proficient, equipped for every good work" (2 Tim. 3:16-17 NRSV). As a woman who has been blessed to travel the world, I have come to appreciate the fact that the women in the Bible each had a heritage, language, ethnicity, and culture different from my own. I am indebted to these Egyptian, Hebrew, Middle Eastern, and Mesopotamian women in Scripture for showing me the riches of a relationship with God. Their examples have literally changed my life, informed my understanding of God's Word, helped me comprehend God as my source of confidence, and enhanced my personal experience with God. My prayer is that their stories will do the same for you and will remind you that God has a calling for you, too.

Regardless of a woman's age, marital status, or background, she will be able to see herself in these stories of biblical women. These women were poor and rich, single and married, childless and mothers, warriors and homemakers, soft-spoken and outspoken, teenaged and elderly. Each of their stories inspires us with principles of resilient confidence. Sometimes, the messages these women's stories convey come through the words they spoke as recorded by the biblical writers. Other times, we may not know their exact words; yet, their behavior implies their spoken messages. Each time I study these women, I am left wondering how my world would be different if *these* stories had been emphasized in the curriculum of my childhood and youth Sunday School classes. Girls and women of all ages need to see themselves in these stories! *Each girl and woman deserves the chance to learn these stories so they can emulate the same God-given confidence exhibited by these biblical women.*

The Harm Caused by the Misinterpretation of Scripture

With more than 30 years of ministry experience and decades of studying and teaching about biblical women, I am offering this fresh look at these women chosen for God-ordained roles. In my opinion, the fact that these women's stories were recorded by *male* writers from such patriarchal cultures makes them especially deserving of our attention. What made these women's words and lives so unforgettable that God ensured these stories would be preserved? God's actions in these stories provide evidence against *any* biblical interpretation that would claim God doesn't want women to lead or that women have to be dependent on men to hear, interpret, or understand God's Word. Even though the truths these women's stories teach have been available to us for centuries through Scripture, many of them are still hidden to most people. As long as people function without the knowledge that all women are created in the image of God and that God places infinite value on their voices, bodies, and abilities, then the disrespect, dismissal, and mistreatment of women will continue. We don't have to look far to see how women are viewed as unequal and/or less-than in many industries, businesses, families, churches, religions, and cultures worldwide.

One of the things I've noticed in my teaching and speaking across the US and in other countries is that many women tend to act as if they are waiting for permission before they speak out with a new idea, stand up for a firm belief, or start toward a new path or role. They are reticent to attempt a big task. They lack confidence. Unfortunately, there's a reason for that. Many women, from the dawn of human history to the present day, have been discouraged—and sometimes, forbidden by both men and women—to fill certain roles simply because they are women! And it is sad to me how the Bible has often been used—wrongly—as a weapon against women's leadership and as a source of an incorrect belief in the inferiority of the female gender. As a serious Bible student, I have come to question such *common interpretations* of certain biblical passages used to discourage women from using their God-given abilities. (Note: I trust the *original,* God-inspired purpose and meaning of the biblical texts; yet, I don't always trust the human *interpretation* of certain texts.)

Contrary to much popular belief, the Bible has many stories which illustrate that God has oftentimes chosen a woman over a man to be the first person to lead out in some way. Sometimes, women were chosen to instruct men with God's message or were sent by God to deliver powerful truths to men in God's name. These examples of God's initiative in choosing women for these roles help me realize that Paul's New Testament writings about the roles of women should be interpreted through the lens of God/Jesus' *intentional actions,* and not the other way around. (Please note: Even though I have tried to do faithful research, I am not saying *my* interpretation is flawless. I am certainly willing to make changes as I learn new things!) In my opinion, the fact that God chose these women for these roles and then made sure their stories were preserved through the ages are reasons enough to silence anyone who considers women "less than" or "unqualified" when compared to men. It is my passion to make these biblical stories come to life to help women see themselves in Scripture, to build their confidence, and to help them realize they already have permission to go forth and fulfill their God-given callings to bring God's kingdom on earth.

The Freedom in God's Call

This book is for the woman who wants to see herself in the pages of the greatest story ever told. This book is for the woman who has a deep desire to know that God's story relates to her story. This book is for the woman needing more confidence—and biblical justification—to pursue the role or task to which she feels God is calling her. This book is for the woman struggling with interpretations of Scripture which make her feel less-than, unworthy, or unqualified due to her gender. This book is for any woman, who, *because of her gender,* has ever

- been told "no"
- been overlooked for a position of leadership in her community, workplace, or church
- had her voice silenced, questioned, or simply ignored

- been bullied out of running or applying for a position of leadership
- been *expected* to fulfill certain responsibilities or tasks
- performed a leadership role without the leadership title
- worked voluntarily at a task for which a man would expect to be paid
- felt less-than or second-class
- watched a man be recognized for his pursuit of a ministry role while her efforts in ministry were ignored
- wondered what the Bible teaches about women as leaders

My guess is that 99% of the women reading this has experienced at least one of those situations, or she knows another woman who has. It is incredible to me that our 21st-century world is still witnessing behaviors caused by people thinking that women are secondary or somehow inferior to men. It is heartbreaking to me that the church has often been the place where this belief has been voiced the loudest when there is so much kingdom work yet to be done for our Lord! *This is why the voices of these biblical women must be heard!*

In the Beginning and Being First

In the beginning, God's ideal was—and is—for women and men to work side by side as equals, sharing dominion over the earth and its creatures according to Genesis 1 and 2. Unfortunately, people chose to second-guess God and to yield to sinful temptation, which brought brokenness into the human experience and into our relationships with God and with other humans. However, as God's image-bearers, we are, through the power of the Holy Spirit, capable of demonstrating God's original ideal even in this broken world.

By being the first *person* to experience or accomplish something makes that person a leader by default. Such a person is often celebrated and honored. Consider Neil Armstrong, the first person on the moon, or Marie Curie, the first person to win a Nobel prize twice. Such a person is a leader who blazes a new trail by example. While these biblical women may not have even been consciously aware of their leadership or status as "first," that title, nonetheless, is theirs to claim. In addition to being the first *person* to accomplish a particular task, some of these Bible characters also hold the "first woman" designation for various roles. Therefore, I see each of these 13 biblical women as a leader who has set a precedent for a variety of women's leadership roles. *Since **God** chose these women to be first, then we need to learn from their stories.* Consider the history-making impact of just a few of the firsts we will study:

- To give God a name
- To authenticate a written document as God's Word
- To break 400 years of God's prophetic silence with a birth announcement of the coming Messiah
- To confess publicly that Jesus is the Messiah
- To be commissioned by Christ to tell the Resurrection news—the hallmark of our faith!

These few examples of the ways God chose women's voices to demonstrate resilient confidence are reason enough to hear these voices again!

My Mission

I'm on a mission to re-introduce these biblical women into the life of the church so that girls and women can get a sense of God's call on their lives and can learn from the leadership examples of their ancient foremothers. I also believe boys and men will benefit from hearing these stories so they can understand better the value of shared leadership and collaboration with women, and of helping women's voices to be heard, as taught by these examples in Scripture.

The Bible provides eye-opening accounts of women who used their voices and lived as examples of confident resilience. Obviously, God wanted these biblical stories preserved for both women and men. Just as women are expected to follow the example of Christ and his male disciples, so should men be expected to follow the examples of Christ's female disciples and the many biblical women God chose for kingdom work. However, people have to be *introduced* to those stories before they can learn from them. The truths these stories teach are universal, yet some of these truths have been overshadowed by the attention we have given to the male protagonists of biblical stories. Consider the last time you heard a sermon or participated in a Bible study about a woman in

Scripture. Hopefully, this book will contribute to the need for more biblical knowledge about the messages in the *women's* stories.

My passion is to awaken today's audiences to the reasons why the voices of biblical women matter! I love to speak and teach on these women and welcome any opportunity to do so. Perhaps I will meet you, my reader, at such an event! Visit my Speaking page on my website at www.WomensMinistryCoach.com and see the page in the back of this book for more information about how to contact me for coaching, consulting, training, or speaking.

How to Use This Book

My approach in writing about these biblical women is to provide several different sections related to each woman. The women are presented chronologically and represent each era of biblical history—from Creation to the Early Church. Here are the types of sections included:

Events That Shaped the Era in Which Each Woman Lived

If you are one of the historically curious, don't miss the "Events" sections sprinkled throughout the book to give you a glimpse of world history as it paralleled the events of each biblical era, placing each woman's story in a global context. I placed a special emphasis on women's accomplishments and status in each of these sections, since such details about women have been overlooked in many of our history books or simply unknown until more recent excavations, and discoveries.

Each Woman's Story Written as Historical Fiction

If you love to read novels, and maybe you're not so interested in history, then you might choose to begin with the story provided about each woman. The goal of these stories is to help the woman come to life outside the biblical text by placing her in a narrative of historical fiction based on the Bible's content and historical background. Historical fiction is based in fact; yet, where details are unknown in the biblical text, I have taken creative license to provide other possibilities.

The Bible Speaks

A Bible study approach of the story is provided in "The Bible Speaks" sections for each woman with excerpts from the biblical text along with commentary and historical notes on particular points.

The Message in Each Woman's Voice

To scan the meaning of each of these women's stories, you can find short summaries entitled, "The Message in the Woman's Voice" toward the end of each woman's chapter.

Biblical Truths Taught through the Story of Each Woman

If you're a list maker and want to see at a glance the nuggets gleaned from each woman's story, you'll find a numerical list of "Biblical Truths Taught through the Story of the Woman" toward the end of each woman's chapter. These are certainly not exhaustive lists. You are welcome to add the truths you glean from the stories as well.

Why the Voice of Each Woman Matters

To consider the different audiences each woman's story may inspire, enlighten, or encourage, be sure to read "Why the Voice of Each Woman Matters" toward the end of each woman's chapter.

Questions Raised by the Story of Each Woman

To explore some of the unanswered questions inspired by each woman's story, you may pursue on your own or with others the "Questions Raised by the Story of Each Woman" toward the end of each woman's chapter.

Each Woman's Keys to Resilient Confidence

The practical applications from these women's stories, are found in the "Key(s) to Resilient Confidence" at the end of each woman's chapter. These sections provide mined nuggets of wisdom exemplified by the woman's words or actions which we can apply in our 21st-century lives as women chosen by God to proclaim and demonstrate God's truth.

Let's listen to the voices of these women whom God chose to be FIRST. . . .

PART ONE

God Chose Eve

THE TIME WHEN EVERYTHING WAS FIRST

ca. THE UNDATABLE PAST

I

Events that Shaped the World of Eve

THE TIME WHEN EVERYTHING WAS FIRST
ca. The Undatable Past

Women's lives do not happen in a vacuum. We are affected by everything going on around us. The same is true for the events of the Bible; they did not happen in a vacuum. Yet, we tend to study them as if they did. The Bible gives us the story of one people group—the Jews—to whom we are forever indebted for giving us our Savior. However, the amazing stories we have been given through Scripture are just *some* of the stories being played out on the world's stage in each of the historical eras represented on the pages of the Bible. In addition, much of the history we have been taught over the centuries has been from a male perspective with seldom a focus on, or even an acknowledgement of, women's contributions. In an effort to make the women in this book seem more real and relevant, I will attempt to recreate that world stage for the time period in which each of them lived.

~

We do not know the exact time of the Creation. The Bible's account of the Creation is not a firsthand account. If the tradition is true that Moses wrote the first five books of the Bible, we know there were many, many generations before him that passed down the story of the Creation through oral storytelling. This was before writing was invented. While we can't pinpoint the moment people first walked the earth, we do know they were created in the image of God, equally, both female and male, according to Genesis 1:26-28.

I was probably out of seminary before I learned that accounts of the Creation are not unique to the Bible. Other cultures, religions, tribes, and people groups have versions of the Creation in their writings and traditions as well. As Christians, we view the biblical Creation account as the foundation for our understanding of why—not how—God set in motion God's activity in the world.

The Bible's Creation story reveals *why* God created everything. God wanted fellowship with humans which would be different from the kind of relationship God could have with other living creatures. Humans are the only living beings on earth who are image-bearers of God. And yet, no individual carries the complete image of God. God's glory is too much for humans to comprehend. God's image is within *each* of us and within *all* of us. That's a wonderful thought—and yet, rather disturbing as well.

When people first appeared, they were the first to experience everything human. They were the first people to experience birth and death—by watching animals be born and die and by experiencing childbirth, aging, and death. Other than spiritual death, the first human death mentioned in the Bible was that of Abel, Adam and Eve's son, at the hand of his own brother, Cain. I think most people of faith assume they understand Eve's role in the first sinful acts committed by humans, yet is that really the only instructive truth we can glean from the story of Eve, the first woman?

Let's listen to the voice of Eve,
when God chose her to be first. . . .

2

Eve's Story

ca. The Undatable Past

God chose Eve's voice to be the first . . .

- To speak as a woman, the first ezer *("helper") in Scripture*

- To have the first theological debate

- To speak directly with both Satan and God

- To acknowledge God's role in the birth of her child

Eve was in the hut preparing some fruit and nuts for supper while waiting for Adam to return. He had gone to the other side of the field to visit their son Cain at his farm. Suddenly, she heard a great rush of birds' wings outside as if there was a disturbance of some kind. She peered through the hut's leafy door covering and saw Adam in the distance staggering toward the hut. Before she could get out of the hut, she heard a painful cry from Adam as if he were hurt.

"Eve! Eve! Come!" Adam sounded breathless and was almost groaning.

"I'm coming, Adam!" a concerned Eve called out as she rushed outside.

Still a ways off, she saw Adam drop to the ground. She had never seen him act this way. He was on all fours sobbing. She rushed to him and knelt in front of him. He reached out to her, but could not raise his head. A deep moan came from deep within him. It stirred a feeling of fear within her, similar to the time when God banished them from the Garden of Eden. She put her face lower and close to his. His face was streaked with dirt and wet as if he had been crying a long time.

"Adam, what is it? Why are you so upset?"

Trying to catch his breath, Adam could barely speak. He just kept saying, "No, no," and pounding his fist into the ground. He finally blurted out, "He's gone, Eve. He's gone."

"Who's gone, Adam, who?" Eve could not imagine what he was talking about and why he was so sorrowful.

Adam placed his head in Eve's lap and cried. After a few moments, he could breathe easily again. Eve gently stroked his curly black hair and held him till he was calm. After a few moments, Adam took a deep breath and was able to sit up. He took Eve's hand in one hand and caressed her face with his other hand. His reddened eyes looked deep into Eve's beautiful dark eyes. "He's gone, Eve. Our son, Abel, is gone."

"Oh, Adam, whatever do you mean?" Eve was so confused and wondered what could be so upsetting about this. "I just saw Abel this morning. He told me about the ewe delivering the twin lambs yesterday."

Adam gently put his finger over her lips to quiet her. He shook his head and looked heavenward with more tears flowing. "Eve, Abel is in the ground. He has no more breath."

"What?! No, that can't be. I just saw him this morning! What are you talking about? What did you do at Cain's today?"

Adam just kept shaking his head and sobbing. When he caught his breath, he said slowly, "Eve, Abel has no more breath because of Cain. Cain made Abel stop breathing."

Eve was puzzled and shocked. She could not understand what this meant. She had never before heard Adam speak such things. "I don't understand, Adam."

Adam struggled to find the right words. "Eve, do you remember when we saw that fox chase that rabbit and catch it? Then the fox made the rabbit stop breathing?"

Eve nodded. As an understanding came to her mind, she began to shake. The tears began to flow and she started yelling, "No, no . . . Not Abel. Gone like that rabbit? No . . . No!" She couldn't breathe. She screamed and pounded the ground with her fists. Adam tried to hold her, but she escaped his grasp. She got up and stumbled back to the hut.

Adam got up, stumbling from dizziness, and followed her into the hut. By the time he got there she was out behind the hut throwing up. He went to her and held back her long hair. She was trembling. She fell back into Adam's strong arms. He helped her up and walked her slowly back into the hut. He found the gourds filled with fresh water from the stream and brought her one. She sipped slowly.

"Cain?! How? Why?" she asked, her thoughts racing.

"All I know is what Cain told me. He said he and Abel took their offerings to the altar and God would not accept his offering, but did accept Abel's. Cain said he got mad. He just wanted to push Abel. Then he wrapped his arm around Abel's neck from behind and pulled with all his strength. Then he heard a cracking sound and Abel fell to the ground. He had no more breath. So he decided he would put him in the ground so the animals wouldn't eat him."

Eve put her face in her hands and sobbed. Adam held her and cried along with her. They did not understand how one son could take the breath from another one. They did not know this kind of anger. They had never seen it before.

"Where is Cain now?" Eve asked.

"He's at his hut, getting ready to leave."

"Leave? Where is *he* going? What is happening? What is happening? Oh, what has Cain done?" her voice became shrill and angry and the sobs began again.

Adam held her close and stroked her hair and tried to calm her. Then he struggled to put into words what he knew. Apparently, when Cain and Abel had brought their offerings to God, Cain's offering was not accepted. Cain got so angry he lashed out at Abel. They had wrestled and then Cain overpowered Abel and killed him. Cain had said he didn't realize what had happened at first. Abel was just lying there, not breathing. When Adam had arrived at Cain's farm, Cain was busy covering something large with straw and dirt. Adam noticed a red splotch across Cain's face and wondered what it was. When he asked him, Cain confessed his deed to his father and told him how God was punishing him. "God is sending Cain away, Eve. He is banished from this place. He said he's going east."

"Oh, my boy, Abel," Eve said with such deep pain. She had never felt this pain before. She had felt the pain of childbirth, of course, but this was a much deeper ache. Her insides hurt. Her head hurt. She leaned over onto Adam's chest and wept. He held her and they sat there, quietly weeping till dark.

Later in the night, she realized she needed to see Cain. She wondered what this feeling was which she was experiencing for the first time. *Am I angry? Am I hurt? Am I sick?* She knew she must try to offer some kind of motherly love to Cain before he left, but she did not know what she would say. She and Adam lit a torch and headed out in the night toward Cain's farm to tell him goodbye. Her feet felt like boulders. She kept stumbling. She and Adam held hands tightly as they trudged the brushy path toward Cain's farm, which had become the burial ground of their dear son, Abel.

The Bible Speaks

Eve's story is found in Genesis 1-4

Most people, even non-believers, who know anything at all about Eve, tend to have her already formed in their mind's eye. The stories we hear place the emphasis oftentimes on either her coming from Adam's rib or being the first to yield to temptation and ushering sin into the world. While those two events are familiar interpretations based on the biblical text, there are other truths about her life that we seldom, if ever, hear mentioned in the church today.

The first few chapters of Genesis are about creation and the way sin entered into our human existence. We need to remember that the stories of creation in Genesis are not a journalistic, eyewitness, or even scientific account. These stories were told orally for centuries before they were ever put into written form. Some read Genesis 1 as more of a poem about creation. Consider it a song, if you will. The repetitive phrases give it organization. The use of seven days gave its first hearers a sense of "wholeness" and "completion." Some scholars see Genesis 1:1-2:4a as the original story of creation as told by the Hebrews and Genesis 2:4b-25 as a later addition, a second story. There are significant differences in the two chapters in the order of creation and in other details. Some people like to read Genesis 2 as events left out of Genesis 1, although it is a challenge to force the two stories together. Regardless of where we fit in our literal, poetic, or allegorical understanding of the stories of Creation, we do know there was a starting point for all the created things around us. As Christians, we believe God existed before everything we know, and God brought it all into being.

Genesis 1 and 2 both introduce us to the fact that at one time there was nothing, no people, no earth, no plants, no animals. The first people, both female and male, were created simultaneously in Genesis 1. They were both created equally in the image of God, making them unique compared to everything else God created. Both the female and the male were given exactly the same responsibilities, as stated in Genesis 1:26-28.

The Creation of Humans in Genesis 1 from Three Translations

I'm providing three different English translations to show how the creation of people—both male and female—is worded similarly in all three translations.

Genesis 1:26-28

26 Then God said, "Let us make mankind in our image, in our likeness, so that they may rule over the fish in the sea and the birds in the sky, over the livestock and all the wild animals, and over all the creatures that move along the ground."

27 So God created mankind in his own image,
in the image of God he created them;
male and female he created them.

28 God blessed them and said to them, "Be fruitful and increase in number; fill the earth and subdue it. Rule over the fish in the sea and the birds in the sky and over every living creature that moves on the ground." (NIV)

Another translation of Genesis 1:26-28

26 Then God said, "Let us make humankind in our image, according to our likeness; and let them have dominion over the fish of the sea, and over the birds of the air, and over the cattle, and over all the wild animals of the earth, and over every creeping thing that creeps upon the earth."

27 So God created humankind in his image,
in the image of God he created them;
male and female he created them.

28 God blessed them, and God said to them, "Be fruitful and multiply, and fill the earth and subdue it; and have dominion over the fish of the sea and over the birds of the air and over every living thing that moves upon the earth." (NRSV)

Another translation of Genesis 1:26-28

26 Then God said, "Let us make humanity in our image to resemble us so that they may take charge of the fish of the sea, the birds in the sky, the livestock, all the earth, and all the crawling things on earth."

27 God created humanity in God's own image,
in the divine image God created them,
male and female God created them.

28 God blessed them and said to them, "Be fertile and multiply; fill the earth and master it. Take charge of the fish of the sea, the birds in the sky, and everything crawling on the ground." (CEB)

According to Scripture, no distinction was made between the genders' responsibilities or relationship to God. That was God's perfect design. It still is! This is the partnership God still wants to see played out on earth: women and men sharing equal responsibility.

Another Account of the Creation of Woman

In Genesis 2, a completely different account of creation is given. Starting in verse 4b, Genesis 2 has all of creation happening in one day and the text implies that God formed a man before God planted the garden in Eden. This is the first time the garden of Eden is mentioned or the two trees: the tree of life and the tree of the knowledge of good and evil. Genesis 1 said that *all* the seed-bearing plants were for food and did not mention the two trees of Genesis 2 nor the rule against eating from one of them. Genesis 2 gives the story of God using dust to create a man and using a man's rib to create a woman, which is different from the act of God speaking things into existence as God did in Genesis 1. Here is one

English translation of the story of God creating a woman using a man's rib.

Genesis 2:18, 21-25

18 Then the LORD God said, "It's not good that the human is alone. I will make him a helper that is perfect for him." . . . **21** So the LORD God put the human into a deep and heavy sleep, and took one of his ribs and closed up the flesh over it. **22** With the rib taken from the human, the LORD God fashioned a woman and brought her to the human being. **23** The human said,

"This one finally is bone from my bones
and flesh from my flesh.
She will be called a woman
because from a man she was taken."

24 This is the reason that a man leaves his father and mother and embraces his wife, and they become one flesh. **25** The two of them were naked, the man and his wife, but they weren't embarrassed. (CEB)

Unfortunately, our English translations do us a disservice by using the word "helper" to describe woman's role in Genesis 2:18. While it is an accurate translation of the literal meaning of the word, it is misleading in our cultural understanding. The original Hebrew term *ezer*, which is translated as "helper" in our English Bibles, has subservient connotations in our Western culture that it did not have in the original language. The only times this particular term *ezer* is used in the Old Testament outside of Genesis 2, is in reference to the kind of strong help God provides to people. A few examples of the Scripture referring to God as this kind of *ezer* "helper" include Deuteronomy 33:7; Psalm 20:2; Psalm 70:5; Psalm 115:11, Ezekiel 12:14; and others. We never envision Almighty God as subservient or second-class or lacking leadership skills, and yet that word "helper" comes with all kinds of negative baggage in our Western Christian culture. **God chose Eve as the first *ezer* "helper" in Scripture.**

And then there's this verse Genesis 2:24, "Therefore a man leaves his father and his mother and clings to his wife, and they become one flesh." Doesn't that sound like the husband is to become part of the wife and her family? Yet, many cultures through the ages—including the biblical characters' cultures and Western Christian cultures—have expected only the woman to become part of the man's family.

We may think we know the story of Eve. After all, artists for more than a millennium have painted Adam and Eve in the Garden of Eden either munching on the forbidden fruit—or about to—or running out of the Garden after being banished from it forever. In every case, Eve is considered the "bad girl." Through the ages, she has been portrayed as the cause of all our problems. Some denominations and churches still view women with a suspect eye because women are descendants of Eve so we must be untrustworthy, easily tempted, and able to tempt others, which somehow makes us lesser persons, in their view. While in reality, every person has those same characteristics. Unfortunately, Eve's legacy in our collective understanding seems to focus on her sin of failing to follow God's instruction regarding one particular tree. Would we want to be remembered that way? Haven't we all committed a first, conscious sinful act?

Eve's story has been misused throughout history by somehow making Eve's sin synonymous with her womanhood. Her story has been used to justify exclusion of women, denigration of women, and even the abuse of women. However, what I want to do here is to help us see Eve as a real woman, a woman who must have been a pretty amazing person if for no other reason except for being the first person—EVER—to experience so many things. Let's ponder some of those firsts for a moment.

The First Person to Live as a Woman

Eve was the first person to express the female/feminine characteristics of the image of God. Since both woman and man were equally created in the image of God, that means that both female and male equally reveal different aspects of the image of God. Is this not reason enough to view women and men as equally valuable and deserving of equal treatment and respect? Neither gender has all the aspects of God, nor could either gender ever have all the aspects of God because humanity is finite. Humans cannot contain all of God. Even Jesus, who was fully God, chose to limit himself and his powers in some ways while he was on earth.

The First Person to Be in a Human Relationship with a Man

Eve was the first person to be in a relationship with a man. (Of course, Adam was also the first person to be in a relationship with a woman.) And just think, their relationship was literally perfect at first because it began before sin had entered into the human experience! None of us can imagine such a thing. Consider how different their communication was—compared to ours today—back when things were still perfect.

The First Person to Be Given Equal Responsibility to Care for the Earth and Its Creatures

Eve was the first, along with her husband who was equally first, to be given responsibility to care for the earth and to be fruitful. The first commandment in Scripture given to humans is the same command God gave to the sea creatures and birds, "Be fruitful and multiply" (compare Gen. 1:22 and Gen. 1:28 in any English translation). Then God gave humans the unique command to "subdue [the earth]; and have dominion over the fish of the sea and over the birds of the air and over every living thing that moves upon the earth" (Genesis 1:28 NRSV). Note that humans were only to have dominion over the earth and its animals, not over one another! That was God's design for the perfect world. That is the world I believe we, as Christians, should be striving to live out, not a world where we are striving to maintain the consequences of sin where people rule over each other.

The First Person to Have a Theological Debate and to Speak with Both Satan and God

When the serpent approached her, **Eve was the first person in Scripture to enter into a theological debate**. The serpent then lied to her about what God had actually said about the consequences of eating from a particular tree. The serpent asked the first question and spoke the first lie in Scripture (Gen. 3:1, 4-5). The exchange between the serpent and Eve was the first conversation recorded in Scripture. Unfortunately, Eve lost that debate and allowed the serpent, believed to be the embodiment of Satan in the Genesis passage, to persuade her to go against God's command. However, it is interesting to note that the man was present during the conversation and said nothing to dissuade Eve from talking to the serpent. He kept quiet when offered the forbidden fruit. He didn't even put forth a question or an argument; he just passively ate what he was given (see Gen. 3:6).

Eve was also the first person in Scripture to speak directly to both Satan and God. The serpent approached Eve in Genesis 3:1 and entered into a theological discussion with her. We can wonder all day long why the serpent approached the woman first instead of the man, yet our answers would only be speculation. We will never know that answer. What we do know is that God gave women the ability to consider and discuss theological issues. When God approached Eve in Genesis 3:13, she answered God directly and blamed the serpent instead of taking responsibility for her actions. So far in Scripture, Eve's voice has only gotten her into trouble.

The First Person to Experience the Brokenness of Relationships

Sin brought brokenness into the world. Eve experienced a broken relationship with God the moment she decided to commit a sinful act (Gen. 3:6). Eve experienced a broken relationship with herself when her nakedness became shameful (Gen. 3:7). Eve experienced a broken relationship with Adam when she misled him (Gen. 3:6), and then he blamed her for his actions (Gen. 3:12). Eve experienced a broken relationship with nature when she misjudged the serpent as truthful and the forbidden fruit as worthy (Gen. 3:4-6), and when an animal's blood had to be spilled to cover her nakedness (Gen. 3:21). Nothing would ever be the same. We all continue to experience aspects of that brokenness.

The First Person to Acknowledge God's Role in Childbirth

Can you even begin to imagine what it was like to be Eve, the first person to give birth?! **Eve was also the first person to acknowledge God's role in childbirth** when she said, "I have given life to a man with the LORD's help" (Gen. 4:1 CEB). Note: Eve said that, not Adam. While Eve's voice previously got her into trouble, this statement illustrated her understanding of God as the source of life.

The pain associated with childbirth was not God's original design; it was a consequence of that broken relationship with God. However, it is important to note that the woman was not "cursed" with the pain of childbirth. The only things that were "cursed" in the Genesis account were the serpent (Gen. 1:14) and the ground (Gen. 1:17). Through the centuries, people made the argument that women *had* to experience the pain of childbirth because it was God's will. Then, in 1853, Queen Victoria chose to use ether during the birth of Prince Leopold and the world took notice. Finally, the doors were open for women to choose *not* to have pain during childbirth and it was no longer an "immoral" choice. Pain in childbirth was a consequence of sin that all mothers have had to face. However, it was not God's original intent. So do we want to model our lives on the consequences of sin or on God's original intent?

The First Mother to Experience the Loss of a Child

Eve was the first mother, along with Adam, the first father, to experience the loss of a child. Any woman who has lost a child to miscarriage or death, or to giving up a child for adoption can relate to Eve's experience on some level. Eve lost her younger son, Abel, to murder when his older brother, Cain, killed him (see Gen. 4:2-8). To be the first parents to know grief must have been a horrifying suffering. Yet, Eve was a survivor. I think this determined spirit of Eve has been forgotten in our retellings of Scripture. Eve went on to have more children. Her next son was named Seth (see Gen. 4:25) and then she had other sons and daughters (see Gen. 5:4). I can only imagine the emotional fortitude that required.

The First Mother to Experience a Child's Murderous Act

Eve was also the first mother, along with the first father, to have a child commit murder when their son Cain killed their son Abel. I cannot begin to imagine the pain of that. I know there are many women since then who have known a similar pain. As a result of Cain's act of killing his brother, God marked him in such a way that would prevent others from killing him (showing God's great mercy) and punished him with banishment to the land of Nod, which also means the land of Wandering (see Gen. 4:16). I would compare that to any parent who has experienced the estrangement or imprisonment of a child. Did Eve ever see Cain again? Did she lose two children that day? We don't know the answers to those questions. Yet, somehow Eve chose to go on and become a mother again to more children. What strength! Anyone who can carry on after such heartache is exhibiting the strong and determined part of the image of God. Our God has endured the betrayal of all God's children and yet continues to let us exist, to know God, to be invited back into fellowship with God, and to anticipate joy. And for some reason, God has allowed created humans to experience and express those godly qualities.

Eve is an enigma in so many ways. Yet, she forged a path of lessons to be learned for all of us. Her story is certainly instructive, yet I also find it inspirational. I cannot imagine the heartache she experienced as a result of being banished from the Garden of Eden—from perfection in 3D—to finding the strength to carry on and build a life with all its hardships and joys and sorrows and surprises. Her story is our story. We are her legacy.

The Message in Eve's Voice

Pondering Eve's existence as the first human expression of the feminine/female characteristics of our Creator God can help us expand our understanding of God. This is an important message we glean from Eve's story. Since both genders originated in God, it is important for us to consider the human—albeit limited—language we use to name God. The English language only offers us two personal singular pronouns (he and she), and most English translations of the Bible use "he" when referring to God the Father or the Godhead. However, the pronoun "he" is theologically incomplete because God is not a human father with physical, human characteristics, nor is the Godhead male in the human sense. Therefore, while "he" is an incomplete term for God, so is "she." The Hebrews had many names for God, which we tend to use only when quoting Scripture, such as Elohim, Yahweh, El Shaddai, etc. So, while most English translations tend to yield to the use of the masculine pronoun "he," considering it the generic term, we need to challenge ourselves to consider names for God that help us express the fact that

God's personhood actually goes far beyond anything we can understand about a God who is completely "other." While both the female / feminine aspects and the male / masculine aspects are equal—but beyond human—in our Creator God, our language simply does not have a pronoun that can communicate that fact. However, one of my concerns is that our language choices for naming God should be compassionate when we consider people who have had painful experiences with abusive men or with cruel, earthly fathers and who, emotionally, cannot relate to a God referred to as "he." Learning to name our infinite God in new finite ways will always be inadequate, yet it can help our hearts and our minds to stretch toward a broader understanding of all God is. Striving to communicate all we know of our loving, merciful God should be our goal when trying to represent God to *all* humans who were created in God's image. Thinking deeply about the creation of Eve will help us do that.

Another message we glean from Eve's story is a picture of God's original intent for relationships. Eve knew something none of us will ever know: the *difference* between a perfect relationship and a damaged relationship with both God and another human being. Before sin entered the world, Eve knew the unimaginable love and had direct communication with God as well as a time of perfect bliss with her husband Adam. We only get "echoes of Eden" today, and while today's relationships can be wonderful, they will never be as they were before the corruption brought by sin.

A message about influence is a part of Eve's story for us. Eve must have discovered just how far-reaching and influential her choices could be. She experienced numerous heartbreaking events in her lifetime involving her family, yet she lived long enough to birth multiple sons and daughters who would become her legacy. Actually, we're all her legacy. Everyone in the world is connected through our common human bond. And just as Eve had a choice, each of us has a choice of how we want to influence those around us and those who will outlive us. I'm sure Eve would encourage us to think carefully about the choices we make today because they will have long-lasting consequences, both positive and negative.

Eve's experiences as a parent also provide some informed messages. Since I have never birthed children myself, I can't relate to the pain of childbirth. According to Genesis 5:4, Eve experienced childbirth multiple more times and had other sons and daughters, as have so many of you! Beyond her courage to continue to go through the birthing process, she also is the first woman in Scripture to lose a child, and actually, she lost two children. She lost her son Abel through murder, and, as painful as that was, the murder was committed by her other son, Cain. Then, Cain was banished from the place where they lived; so, it is possible that Eve never saw Cain again either. Eve somehow survived the pain, the heartache, the grief, and the anger. Hopefully, she also experienced and extended forgiveness with God's help, which can be offered even in the midst of such horrible circumstances. And she did it all without many people to support her.

Eve's message to us through her voice and her story is both the sad consequences of sin and the triumphal demonstration of survival, which has continued throughout the ages. Let Eve's voice remind you to keep going on in spite of family tragedy and broken relationships, and to keep returning to your Creator God, whose image you bear, for forgiveness and strength.

Biblical Truths Taught through the Story of Eve

1. God created woman in God's image just as much as man was created in God's image.
2. God is beyond our culture's (or any other culture's) definitions and descriptions of gender.
3. God is more expansive than we could ever hope to imagine.
4. God values and views women and men equally.
5. God gave dominion of the earth equally to women and men.
6. God gave women the ability to choose their own spiritual paths and to discuss them intelligently.

7. God's gift of freewill to humans means our choices today affect not only our lives but also the lives of the people around us and those of future generations.
8. God's instructions for life are knowable and attainable, yet there is always the potential that our understanding of them can be manipulated, which can lead to our downfall.

Why the Voice of Eve Matters . . .

To women: because Eve's story shows how a woman's voice can be used for both evil and blessing since her voice—the first woman's voice—was the first human voice recorded in Scripture as a participant in a conversation—albeit with a bad influence—and yet, Eve's voice was also the first human voice in Scripture to acknowledge God's role in childbirth!

To men: because Eve's story illustrates how important it is for men to be engaged in spiritual conversations as much as women. If Adam had stepped up and entered into that conversation with Satan and Eve, would our world be different today? When presented with spiritual challenges, men should take that responsibility seriously because of the potential negative and positive consequences.

To mothers: because Eve's story shows that acknowledgement of God's role in childbirth is a universal truth all mothers can speak. Eve's story also reminds us that pain in childbirth was a consequence of sin and not God's original intent nor God's curse on women.

To anyone who has lost a child to death, estrangement, or imprisonment: because Eve's story illustrates how in spite of the indescribable pain, she was able to keep moving forward for the sake of her husband and other children, and she was able to praise God for the other children she had.

Questions Raised by the Story of Eve

What can we learn from the fact that the Bible teaches that the image of God is equally present and yet still incomplete in both genders?

Why is the Genesis 2 creation story so often emphasized over the Genesis 1 creation story in regard to the creation of people?

Why do so many people assume the Genesis 2 creation story is a filling-in of the details of the Genesis 1 creation story when the Bible presents them as two separate accounts of creation with different details?

Why do some religions and denominations still teach that it is woman's fault that sin came into the world when Adam sinned just as much as Eve? Who was more easily persuaded: Eve after a long conversation with the serpent or Adam with a simple offer of a piece of fruit?

What was it like to be the first human to experience childbirth?

What was it like to have a perfect relationship with both God and spouse?

What could you change to make your relationship with God more like God intended?

What could you change to make your current relationship with your spouse more like the original ideal?

Why has there not been much emphasis on the fact that the first person to sin was also the first person in Scripture to acknowledge God's role in childbirth?

Eve's Key to Resilient Confidence

Eve's story is so intertwined with our understanding of sin and the fallen world that it is difficult to imagine Eve as someone who demonstrated resilient confidence. Yet, when you consider her experiences of birthing two sons, Cain and Abel, then the murder of one by the other, the banishment of Cain, and the birthing of more children, resilience is a word that comes easily to mind.

I can only imagine how Eve instructed her children about the consequences of the choices they made. Eve did not have two of the blessings we have today: the Holy Spirit living within us or the written word of God. Therefore, we have access to truth in ways that she didn't and we can be held accountable for knowing that truth. This is why I believe **Eve would say her key to resilient confidence was learning to think carefully about the extent of one's influence in the world.**

Here are some ways you can seriously consider your influence:

1. Uphold biblical truth.

When presented with spiritual knowledge of any kind, take the time and responsibility to compare it to the biblical truth you know and to which you have access. Don't assume someone else is telling you the truth just because they are speaking from a place of authority, from a pulpit, or in a publication. All humans are fallible and have the potential to be manipulated to believe lies.

2. Make careful decisions.

When making decisions, determine how your choice will affect you and those around you and whether your choice will bring God glory or disappointment. This takes discipline and a willingness to deny yourself something in the present to receive benefits in the future. This requires the spiritual discipline of humility.

3. Consider the potential positive consequences of your choices.
Just as our bad choices can have negative consequences for years to come, so can our good choices have positive consequences for years to come. Focus on how you are relating to the next generation in positive, constructive, and encouraging ways.

4. Develop your friendship with God.
Take your relationship with God seriously and do whatever you can to cultivate that friendship. Take time to develop your understanding of God's almighty power, grace, and mercy which coexist with God's desire to commune with you on a moment-by-moment basis.

5. Praise God *in* every circumstance—not *for* every circumstance.
We will all experience pain and grief in our lives. Some will experience horrible things. Yet, no matter how horrible the situation, we know we can still praise God *not* for the situation itself, but for being with us, for being the God who grieves with us, and for being the God who can bring people into our lives to comfort us. Your confidence for any task or role is rooted in your ability to praise God, to acknowledge God's role in your life and accomplishments, and to trust God's purpose for your life.

6. Pray continuously.
While Eve had the privilege of walking with God in the Garden, you have the privilege of prayer. Learning to talk to God and to hear God throughout your day will help you know when you are having a godly influence in a situation. Praying continuously is more of a mindset than a posture. You can pray silently with your eyes open in the midst of a busy task or you can pause what you're doing, bow your head, and voice a prayer. The method and motions are not the important things. Your continuous communication with God and constant sense of God's presence are the goals.

Every decision we make has consequences, sometimes more far-reaching than we could ever imagine. Resilient confidence grows when we yield our decision-making power to the Holy Spirit and allow God to direct us even in the relatively small moments of our lives.

"She said, 'I have given life to a man with the LORD's help.'"
—Genesis 4:1 (CEB)

PART TWO

God Chose Hagar

THE TIME OF ISRAEL'S PATRIARCHS

ca. 4000 - 1800 BCE

3

Events that Shaped the World of Hagar

THE TIME OF ISRAEL'S PATRIARCHS
ca. 4000 - 1800 BCE

With stories of the Creation, the Flood, and the Tower of Babel, the first 11 chapters of Genesis are a wide-lens perspective of the beginnings of life on earth in the undatable past. Archaeological and scientific discoveries have revealed the advancements of civilizations around the world which were occurring between the time of the Tower of Babel and the time of the biblical Abraham. Beginning in Genesis 12, God pursued a relationship with one particular man, Abraham, through which God blessed the whole world. The rest of the biblical epic is the story of God's relationship with the Hebrew people—the Chosen People—who would bring our Savior, Jesus Christ, into the world 2,000 years after the time of God's first promise to Abraham.

Happenings in the Rest of the World

Note: The historical highlights listed below and on all the following "Events" pages can be found in many easily accessible sources, yet the books listed on the "For Further Reading" pages were my best guides.

Scientists, archaeologists, and biblical scholars have told us that by the time the first biblical patriarch, Abraham, walked the earth, which was sometime between 2200 and 1800 BCE, the rest of the world had witnessed these advances:

- Civilizations had established farming communities in China, the Americas, and across the Fertile Crescent (the crescent-shaped area of the ancient world that went from the Persian Gulf in the East and upward through Mesopotamia and down toward Canaan and Egypt along the Mediterranean Sea).

- Most of the civilized world was already well into the Bronze Age, making use of the alloy of copper and tin to fashion tools.
- South America had complex societies and had developed their own temple architecture.
- The Sumerians of Mesopotamia invented the wheel and developed the first writing known as cuneiform, wrote an Epic of Creation, and provided the world's first female poet who wrote a hymn to the Great Goddess. One of Sumer's great cities was Ur, Abraham's hometown according to Genesis, grew into a bustling metropolis of more than 200,000 people by 2000 BCE with a central temple built atop one of the earliest step pyramids (called a ziggurat), had a thriving trade—with countries as far away as India; wealthy citizens; and two-storied houses; among other characteristics of an opulent and highly developed civilization.
- The British Isles saw the building of Stonehenge and other stone circles, thought to be for religious ceremonies.
- China's history already included the development of Emperor Fu Hsi's yin and yang philosophy of nature; the discovery of silk production by Leizu, wife of the Yellow Emperor; and the Chinese government's employment of women as leaders of armies, regulators of agriculture, and supervisors of religious activities.
- Babylon's Code of Hammurabi, one of the world's early law codes—established at least 500 years before the time of Moses and the Ten Commandments—addressed regulations for women wine sellers, indicating that women in the ancient world were already known for their business endeavors.
- Egypt became the world's first nation-state, produced a female ruler (Queen Merneith, maybe the world's first female ruler), and provided the first female doctor (Merit Ptah), built the Sphinx and the Great Pyramids—an expression of their well-established beliefs in the afterlife—and went through 12 dynasties of pharaohs. Culturally, Egyptians were already designing beads for jewelry, wearing wedding rings, sculpting great artworks, and cultivating wine.

Focusing on the Bible's Story

All that and more had occurred by the time God called Abraham! While the whole world was advancing in so many remarkable ways and women throughout the world were making contributions to their communities and cultures, the Bible's story gives us a glimpse of a moment in time when God broke into the life of a throw-away young woman and changed the world through her. Her story is part of the story of Abraham and Sarah, who are first known by the names Abram and Sarai, and the beginnings of the Israelite/Jewish people group. These stories were memorized and passed down for about a thousand years before they were put into a written form around 1000 BCE. Amazingly, that original written form would one day be translated into multiple languages and become part of the Bible we are still reading in the 21st century.

This story occurred sometime between 2000 and 1800 BCE. While the details of ancient history are hard to pinpoint, we do know it was two generations before the birth of Jacob who became Israel, the father of the Twelve Tribes, and centuries before God chose Moses to lead the Hebrews' exodus out of slavery in Egypt. Yet, the writer of Genesis, the beginning of the Bible's great epic, made sure to preserve the story of Hagar, this particular Egyptian woman, an "outsider" to the Covenant, one we would call a sex slave today, and one who, according to the biblical text, heard her name spoken *only* by the God who visited her.

Let's listen to the voice of Hagar,
when God chose her to be first. . . .

4

Hagar's Story

ca. 2000 - 1800 BCE

God chose Hagar's voice to be the first . . .
- Human voice to encounter the angel of the LORD
- With whom God would discuss the gender and name of an unborn child
- To give God a name
- To communicate her son's name to his father, Abram

Hagar, hot and hungry, wearily dropped her sheepskin bag and her wineskin as she knelt down by the desert spring to get a drink of cool water. She found a place to sit and rest in the shade of a big boulder on a rocky hillside not far from the spring. She knew she would need a safe place for the night if she had to sleep outdoors. *How did I get here?* she wondered. Not that she wondered where she was—she was very intentional on choosing this long, dusty road back to her homeland of Egypt. *Why couldn't I just endure a while longer? Then Abram would have his child and Sarai might make things easier for me. She already has claim to this baby I'm carrying inside me!* Hagar started to doubt her decision to run away. Then with a fresh resoluteness, she reminded herself, *No, she can't treat me this way. I have been her faithful slave for more than ten years. Now, all this constant badgering and her threats; it's all just too much. Abram didn't even take up for me! He looked at me as if I were some rag doll. He'll be sorry when he realizes I'm gone. I'm going back home to Egypt. I don't belong in this land of Canaan!* Hagar rested her head against the rock and enjoyed a cool, momentary breeze.

As the afternoon sun brightened and the clouds were no longer shielding her from the hot rays, she decided to look for shelter. She stood up to go fill her wineskin with the spring water. Walking toward the spring she thought she saw the shape of a man approaching from the far side of the stream. She wondered if she were seeing a mirage. He was getting closer. He was alone. He was walking with a shepherd's staff, but no sheep were following him. Her eyes darted around the landscape, quickly planning where she would run if he threatened her. Keeping an eye on the approaching stranger, she crouched down cautiously by the stream to fill her wineskin. He knelt down slowly on the other side of the narrow stream and laid down his shepherd's staff. He used both hands to cup the cool spring water to his mouth. He looked up and smiled at Hagar. He acted as if he knew her, but she knew she didn't recognize him.

When he sat up, still smiling, he looked at the guarded young woman and said, "Hagar, Sarai's servant!"

Startled, she said, "Yes, how did you know my name? Do I know you?" Inside, she was thinking, *It's nice to hear my name. Abram and Sarai never call me by my name!*

Ignoring her questions, the man asked her, "Where did you come from and where are you going?" He held his hand up to his eyes and looked down the long road both directions. There wasn't much around. A person had to *want* to be on this road.

She wondered if she should answer him. Then, she thought, *Oh, I guess Abram paid this man to come find me. Well, it's not going to work!* She decided she would tell him what she assumed he already knew, still wondering if she should reveal anything else. "I came from Sarai, my mistress."

He patiently waited for her to answer his other question.

After an awkward silence, she finally announced with great determination, "I'm running away."

The man looked up at the blazing sun and around the area at the sparse vegetation and the long, dusty and rocky road ahead of Hagar. She began to doubt herself again.

His reply was difficult to hear: "Go back to your mistress. Put up with her harsh treatment of you."

"Why would I do that?" she asked and then wondered, *Wait! How does he know about that?!*

The man stood up and leaned on his shepherd's staff. "Hagar, God promises to give you many children, so many children they can't be counted!"

"How do you know that?" asked a very curious Hagar who was beginning to wonder just who this man could be.

"I know that you are now pregnant and will give birth to a son."

Hagar clutched her belly and smiled. "A son? I'm going to have a boy?" She was beaming. Then she wondered silently, *How does this man know all this? Is he a prophet?*

When she looked back into his kind face, he was nodding joyfully. "You will name him Ishmael."

She patted her belly and smiled. "That means, the LORD hears. . . . Ishmael." She repeated the name several times. She looked again at the stranger before her. "That's a good name. . . . So, the one true God—the one Abram worships—really hears *me*?"

The stranger nodded. "Yes, the LORD has heard about your harsh treatment. The LORD understands."

"Do you know anything else about this baby? What he will become one day?" Hagar's mind began to overflow with questions. But the next one was like a stab to her already-wounded heart: *What will become of me?* Hagar had kept this fear pushed to the far corners of her mind ever since she realized she was pregnant with Abram's child. By all rights, her baby would become Sarai's property, just as she was Sarai's property. But her son would have a better place as the master's firstborn son. He would become Sarai's son, just as if she had birthed him herself. Hagar knew that if it pleased her mistress, she could be tossed away, sold to the next shepherding clan, and she would never see her baby boy again.

The intriguing stranger answered her first questions. "The LORD says that he will be a wild mule of a man; he will fight everyone, and they will fight him. He will live at odds with all his relatives."

With an agreeing nod, Hagar said, "I can believe that. He already keeps me awake at night with all his jumping!"

Then a sudden realization occurred to Hagar. She now knew what was happening. This was a sacred moment. It felt like the air stood still and the bubbling spring sounded like soft music. She now understood this was God visiting her. This messenger before her was from the one true God. *Oh my! Am I dead?* she wondered, because she knew that if anyone saw God face to face, that person would die. Coming to her senses, she said out loud to reassure herself, "No, no, I'm not dead." She looked up at the man who was smiling broadly.

Almost breathless with excitement, and falling to her knees, Hagar spoke as she pointed to the man, "You . . . You . . . You are . . ." stammering for words, she finally spoke the name, "El Roi, yes, yes . . . You are . . . You are the God Who Sees . . . You . . . You are the God Whom I've seen."

The man nodded and held up his hand as if he was going to bless her and then . . . he was gone. He didn't walk away. He was just . . . gone.

Hagar stood up, looking all around. He was nowhere to be seen. She gathered up her wineskin and balanced her bag on her head and looked toward Egypt once more. Then she felt a kick inside her and clutched her belly. "Ishmael," she spoke tenderly to her unborn child as she began back down the road that brought her to this place. "I can't wait to tell your father about this!"

With all that had happened in those moments, her thoughts could no longer echo silently in her head. Instead, they seemed to pour out of her mouth—audible, excited, spoken words that only the rocks, the stream, and her unborn child witnessed. "Oh, Ishmael, your father will be so proud that you're a boy! And I think he'll like the name El-Roi gave you! Just think, Ishmael, the one true God has seen me . . . *me!* . . . And has *heard* me. Not even my mistress Sarai has *seen* the one true God. She has often talked about the promise God spoke to Abram, but she has never said God spoke to her. Now I believe that God knows *me*—and *you,* Ishmael! Every time I say your name, I'll remember this moment when God told me that God *hears* me! Oh, Ishmael, this changes everything! I think I can endure anything now!"

The Bible Speaks

Hagar's story is found in Genesis 16, 21, and 25

Hagar's owner, Abram, grew up in eastern Mesopotamia in the city of Ur, possibly toward the southern end of the Euphrates River which joins with the Tigris River before they both drain into the Persian Gulf. After he was grown and married to Sarai, he moved with his father northwest to Haran. In Genesis 12:1-7, we are introduced to God's plan to give Abram the Promised Land, where the Canaanites lived, and to God's choice of Abram to be the father of God's Chosen People—a great nation through whom the rest of the world would be blessed. Abram followed God's call to move farther southwest to Canaan on the Mediterranean Sea.

After Abram arrived in Canaan, a severe famine struck the land, so he picked up his family and moved even farther south to Egypt. At this point, Abram had traveled more than 1,200 miles from his homeland in Ur to eventually end up in Egypt. While in Egypt, he became wealthy and acquired numerous male and female slaves. This was the likely time when Abram acquired Hagar, an Egyptian maidservant whom he gave to his wife Sarai. After a run-in with Pharaoh (see Gen. 12:17-20) over the beautiful Sarai, Abram and Sarai were expelled from Egypt with all they had accumulated. Together with their entourage, they turned their caravan northeast toward Canaan. This is where and when our story about Hagar took place.

The Bible gives us some wonderful details about Hagar and the role in history God chose for her. What I especially love about her story is that it shows God working outside the boundaries we tend to place on God. We all like to read—and hold onto—promises in the Bible about how God blesses those who love God and follow God's commandments. We need to ask ourselves if we tend to overlook the passages that remind us that *all* of God's created beings are loved and blessed by God. For example:

"He makes the sun rise on both the evil and the good and sends rain on both the righteous and the unrighteous. . . . Therefore, just as your heavenly Father is complete in showing love to everyone, so also you must be complete" (Matt. 5:45b, 48 CEB).

"Praise the LORD, all you nations! Worship him, all you peoples! Because God's faithful love toward us is strong, the LORD's faithfulness lasts forever! Praise the LORD!" (Psalm 117 CEB)

"So circumcise your hearts and stop being so stubborn, because the LORD your God is the God of all gods and Lord of all lords, the great, mighty, and awesome God who doesn't play favorites and doesn't take bribes. He enacts justice for orphans and widows, and he loves immigrants, giving them food and clothing. That means you must also love immigrants because you were immigrants in Egypt" (Deut. 10:16-19 CEB).

Now that you've read a fictional account of this woman named Hagar, the following section will provide the biblical text on which that scene was based. As you read, consider the fact that Hagar had grown up in Egypt, the land where pharaohs were worshipped as gods and their culture had a well-established belief system regarding an afterlife. Each of the stone pyramid structures built by the Egyptians took decades to construct and were for the purpose of ushering their rulers into the next world. Hagar had been taken as a slave away from all that was familiar to her and forced to comply with the wishes of a desperate, infertile couple in Canaan who impatiently got ahead of God's timing. Abram had tried to name Eliezer, his slave, as his heir, but God said, "No," and reminded Abram his heir would be his own flesh and blood (see Gen. 15:1-5). Then Sarai took matters into her own hands.

Sarai's Decision
Genesis 16:1-6

1 Sarai, Abram's wife, had not been able to have children. Since she had
an Egyptian servant named Hagar, **2** Sarai said to Abram, "The LORD has
kept me from giving birth, so go to my servant. Maybe she will provide
me with children." Abram did just as Sarai said. **3** After Abram had lived
ten years in the land of Canaan, Abram's wife Sarai took her Egyptian
servant Hagar and gave her to her husband Abram as his wife. **4** He slept
with Hagar, and she became pregnant. But when she realized that she
was pregnant, she no longer respected her mistress. **5** Sarai said to
Abram, "This harassment is your fault. I allowed you to embrace my
servant, but when she realized she was pregnant, I lost her respect. Let
the LORD decide who is right, you or me."

6 Abram said to Sarai, "Since she's your servant, do whatever you
wish to her." So Sarai treated her harshly, and she ran away from Sarai.
(CEB)

According to Old Testament scholar Theodore Hiebert, in his commentary on Genesis in *The CEB Study Bible,*

> This kind of slavery was common in ancient Near Eastern and biblical society (Exod. 21:1-11). Frequently servants were outsiders, as was the Egyptian Hagar. Ancient Near Eastern legal texts describe similar situations where an infertile wife gives her servant to her husband, hoping that children will be born through that union. In such cases, the principal wife may possess legal rights to the children of her servant (cf. Gen. 30:1-13). Sarai's proposal follows accepted practices and shouldn't necessarily be considered an act of faithlessness in God's promises of descendants. God hasn't yet prescribed the line through which Abram's heirs will come. (Hiebert 2013, 27)

Hiebert also stated, "In biblical society, pregnancy was highly regarded, while childlessness was shameful. Because of these cultural values, Hagar uses her new status to challenge Sarai's authority, even though Hagar is the secondary wife" (Hiebert 2013, 27). Hiebert continued to explain, "Sarai blames Abram, the male head of the household, for allowing Hagar's harassment and lack of respect. He hasn't protected Sarai's status as the principal wife" (Hiebert 2013, 28).

While culturally acceptable at the time, using a maidservant to have a child with one's husband would certainly cause discord in the home. Apparently, the relationship between Hagar and Sarai deteriorated to unbearable misery for Hagar and she decided to run away.

This next scene is the **first time in Scripture where we see an appearance of "the angel of the LORD,"** as the phrase appears in most English translations. The CEB translates it as "the LORD's messenger." Some scholars believe this was a reference to Jesus appearing to someone on earth before he became human through Mary. Appearances like this are known as the pre-incarnate Christ. For example, according to Bible commentator David M. Carr in his notes in *The New Oxford Annotated Bible Third Edition,* "Here the angel of the LORD is not a heavenly being subordinate to God but the LORD (Yahweh) in earthly manifestation, as is clear from v. 13 (cf. 21.17, 19; Ex 14.19)" (Carr 2001, 33). Also, Bible commentator Ronald Youngblood stated in *The NIV Study Bible* that

> since the angel of the Lord speaks for God in the first person (v. 10) and Hagar is said to name "the LORD who spoke to her: 'You are the God who sees me' " (v. 13), the angel appears to be both distinguished from the LORD (in that he is called "messenger"—the Hebrew for "angel" means "messenger") and identified with him. Similar distinction and identification can be found in 19:1,21; 31:11,13; Ex 3:2,4; Jdg 2:1-5; 6:11-12,14; 13:3,6,8-11,13,15-17,20-23; Zec 3:1-6; 12:8. Traditional Christian interpretation has held that this "angel" was a preincarnate manifestation of Christ as God's Messenger-Servant. It may be, however, that, as the Lord's personal messenger who represented him and bore his credentials, the angel could speak on behalf of (and so be indented with) the One who sent him (see especially 19:21; cf. 18:2,22; 19:2). Whether this "angel" was the second person of the Trinity remains therefore uncertain" (Youngblood 1985, 29).

Regardless of the translation, this is the first time the word "angel" appears in Scripture. This is also the first of 50 times the phrase "the angel of the LORD" appears in the Hebrew Scriptures (Davidson 2006, 150). The fascinating aspect of this is to whom this first-time appearance occurs—to an Egyptian woman, an outsider to the Covenant, a pregnant slave, an abused surrogate, and a runaway!

The Angel of the LORD Appears
Genesis 16:7-9

7 The LORD's messenger found Hagar at a spring in the desert, the spring on the road to Shur, **8** and said, "Hagar! Sarai's servant! Where did you come from and where are you going?"

She said, "From Sarai my mistress. I'm running away."

9 The LORD's messenger said to her, "Go back to your mistress. Put up with her harsh treatment of you." (CEB)

One of the most beautiful details in this story is the first word spoken by this angel/messenger: Hagar's name! This messenger was the *only* person who ever addressed Hagar by her name in the entire biblical account. Abram and Sarai only referred to her as a slave, never once calling her by name. This one encounter apparently empowered Hagar to return to the harsh treatment of Sarai. Our 21st-century, Western mindsets cannot really grasp the logic of expecting a slave to return to any kind of slavery, let alone harsh treatment, yet Hagar felt compelled to obey.

It is also interesting to note, that just as with men in Scripture who encountered God in dramatic ways, God took the initiative in communicating with Hagar. God found her. God called her by name. God made it clear that she was the specific intended audience. And God started the conversation. God did not approach her with a command or a judgment. The Creator of the universe approached this Egyptian servant girl with an invitation to a dialogue.

Hagar Learns about Ishmael

The next few verses reveal **the first time in the biblical record God revealed to someone the gender and name of an unborn child.** God had spoken and appeared to Abram before (see Gen. 12), but not in this form and God had not yet told him the gender or name(s) of the offspring promised. Once again, God communicated directly to this "outsider," giving her prophetic knowledge with which she would go home to share with Abram.

Genesis 16:10-12

10 The LORD's messenger also said to her,
"I will give you many children,
so many they can't be counted!"
11 The LORD's messenger said to her,
"You are now pregnant and will give birth to a son.
You will name him Ishmael [or *God hears*]
because the LORD has heard about your harsh treatment.
12 He will be a wild mule of a man;
he will fight everyone, and they will fight him.
He will live at odds with all his relatives."
[or *He will reside near all his relatives*] (CEB)

The promise in verse 10 is similar to the one God gave Abram and is **the first time such a promise is given to a woman in Scripture.**

Hagar Names God; Abram Names Ishmael

In response to God's promise, Hagar became **the first person ever to give God a name.**

Genesis 16:13-16

13 Hagar named the LORD who spoke to her, "You are El Roi"[or *God who sees me* or *God whom I've seen*] because she said, "Can I still see after he saw me?" [Heb uncertain; or *Have I really seen God and survived?*] **14** Therefore, that well is called Beer-lahai-roi [or *the Well of the Living One who sees me* or *whom I've seen*]; it's the well between Kadesh and Bered. **15** Hagar gave birth to a son for Abram, and Abram named him Ishmael. **16** Abram was 86 years old when Hagar gave birth to Ishmael for Abram. (CEB)

While her son's name would be "God hears," she chose the name "El-roi" for the angel before her, which means "God who sees." These two names in these few verses—*God hears* and *God who sees*—give us a wonderful picture of the nature of our personal God: God hears us and God sees us as named individuals with unique purposes.

The last two verses (15-16) of Genesis 16 reveal two things:

1. Hagar returned to Sarai as the angel instructed her to do. That one encounter with the angel must have empowered her to be willing and able to endure the treatment she knew she would receive from Sarai.
2. She bore Abram's firstborn son and **Abram must have believed the testimony of Hagar because he named his firstborn son Ishmael. God used Hagar's voice to inform Abram that God heard *her* and knew *her*, too.** Can you imagine that conversation? I can just hear Hagar telling Abram, "I know we're having a son. I know we have to call him Ishmael. And oh, by the way, I saw and talked to your God out there!"
   I would love to have a picture of Abram's face in that moment!

Regardless of her faith experiences (or lack of) during her upbringing in Egypt, Hagar's experience with the one true God was as real for her as it was for Abram. Her story includes a unique, first-time encounter with the angel of the LORD that no one else in Scripture, not even Abram, had experienced to that point.

Apparently, this first encounter with God gave Hagar all the determination she needed to return to an abusive situation. They say knowledge is power, and for Hagar, that was absolutely true. Hagar was promised that her descendants would be "too numerous to count" just as Abram had been promised. Hagar was told she would have a son. She was also told that God had already named this child Ishmael, and his name meant "God hears" or "God heeds." Every time she would say her son's name, she would remember that the God of the universe *heard* her and *came* to her to *talk* to her and to help *her*. The fact that Hagar did indeed return to Abram and Sarai's household reveals that she trusted God to fulfill the promise given to her. She must have felt empowered to endure any mistreatment because she believed what God told her.

The same God who had made the covenant with Abram also knew Hagar, cared about her, initiated a relationship with her, and gave her a personal promise of blessing beyond her wildest imagination. Our God is still capable of that today! God's personal promise to an Egyptian slave woman has grown into a mighty nation indeed—the Arabs—of which Hagar and Abraham are the original parents. How well do we know the people who have fulfilled this other promise of the same God we serve?

Ishmael Grows

Genesis 17:17-27 moves us quickly to 13 years later. Ishmael was a teenager and Abram still had not had any other children. He also received another visit from God, his name was changed to Abraham, and he received more information about his firstborn son, Ishmael, and his yet unborn son to be named Isaac. God renewed the original promise and told Abraham that Sarai would have a son and her name would be changed to Sarah. From these verses we also learn of God's promise that Ishmael would become the father of twelve princes and would also become a great nation. The fulfillment of the prophecy of Genesis 16:12 is seen in our news headlines today.

Arabs today are from many ethnic groups and many different countries, yet many share the common language of Arabic. While the majority of Arabs are Muslim, there are many Arab Christians as well, numbering more than 20 million. Muslims revere Hagar as the mother of Ishmael, yet the Quran does not mention her name. When you meet someone of Arab descent or from Egypt or an African, or Middle Eastern country, consider asking them if they grew up in a Muslim or Christian community. It might possibly open the door for a longer conversation about your faith and/or knowledge of Jesus.

Fast forward another few years. Ishmael was in his mid-teens and he now had a half-brother, Isaac. Abraham and Sarah had finally had the heir God promised them. Can you imagine the turmoil that Isaac's birth must have added to the household when Sarah and Hagar already weren't getting along? Read about how bad it got in the next passage.

Hagar and Ishmael Sent Away
Genesis 21:8-16

8 The child [Isaac] grew and was weaned, and on the day Isaac was weaned Abraham held a great feast. **9** But Sarah saw that the son whom Hagar the Egyptian had borne to Abraham was mocking, **10** and she said to Abraham, "Get rid of that slave woman and her son, for that woman's son will never share in the inheritance with my son Isaac."

11 The matter distressed Abraham greatly because it concerned his son. **12** But God said to him, "Do not be so distressed about the boy and your slave woman. Listen to whatever Sarah tells you, because it is through Isaac that your offspring [or *seed*] will be reckoned. **13** I will make the son of the slave into a nation also, because he is your offspring."

14 Early the next morning Abraham took some food and a skin of water and gave them to Hagar. He set them on her shoulders and then sent her off with the boy. She went on her way and wandered in the Desert of Beersheba.

15 When the water in the skin was gone, she put the boy under one of the bushes.**16** Then she went off and sat down about a bowshot away, for she thought, "I cannot watch the boy die." And as she sat there, she [Hebrew; Septuagint *the child*] began to sob. (NIV)

Next, we see the compassion of God enter the story once more. Genesis 21:17-21 provides another example of God responding to the specific needs of a woman in a desperate situation. Note the promises God made to Hagar in the following passage.

Hagar and Ishmael's New Life
Genesis 21:17-21

17 God heard the boy's cries, and God's messenger called to Hagar from
heaven and said to her, "Hagar! What's wrong? Don't be afraid. God has
heard the boy's cries over there. **18** Get up, pick up the boy, and take him
by the hand because I will make of him a great nation." **19** Then God
opened her eyes, and she saw a well. She went over, filled the water flask,
and gave the boy a drink. **20** God remained with the boy; he grew up,
lived in the desert, and became an expert archer. **21** He lived in the Paran
desert, and his mother found him an Egyptian wife. (CEB)

I wonder if the words of Genesis 21:20-21 are letting us know that Hagar was also the first single mother we read about in Scripture. The promise of Ishmael becoming a great nation with 12 sons was confirmed in Genesis 25:12-18. Hagar believed what God told her, obeyed God's command, endured a difficult home situation, cared for her son, and even got him a wife from Egypt—because apparently, Abram did not consider it necessary to get this son a wife from among his relatives.

Hagar's story is a beacon for anyone who feels alone or overlooked, abused or mistreated. God's personal appearance to her makes it clear that God is aware of each individual's circumstance, regardless of gender, status, or creed. God's promise to her reveals that God has a purpose for each of us.

The Message in Hagar's Voice

In all its rich details, carefully chosen by the Hebrew author of Genesis, this story lets us hear Hagar's voice while she had a conversation with the God who *chose* to take the initiative in reaching out to her. God made promises directly to her, including a secure future *without* a husband. God did all this with a woman who was not part of the Chosen People. She was Egyptian, not Hebrew—yet her story was preserved through storytelling by the *Jewish* people for centuries. The story was eventually written and, centuries later, became part of the Bible we hold in our hands today. Hagar was named. Hagar is remembered.

This story teaches us so much about how God loves and is attentive to all people, especially those in desperate situations. The Arab people of today's world are living proof of God's promises and purpose. As modern-day Christians, we don't hear much about Hagar and her role as the mother of Abraham's firstborn or as the ancestral mother of the people known as Arabs.

Hagar would be considered an "outsider" on several levels. She lived and worked outside her homeland/culture/ethnic group. She was used and abused as a slave. She had no social or legal status. She was cast aside and ignored by the people around her. And yet, according to the Bible, our Great God chose her . . .

- To be the first person to be visited by the angel of the LORD, whom many scholars believe to be the pre-incarnate Jesus (before he became human).
- To be the first person ever to be told the gender and name of an unborn child.
- To be the first person to give God a name: "The God Who Sees Me."
- To be the mother of a great nation—the people known today as the Arabs.

Let Hagar's voice remind you that God wants a personal relationship with each person, that each person's pain is known by God and, regardless of your station or situation in life, God may choose to speak through you to bring God's truth or blessing to others.

Biblical Truths Taught through the Story of Hagar

1. God appears and communicates to people other than Jews and Christians
2. God communicates directly to and through women.
3. God does not place value on people based on their status (or lack thereof), heritage, religion, or life circumstances.
4. God instructs and informs women who, in turn, share their knowledge with powerful men.
5. God knows each person by name and wants a personal relationship with each person. Such a relationship empowers individuals to do seemingly impossible things.
6. God listens to people regardless of their gender, ethnic or religious backgrounds, or status in life.
7. God can change even dire circumstances into blessings.

Why the Voice of Hagar Matters . . .

To women: because Hagar's story provides evidence that women can speak directly with God since Hagar spoke to God in this biblical account and was the first human voice which gave God a name in the biblical record.

To men: because Hagar's story shows how compelling a woman's influence can be when sharing God's instructions with men, since Scripture implies it was Hagar's voice that informed Abram of the name to be given their son, and he agreed.

To outsiders: because Hagar's story shows that God blesses people outside "The Chosen" since she was not one of "The Chosen" and yet, God specifically chose Hagar for a significant role with its own unique blessings.

To the abused, mistreated, forgotten, and overlooked: because Hagar's story says God sees you; God hears you; God has a unique purpose only you can fulfill; and God wants a relationship with you.

Questions Raised by the Story of Hagar

How did the author of the book of Genesis get the details of this story of Hagar and her encounter with the angel since the author was not an eyewitness?

Why do some people assume Christians are the only ones who can hear directly from God?

Why do some men think they cannot be taught spiritual truths by women?

Who are the outsiders in your church, workplace, community, and/or family who need to be acknowledged for their valuable contributions or helped to understand that God hears them individually and wants a relationship with each of them?

If you had been the person writing the book of Genesis, why would you think it was so important to include this story about an Egyptian woman even though the rest of the book is more about God's relationship to the Hebrews/Israelites?

What are two ways you can help or encourage "outsiders" in your church or community?

What has been the most empowering encounter you have ever experienced? What kind of resilient confidence did it give you?

Considering the fact that the angel of the LORD chose to appear *first* to this Egyptian slave girl instead of to any of the male patriarchs we know from Scripture, what can you learn from that?

Since the biblical record has preserved this story of a woman on the outside of the promise given to Abram in Genesis 12:1-3, what does this tell you about those with whom God chooses to communicate?

How does this story empower you—as a woman or an outsider—to know there is a God who sees you, who hears you, who wants to have a relationship with you, and who wants to bless you?

If you are in a leadership role of any ministry, how does this story challenge you regarding the types of women who are already involved in your ministry and those who are not yet involved? Why do you think some of those women not yet involved may feel like outsiders?

Hagar's Keys to Resilient Confidence

She had no control over her circumstances. Hagar was the slave girl in a home where she was misused by Abram and Sarai when they chose to get ahead of God's promise to them. Sarai's plot to give Hagar to Abram to become a surrogate mother—while culturally appropriate—was not God's Plan A. When Hagar got pregnant, she started looking down on Sarai and then Sarai harshly mistreated Hagar, causing Hagar to run away into the wilderness. And that's when **God chose Hagar—the pregnant, Egyptian slave girl—to be the first person to encounter the "angel of the LORD,"** which many scholars believe to be an *appearance of Jesus before he became human!*

The angel initiated a conversation with her by calling her by name—the *only* one in the story who *ever* called her by name. Then, **God gave her a personal promise and a responsibility.** Hagar responded with obedience.

1. An Empowering Encounter

Hagar's first key to resilient confidence was her empowering encounter with God. In that encounter, **Hagar gave God a name—the first person *ever* to do so in the Bible!** The name she gave God means "The God Who Sees Me." Hagar—the outsider, the foreigner, not even part of the Covenant People—experienced the *personal* attention of God—the Creator and Ruler of the Universe—regardless of her nationality, her gender, her social status, or even her religious beliefs. No matter *who* you are or *where* you are:

- God sees you
- God knows your name
- God hears you
- God has promises for you
- And God wants a personal encounter with *you*!

2. A Purpose Grounded in a Relationship with God

Hagar was a sex slave with no claim to the Chosen People, and yet, God's gift to her was a purposeful and secure future. **Hagar's second key to resilient confidence was a purpose grounded in relationship with God.** And it's in the context of such a relationship with God, that God's gift to you will be security.

Since God was willing to make a special appearance to endow a young, pregnant, foreign slave girl with a personal promise and the courage to return to less than ideal circumstances, what do you think God is willing to do for someone who has already committed to serve in Christ's name? (See Ephesians 1 for starters.)

I believe Hagar would tell us the path to resilience is this:

- Believe God knows you and calls you by name
- Trust God's promises
- Encounter God personally.

When you embrace the fact that the Creator of the universe knows you by name and that the truth of God's promises apply to you personally, you have all you need to withstand anything: family crises, health scares, tragic news, devastating events, even death! When you know you have encountered the Savior and have allowed him to become your Lord, then that *one* encounter will change the rest of your life and give you the kind of resilient confidence that will carry you through anything and everything.

"Hagar named the LORD *who spoke to her, 'You are El Roi [*Or God who sees *or* God whom I've seen*].'"*
—Genesis 16:13 (CEB)

PART THREE

God Chose Miriam

THE TIME OF ISRAEL'S EXODUS

ca. 1800 - 1200 BCE

5

Events that Shaped the World of Miriam

THE TIME OF ISRAEL'S EXODUS
ca. 1800 - 1200 BCE

After the stories of Hagar and Ishmael, the biblical record focuses on the lineage of Abraham through his second son, Isaac. Isaac grew up as the delight of his parents Abraham and Sarah. He married Rebekah and they had twin sons, Jacob and Esau. Jacob would later marry Leah and Rachel and have twelve sons and one daughter with his wives and their two maids, Bilhah and Zilpah. God later changed Jacob's name to Israel. Later, ten of Jacob/Israel's sons and two of his grandsons became known as the twelve tribes of Israel which would make up the nation of Israel. They are also known as the Hebrews, the Israelites, or the Jewish people —the people group of the Bible—from which the Messiah would one day be born. (That select people group is not quite the same as the broader political and geographical borders we know today as the nation of Israel. The nation of Israel today is a modern political entity—a country with disputed borders—comprising many different ethnic groups.) Due to a famine in Palestine, Jacob/Israel's family eventually settled in Egypt and continued to grow for multiple generations over 400 years.

Happenings in the Rest of the World

Those things occurred in Palestine sometime between 1800 and 1200 BCE. During this time in the rest of the world:

- The Chinese developed their system of written characters.
- Hammurabi of Babylonia became the ruler in Mesopotamia.
- Syrian and Palestinian armies invaded Egypt.
- Egypt was ruled by a female pharaoh, Hatshepsut, 1507-1458 BCE; Egyptian artists created the masterwork portrait sculpture of Queen Nefertiti; the Egyptians established an understanding of

the afterlife; Egypt ruled most of Canaan, including Palestine (1550-1200 BCE).

- The Aryan peoples arrived in the Indus Valley (modern-day Pakistan) around 1500 BCE; their priests sang hymns that became part of the Hindu religion; the caste system was developed.
- Eurasian had two-wheeled chariot as supreme military weapon.
- Script alphabets developed in the Mediterranean region.
- The first settled communities appeared in the Americas, and by 1200 BCE, the Chavin people were the first civilization in South America and the first to make things from gold. As skilled stone workers, they built temples to their gods.
- In Central America, the Olmecs built temples to their gods at San Lorenzo and La Venta, and sculpted unique, huge stone heads.
- Zoroaster was born in ancient Persia (modern-day Iran) and became a prophet. The growth of his philosophy became the religion known as Zoroastrianism and was the national religion of Persia. The historical dates of Zoroaster's life are questioned by scholars. Some place Zoroaster in this millennium and others place him around 600 BCE. Some scholars have speculated that the wise men who visited the infant Jesus sometime around 4 BCE may have been followers of Zoroaster.

Focusing on the Bible's Story

Also in this era, the Egyptian pharaohs, out of fear of the growing population of the Israelites, began to enslave them. After 430 years, according to the biblical text (see Exodus 12:40), God helped Moses lead the Israelites out of slavery in Egypt toward the Promised Land, the land of Canaan promised to Abraham more than six centuries earlier. Scholars have estimated the Exodus occurred sometime between 1500 and 1200 BCE. And that's where the story of Miriam, the older sister of Moses, will commence.

Let's listen to the voice of Miriam, when God chose her to be first. . . .

6

Miriam's Story

ca. 1600-1200 BCE

God chose Miriam's voice to be the first . . .

-Woman prophet among the Israelites

- Praise and worship leader

Miriam's heart was full. She stood tall with her brother Moses on the hillside watching as the last of the Israelites crossed through the dry seabed to safety on the other side of the Red Sea. Guided by the light of the pillar of fire provided by God Almighty, it had taken all night for the throngs of people to get across. Moses had sent his older brother Aaron on ahead to lead the people toward the place they would set up camp. Miriam and Moses would bring up the rear to be sure everyone made it across. They started down the rocky path to join their people who had just experienced another miracle of God's protection. Miriam's mind was swimming with memories of recent weeks of all the plagues their people had survived as God had used more and more threatening efforts to get Pharaoh's attention. The results had been tragic for the Egyptians, but now her people were walking out of slavery and into freedom and her "baby brother" was the one God had chosen to lead them to a new home. She and Aaron were close at hand to lend support and help.

"Mother would have been so proud of you, Moses. I'm sorry she's not here to see how God is using you to help our people."

"Thank you, Miriam," a humble Moses replied. "I can take none of the credit. This is God's doing. I didn't want this job. I argued with God about taking it, but God had a plan that wouldn't be changed." He helped his elder sister navigate the rocks and boulders down the hillside.

"Moses, I know God will make a way for us to get to safety, but I don't understand how God is going to protect us once we're out in the wilderness."

He didn't want to add to his sister's worry, but Moses wondered the same thing—*How would God protect this massive, defenseless throng of people from one of the strongest armies in the world?* Laden with wagons for the very young and the very old, carrying bags and bundles filled with the riches of Egypt, more than two million people couldn't help but move at what seemed a snail's pace. Keeping them safe was just one of the reasons Moses felt he was the wrong guy for this job, but like everything else in this experience, God always seemed to appear in the most unusual ways. Moses had no choice but to pray God would do the same thing now—and soon.

As the morning sun rose in the east, the Red Sea was still parted and stood in two walls on either side of the path through the dry seabed across which the Israelites had walked. Just as God had promised, the pillar of cloud that was leading them through the wilderness had moved behind them to shield them from Pharaoh's army. Moses and Miriam walked by faith toward the east, knowing that Pharaoh's minions would soon be in sight again coming behind them. They didn't know exactly what God would do to protect them from the Egyptian army, but they trusted the God who had led them this far.

The sun shone down onto the dry seabed and reflected off the walls of water on either side. Moses and Miriam stopped to look back and were stunned to see that the army had stopped advancing. They were still quite a distance away, but from Moses and Miriam's vantage point high above the seabed, they could see that the horses and chariots were running into each other. They were falling and stumbling and being blocked from going forward by some unseen force.

Suddenly Moses was standing firm in place. Miriam wasn't sure what was happening. Moses looked like he was listening to someone. Then she saw Moses stretch out his hand over the sea. As they stood there, Moses with his hand extended and Miriam trying to understand what was happening, the walls of water fell onto the Egyptian army. Miriam hid her face knowing she had just witnessed another tragedy for the Egyptians. Yet, she also knew that God Almighty was making a way for them to be released forever from their cruel slave masters.

~

Soon, Moses and Miriam were back among the Israelites who were setting up camp on this first day of freedom. Even though he was exhausted from the long night's events, Moses recounted for the people what had happened. Some scouts were sent to survey the results at the shore of the Red Sea. They returned with reports of dead soldiers and horses scattered along the sea banks. Because of what the LORD did against the Egyptians, the people feared the LORD and trusted Moses, the LORD's servant.

With great joy, Miriam grabbed her tambourine and gathered her women singers. Together, they sang the whole story in song. Moved by the music and lyrics, Moses called Miriam to the side. "Teach them," Moses said. "Teach all of us the song you've just been given by the LORD. Teach it so our people will teach their children and their children's children."

Miriam could barely believe it. Her song was just an act of worship that she couldn't keep herself from sharing, from proclaiming. She was humbled to think that this song was seen by Moses as a gift from God that was to inspire and bless and be repeated for generations to come. How exhilarating!

"Yes, yes, of course!" she said, so excited that her words seemed to tumble over themselves as her heart tried to absorb the enormity of the moment.

After a time of great celebration with all the people, Moses and Miriam sat down by a fire. They were so tired, they couldn't sleep. They rehearsed all that God had done for them in recent weeks. They talked about the plagues and how the angel of death had passed over Egypt, finally persuading Pharaoh to free their people from slavery. Moses and Miriam recounted incidents of God's grace and protection and the tears flowed freely from hearts overwhelmed with gratitude.

Since Moses was the youngest of his siblings and had grown up in Pharaoh's household away from his birth family, he had questions about his older sister. "Miriam, when did you know you loved to sing?"

Miriam thought back to her childhood. "I guess I have always loved to sing. As a very young child, I remember how Mother would sing whenever she was happy or busy around the house. Do you remember her singing?"

"Not really," Moses replied sadly. "I was still so young when she weaned me and I went to live in Pharaoh's palace."

Miriam nodded and then went back to her memories, "Mother would make up tunes and words and then I guess I just began to do that for myself. I soon discovered how comforting it was to sing when I was scared or lonely. Of course, I wasn't lonely long. First, Aaron was born and I helped Mother by singing to him so she could get her chores done. Then, when you came along, it was a very scary time. Pharaoh had given the edict that all Hebrew baby boys were to be killed. As you know, he was trying to keep our people from increasing in number. Mother hid you for as long as she could. I sang a lot during that time. She was able to muffle most of your whimpers, but anytime she could not stop you from crying, she would ask me to sing loudly so no one would suspect there was a baby in the house."

"I'm sure that's what kept me alive during those first few months!" Moses reached out to squeeze Miriam's hand.

Miriam smiled and was grateful for her brother's humble attitude. As she looked at the face of this aged man in the firelight, it was hard to believe he was her younger brother! She saw him now as a strong, confident leader. She was ashamed of her previous doubts about Moses being chosen to lead their people out of Egypt since he had been gone so long and had established roots in another country with a family there. Yet, when she stopped to think about the miraculous events that had occurred to get Moses into Pharaoh's household as a young child and for him to be educated in the affairs of state, she remembered how God had prepared him for this specific role. She looked around at a quiet campsite where almost everyone was sleeping and resting after the events of the past few weeks and months. She almost had to pinch herself to believe that her people were finally free from Pharaoh's oppression and that her family had been chosen to be part of God's perfect plan.

She knew she would have much to sing about in the days ahead!

The Bible Speaks

Miriam's story is found in Exodus 2, 15; Numbers 12, 20, 26; Deuteronomy 24:9; I Chronicles 6:3; and Micah 6:4

The story of Miriam—the only woman in the Bible whose story starts in childhood and ends with her death—begins in Exodus 2:1-10. In that passage she is not even given a name, yet most scholars identify the big sister of Moses in Exodus 2 as Miriam based on later verses, such as Exodus 15:20. Miriam was born in Egypt to an Israelite slave family. At that time, her people had been slaves in Egypt for 400 years. The stories the Israelites knew of their forefathers Abraham, Isaac, Jacob, and Joseph were centuries old! Read Exodus 1:8 and you'll see that no one else—and especially not the new Egyptian pharaoh—shared the same memories the Israelites held of their ancestors.

Today, many people in our American culture know the story of the Exodus thanks to the 1956 classic movie, "The Ten Commandments," and could probably tell you that the one who led the Israelites out of Egypt was Moses. Children growing up in Sunday School may hear the story of Moses as a baby in the bulrushes. Some children may have learned the detail that it was Moses' big sister, Miriam, who stood by her baby brother's basket in the Nile River until the Egyptian princess found him and saved his life. What other details and biblical truths can the life of Miriam teach us almost 3,500 years after the time God chose her to be first?

Miriam's Emerging Leadership
Exodus 2:1 - 10

1 Now a man from Levi's household married a Levite woman. **2** The
woman became pregnant and gave birth to a son. She saw that the baby
was healthy and beautiful, so she hid him for three months. **3** When she
couldn't hide him any longer, she took a reed basket and sealed it up with
black tar. She put the child in the basket and set the basket among the
reeds at the riverbank. **4** The baby's older sister stood watch nearby to see
what would happen to him.

5 Pharaoh's daughter came down to bathe in the river, while her women servants walked along beside the river. She saw the basket among the reeds, and she sent one of her servants to bring it to
her. **6** When she opened it, she saw the child. The boy was crying, and she felt sorry for him. She said, "This must be one of the Hebrews' children."

7 Then the baby's sister said to Pharaoh's daughter, "Would you like me to go and find one of the Hebrew women to nurse the child for you?"

8 Pharaoh's daughter agreed, "Yes, do that." So the girl went and
called the child's mother. **9** Pharaoh's daughter said to her, "Take this child and nurse it for me, and I'll pay you for your work." So the woman
took the child and nursed it. **10** After the child had grown up, she brought him back to Pharaoh's daughter, who adopted him as her son. She named him Moses, "because," she said, "I pulled him out of the water." (CEB)

Biblical historians have estimated the time of the Exodus somewhere between 1500 and 1200 BCE. They have also helped us determine that Miriam was about seven years old when she boldly approached the Pharaoh's daughter that day. She stood watch over the basket her mother Jochebed had waterproofed and placed into the Nile River. What an empowering responsibility Miriam had been given by her mother. Her ability to approach confidently the princess and to voice a strategic request in the face of power and privilege gives us several insights into Miriam's characteristics.

1. She was courageous—in spite of the risks—for the sake of a bigger purpose.
2. She had a voice and was not timid in using it, even though she was a slave speaking to a member of the ruling family.
3. She was cunning—or had the cleverness to fulfill her mother's plan—which resulted in their family being able to keep Baby Moses until he was weaned.

If we fast forward through Exodus 3-14 to get the Israelites out of Egypt, we'll come to Exodus 15 which begins with a wonderful song of praise to God for the deliverance of the Israelites out of the hand of Pharaoh. We are then reintroduced to Miriam.

The Prophet Miriam Serves as the First Praise and Worship Leader
Exodus 15:20-21
20 Then the prophet Miriam, Aaron's sister, took a tambourine in her hand. All the women followed her playing tambourines and dancing. **21** Miriam sang the refrain back to them:

Sing to the LORD, for an overflowing victory!
Horse and rider he threw into the sea! (CEB)

This song, one of the oldest pieces of Hebrew poetry, would be memorized and passed down through the generations before it was ever written down. While Exodus 15:20-21 appear to be the only verses to Miriam's song, biblical scholar Phyllis Trible explained that other "historical and literary studies" of this passage show that the whole song beginning in Exodus 15:1 "is itself the Song of Miriam" and belongs to Jewish "women's traditions that include the long Songs of Deborah (Judges 5:1-31) and Hannah (1 Samuel 2:1-10)" (Trible 2001, 128).

Since I am married to a worship leader with a passion for beautiful, sacred choral music, it is fascinating to me that this is the first place in the Bible where anyone is noted for composing a song and playing a musical instrument while leading others to sing and praise God. **This makes Miriam the first praise and worship leader mentioned in the Bible.**

Miriam is also called a prophet in these verses. Prophets were primarily people who were given divine authority by God to communicate messages to the people. Sometimes their messages had predictive qualities to them, but that was usually secondary to their main purpose of communicating God's will. While Miriam is not the first prophet mentioned in the Bible, **she is the first *woman* prophet mentioned in the Bible**. (The Bible identifies at least five other women prophets: Deborah, Huldah, Noadiah, Anna, Philip's daughters, and some unnamed ones; and other women make prophetic statements, but are not identified as prophets.)

Interestingly, women prophets were common among other people groups surrounding the Israelites during this same time period. During this period of history between 1600 and 1200 BCE, many people groups around the world worshipped goddesses or revered their rulers as gods on earth. The Israelites had spent 400 years in Egypt among people who worshipped the pharaoh as a god. Most other people groups were also polytheistic, worshiping many gods. One of the distinct characteristics of the Israelites was their monotheism, the worship of one God.

Miriam's Leadership—The Good, the Bad, and the Ugly

Miriam's leadership was not without its flaws. One of the indicators that biblical stories are true is that they reveal both the good and bad qualities of the leaders portrayed. Most other histories of ancient people groups leave out the negative events or character traits of leaders. In the years to come, Miriam would have an episode in her life when she questioned the actions of Moses and God punished her for seven days with leprosy. She was restored to health, but she had to suffer some consequences for her behavior. This story is found in Numbers 12. Verse 15 from that chapter indicates just how much the people loved and respected Miriam:

Numbers 12:14-16

14 The LORD said to Moses, "If her father had spit in her face, would she not be shamed for seven days? Let her be shut out of the camp for seven days, and afterward she will be brought back." **15** So they shut Miriam out of the camp seven days. And the people didn't march until Miriam was brought back. **16** Afterward the people marched from Hazeroth, and they camped in the Paran desert. (CEB)

The people stayed near to Miriam until her punishment was over and then they marched on to the next place. Obviously, they did not want to abandon Miriam. This act on the people's part demonstrated their acknowledgement of the shared leadership between Moses, Aaron, and Miriam. And I'm sure it took all three of them. They must have been extremely organized because it is estimated that the number of Hebrews who crossed the Red Sea on their way to freedom numbered approximately 2.4 million—that is compared to the whole population of Houston, Texas, plus another 100,000 or so! The numbers may be difficult for us to imagine in the literal sense; the point is that it took a series of miracles to get all the Hebrews out of Egypt and on their way to the Promised Land.

Sadly, as revered as all three of these siblings were, none of them would actually get to enter the Promised Land. We learn first of Miriam's death in Numbers 20:1, "In the first month, the entire Israelite community entered the Zin desert and the people stayed at Kadesh. Miriam died and was buried there" (CEB). She was the eldest of the three siblings and the first to pass away. Yet, when you skip over to the small book of the prophet Micah among the 12 Minor Prophets in the Bible, you'll see that even 500 years after Miriam's death, the Jews still remembered her as an important leader along with Moses and Aaron. As a prophet, Micah spoke for God, "My people, what did I ever do to you? How have I wearied you? Answer me! I brought you up out of the land of Egypt; I redeemed you from the house of slavery. I sent Moses, Aaron, and Miriam before you" (Micah 6:3-4, CEB). All three siblings were remembered for their leadership.

We have a record of Moses' and Aaron's descendants, but none are mentioned for Miriam in the biblical text, and neither is a husband named. If Miriam was single, what a great example of spiritual leadership by a single woman in ancient times.

The Message in Miriam's Voice

Miriam's story inspires me to seek out the voices of women who sing praises and write hymns and Christian literature and who are women theologians. When the church does not hear the voices of both women and men in leadership and in worship, we are missing out on distinct gifts and perspectives with which God has blessed people and through whom God wants to speak. Let Miriam's voice remind you that all voices are welcome in worship and the people with gifts of music, songwriting, poetry writing, dramatic reading, acting, hymn writing, visual, and other creative arts should be invited to share their gifts in worship in some way.

Biblical Truths Taught through the Story of Miriam:

1. God's praise is sometimes best expressed through a woman.
2. God has been choosing women—at least since the time of the Exodus—to compose hymns of faith and to lead both women and men in singing them.
3. God sometimes chooses girls and women to enter difficult situations to provide the necessary leadership.
4. God often provides a team of leaders to share the load. Teams made up of both genders is a good thing for both the leaders and those they lead.

Why the Voice of Miriam Matters . . .

To women: because Miriam's story shows how she was empowered even as a child to use her voice among the powerful and mighty ruling classes. Consider how this prepared Miriam for her future leadership roles.

To men: because Miriam's story demonstrates that male leaders would do well to seek out women's unique perspectives and abilities and learn to share leadership roles, just as the great leader Moses depended on his sister Miriam's leadership gifts.

To singers and musicians: because Miriam's story shows that praising God for provision, leadership, and mercy is sometimes led best by the voice of a woman.

To preachers: because Miriam's story illustrates how a woman's perspective on God's activity in the world is necessary to be able to communicate God's *whole* message to the people.

To singles: because Miriam's story helps us see that single women have much to offer as spiritual leaders. The Bible gives no indication that

Miriam was married, yet it was her leadership *as a single woman* that was remembered and appreciated by her people all those years.

Questions Raised by the Story of Miriam

How can knowing that the first praise and worship leader in the Bible was a woman help you encourage other women to take on leadership roles in the church?

Are there women in your church whose voices need to be heard in leadership and/or worship? How would their voices make a difference in the way a message is received or delivered?

What do you imagine Miriam's other leadership duties may have been as she worked with Moses and Aaron?

Consider the leaders of praise and worship in your church. Is there a balance of female and male voices? Does the music ministry provide a place for both female and male singers and instrumentalists?

What do you think Moses would say about the need for women's leadership in praise and worship today?

Why do some churches still insist on male-only worship leadership or continue to suppress girls' and women's voices as leaders?

Why do you think it is important for praise and worship leaders today to know that Miriam, the first woman prophet, was also the first-ever praise and worship leader for God's people?

When does your ministry leadership team—or you, personally—take time to celebrate what God is doing in your midst?

Miriam's Key to Resilient Confidence

I believe Miriam would tell us that praising God with song reminds us that God is the source of our confidence and that learning to praise God is a path to resilient confidence.

The Power of Praising God

We know that praising God is powerful! Many of the psalms of David illustrate how the process of starting out fearful or angry can end up strong, confident, and joyful if we take our focus off ourselves or our situation and shift our gaze toward the God of the universe. A wonderful thing happens in this process: the more we voice our praises to God, the closer we feel to God. Also, the more room we give the Holy Spirit in our hearts and minds, the more we will be able to release those negative feelings and emotions.

Praise is different from gratitude. It is so easy to thank God for our blessings. We can rattle those off without even thinking. Praise is not a "thank you." Praise is an acknowledgement of WHO God is: the Almighty, our Savior, our Heavenly Father/Parent, our Shepherd, our Great Physician, our Creator, and our Sustainer (you can add to the list).

Praising God is an act that reminds you to WHOM you are talking. It establishes your relationship to God and helps you remember that you are the created one. Focusing on praise can be difficult because it is so much easier to slip into thanking God for what God has done. Bring yourself back to praise by filling in this blank, "God, you are the ______________."

Empowering People with Praise

Business gurus of our day have discovered that people can be much more productive if they focus on their strengths instead of their weaknesses. (See the book *StrengthsFinder 2.0* by Tom Rath.) I like this approach. I know it works in my own life. When I am doing what I do best, I work harder, enjoy it more, and the time flies. I definitely get more done and feel more fulfilled when I am in my element.

I learned years ago to keep a "rose file" where you store those memories and notes of encouragement or gratitude. Then, when you're having "one of those days," you can pull them out to be reminded that you have brought value to others in the past and it will happen again. We all have "those" days! (Even Miriam had "one of those days" in Numbers 12.)

How can we praise others in such a way that they will feel empowered to function more in their strengths? Remember, we are striving to point out details about their unique qualities more than thanking them for a task.

Here are 3 principles for empowering people with praise:

1. Notice the positive details of their personalities.

Acknowledge the joy their laughter brings. Mention the encouragement produced by their listening skills. Use them as examples of bringing organization or harmony to your group. Give them credit for their curiosity by repeating aloud points they made or questions they asked.

2. Recognize their specific strengths by matching them to roles that will use those strengths.

Brag on their friendliness and ask them to help welcome newcomers. Acknowledge their attention to detail and ask them to proofread your report. Tell them that their abilities to see the potential in plans or people could be helpful in forming new teams or planning a new project.

3. Ask them when/how they realized they had an interest/ ability in ______.

This will help them talk about themselves and will give you a chance to learn more about them so you can go back and apply Principle 1.

As with most things in life, these principles really boil down to relationships. How much effort are you investing in others? Are you taking the time to really get to know the people serving and working alongside you? Knowing their strengths and making sure they are functioning in those strengths will make your organization much more productive and more joy-filled.

How Do Your Prayers Praise God?

Taking time in your prayers to acknowledge WHO God is reminds you who you are *not* (and that *is* humbling). Praising God's omnipresence, omniscience, and omnipotence keeps things in perspective. Here are a few more examples of ways other women have praised God through the centuries:

"There is no Holy One like the LORD; no one besides you; there is no Rock like our God" (prayed by Hannah, 1 Samuel 2:2 NRSV).

"My spirit rejoices in God my Savior" (spoken by Mary, the mother of Jesus, Luke 1:47 NRSV).

"Yes, Lord, I believe that you are the Messiah, the Son of God, the one coming into the world" (spoken by Martha of Bethany as the first public messianic confession allowed by Jesus, John 11:27 NRSV).

Let your voice praise God in song, in prayer, and in daily conversation, and you will develop resilient confidence.

"Miriam sang . . . :
'Sing to the LORD, for an overflowing victory!"
—Exodus 15:21 (CEB)

PART FOUR

God Chose Deborah and Hannah

THE TIME OF ISRAEL'S JUDGES

ca. 1400 - 1100 BCE

7

Events that Shaped the World of Deborah and Hannah

THE TIME OF ISRAEL'S JUDGES
ca. 1400 - 1100 BCE

After the death of Moses, Joshua led the Israelites into the Promised Land sometime between 1400-1200 BCE. The biblical account in the books of Joshua and Judges tells how the Israelites drove out the people who were already in the land so they, themselves, could possess it; yet, they did not drive out everyone. The Philistines were one group which remained. The Lord warned the Israelites if they did not do a complete job, they would be tempted to follow the other gods of the people they let remain. And that is exactly what happened. The Israelites were oppressed by surrounding kings and nations who were bigger, stronger, and had a more powerful military. The people quit obeying the Lord's commands and disaster overtook them. The Israelites started a cycle of disobedience, disaster, crying out to the Lord for deliverance, and the Lord providing a new leader—a judge—to guide them to victory and peace. Then the Israelites would get comfortable and forget about the Lord again and the cycle would repeat. This went on for generations over the course of about 300 years during which Israel had 13 judges. The stories of the time of Israel's judges are recorded in the biblical books of Judges, Ruth, and 1 Samuel.

Happenings in the Rest of the World

While all of that was going on in the land of Palestine between 1400 and 1100 BCE, other parts of the world were seeing the following things happening:

- The Trojan War occurred in what we know as modern-day Turkey (if it was historical; many think the war was just mythical).

- In Egypt, Pharaoh Rameses II led an immense building program, and the last ruler of the 19th dynasty was Queen Twosret. Women in Egypt were advancing in the arts as professional musicians. The Egyptian woman poet, Phautasia, wrote about the Trojan War. This may have been the source used later by Homer.
- In Europe, the Slav peoples became established in Poland.
- China's bronze production developed to include musical instruments such as drums and bells and elaborate vessels for food and wine. One of China's queens, Fu Hao, was buried at this time and her burial chamber revealed that she served as a military general and a high priestess.

Focusing on the Bible's Story

Apparently, women leaders were emerging around the world, so it's not surprising, then, that a woman would also lead Israel. Scholars have estimated the forty-year span of the prophet Deborah's leadership as a judge over Israel was around 1209-1169 BCE. Deborah was the fourth in the line of Israel's 13 judges and the first prophet among the judges, as well as the first and only woman judge. The last judge, Samuel, was only the second prophet among all the judges. Samuel's mother was Hannah who lived shortly after Deborah and in the same territory of Ephraim, in central Palestine, where Deborah lived. Since it is estimated that Samuel was born around 1105 BCE, Hannah's life spanned the years sometime between 1150 and 1050.

Let's listen to the voices of Deborah and Hannah, when God chose them to be first. . . .

8

Deborah's Story

ca. 1250 - 1150 BCE

God chose Deborah's voice to be the first . . .
- Prophet's voice to judge Israel
- And only woman's voice to judge Israel

Deborah and her assistants appreciated the westerly breeze from the direction of the Great Mediterranean Sea. It provided a welcome respite at the end of a long day of hearing difficult discussions between disagreeable people. The palm tree grove in this arid land was an oasis in this hilly area in the territory of Ephraim. The people from the various tribes of Israel came to this particular place to meet with the judge, Deborah, the prophet. There, under the large, colorful awnings, and with the help of servants to fan the people with wide palm leaves, the people waited to ask the judge to decide their legal disputes. Some days were easier than others, yet this had not been one of those days.

~

Deborah arrived home at the end of that long day in the judge's seat and plopped herself down on the bench at the table. Her role was fulfilling and purposeful, yet, the difficult cases had developed within her a keener understanding of God's frustration with a sinful people.

"How many cases did you hear today?" asked Lappidoth, her husband, as he put down his tool cleaning project.

"I think there were six today . . . no, seven. A case came in just as we were preparing to leave."

"So, which one was the most interesting today?"

Deborah sighed, "Unfortunately, most of today's cases were typical: land allotments in the case of a marriage, disagreements over livestock ownership, and the distribution of property after a father's death.

However, there was one bright spot." Deborah stretched to soothe her tired body.

"Oh? What was that?" asked an attentive Lappidoth.

"A young couple came in on the brink of divorce. After a long discussion and some tearful confessions, the young man withdrew his divorce decree. We talked about some better ways to express misunderstandings and some kinder ways to show feelings of frustration. I think they're going to make it."

"I bet that felt good, knowing you helped a marriage survive," Lappidoth said with his usual encouraging tone.

Deborah smiled and squeezed his hand across the table.

"I think there is some of your favorite dried fish we can have for supper. And our neighbor brought us some of her date cakes just before you got home," Lappidoth said as he got up to clear his project from the table.

"You know, I think I'm too tired to eat tonight. I think I'll just have some tea out in the courtyard, if you don't mind."

Lappidoth knew how draining his wife's work as a judge was. He also couldn't be more proud of her. To think, their God Yahweh had chosen his wife to guide, direct, and lead their people Israel. The three previous judges had helped Israel through some difficult times as good military leaders but they had not been God's spokespersons. Deborah was the first prophet God had chosen to lead the people since the time of Joshua when he led the Israelites as they entered the Promised Land.

At this time, however, it seemed the people needed spiritual guidance as much as military leadership in their judge. Deborah had followed in the footsteps of another great woman prophet from a much earlier time: their foremother Miriam, Moses' sister. Deborah's reputation as a prophet had traveled far and wide and the people had grown to respect her compassionate, godly wisdom she so generously shared. Lappidoth would leave her in peace in her favorite corner of the courtyard where she often heard God's voice the clearest.

~

The next morning, Lappidoth awoke to an empty bed. He soon found Deborah at the table writing diligently by the light of the oil lamp as the dawn crept in through the shutters.

"You are up early," greeted a sleepy Lappidoth.

"Oh, I hope I didn't wake you," Deborah said as she looked up from her papyrus, dipping her quill in the ink pot. "I heard a message from Yahweh last night and I must send a message to Commander Barak today. God has finally promised us a victory over King Jabin!"

"After these 20 years of oppression, surely that will be welcome news to Barak!" Lappidoth exclaimed.

"Well, I'm afraid he may be a bit reluctant to fulfill this command."

"Oh, I'm sure you can persuade him, Deborah. You always do."

Deborah put the finishing touches on her message, tied it up in a roll and sealed it. She slid it into a leather pouch and got ready to take it to her messenger. "I'll return shortly and then we'll have breakfast. I need to get this off to Barak as soon as possible." With that, she headed out into the early morning light. The pebbly path crunched beneath her sandals as she hurried to summon her messenger. He would then take a day or so to deliver the leather pouch north to the territory of Naphtali where her military commander Barak lived.

Barak would need several days to make the journey southward to meet with Deborah, which would give her some time to develop a way to convince Barak of the power of God's prophetic word.

It had been several generations since the people of Israel had heard a prophet among them. The three previous judges God had chosen to lead the Israelites were great military leaders, but they were not known for speaking God's message to the people.

The last prophet her people had known was Joshua who had succeeded Moses. Deborah had questioned God many times why she was chosen to be the first woman and the first prophet among the judges that God appointed to lead the Israelites, but God was silent in response to that particular question. So she tried to focus on serving God with the gifts she was given: discernment, wisdom, courage, and patience. She knew the military battle before them would require all those gifts and more. She knew she was completely dependent on the God who had chosen her. And she had also learned the value of allowing others to share in the efforts of accomplishing God's purposes. While God alone would receive the glory, she and her co-laborers could share the joy of being part of God's work.

The Bible Speaks

Deborah's story is found in Judges 4-5

God *chose* Israel's 13 judges listed in Scripture; they were not elected by the people nor did they inherit their role. This period of the Judges lasted about 300 years. Judges were often the military leaders of the people who led the Israelites to victory over the neighboring nations. These stories were told to each succeeding generation as a way to forge them into a people who knew they were chosen by God and who knew they had a relationship with the Almighty. Of all the stories told about the judges, the ones we have in our Bible were the ones finally written down many years after the actual events. Their purpose was and is to remind the Israelites of God's protection and provision for them as a nation. Judges were God's original plan for the Israelites. God filled the role of King for the nation.

Deborah, God's Choice for Israel

Deborah was appointed by God to be the ***first of only two prophets and the only woman in the line of judges*** who would lead Israel to victory over their enemies. In Scripture, God-chosen prophets had the role of being God's messengers and interpreting the people's circumstances in light of God's laws more than they foretold the future. Deborah's story is found in two chapters in the Bible, Judges 4-5.

Judges 4:4-5

4 Now Deborah, a prophet, the wife of Lappidoth, was a leader of Israel
at that time. **5** She would sit under Deborah's palm tree between Ramah
and Bethel in the Ephraim highlands, and the Israelites would come to
her to settle disputes. (CEB)

Deborah was the fourth of the 13 God-chosen judges Israel had before the nation had its first king. Her leadership, which lasted 40 years, brought peace to the nation. One of the keys to her confidence and success was her willingness and ability to collaborate with God and others to accomplish things beyond their individual abilities.

Deborah Prophesies a Military Victory
Judges 4:1-3, 6-7

1 After Ehud had died, the Israelites again did things that the LORD saw
as evil. **2** So the LORD gave them over to King Jabin of Canaan, who
reigned in Hazor. The commander of his army was Sisera, and he was
stationed in Harosheth-ha-goiim. **3** The Israelites cried out to
the LORD because Sisera had nine hundred iron chariots and had
oppressed the Israelites cruelly for twenty years. . . .

6 [Deborah] sent word to Barak, Abinoam's son, from Kedesh in
Naphtali and said to him, "Hasn't the LORD, Israel's God, issued you a
command? 'Go and assemble at Mount Tabor, taking ten thousand men
from the people of Naphtali and Zebulun with you. **7** I'll lure Sisera, the
commander of Jabin's army, to assemble with his chariots and troops
against you at the Kishon River, and then I'll help you overpower
him.'" (CEB)

Deborah's story occurred during the nation of Israel's 20-year period of servitude to a Canaanite ruler who had a well-equipped military with 900 iron chariots. The Israelites were not so well equipped with weapons. God spoke to Deborah with a command for her military leader, Barak, to fight against the wicked ruler and God would give the victory.

Deborah Prophesies How the Military Victory Will Be Won
Judges 4:8-10

8 Barak replied to her, "If you'll go with me, I'll go; but if not, I won't go."

9 Deborah answered, "I'll definitely go with you. However, the path
you're taking won't bring honor to you, because the LORD will hand over
Sisera to a woman." Then Deborah got up and went with Barak to
Kedesh. **10** He summoned Zebulun and Naphtali to Kedesh, and ten

thousand men marched out behind him. Deborah marched out with him too. (CEB)

Barak agreed to go into battle *only* if Deborah accompanied him. She agreed and prophesied that the victory would not be credited to Barak, but instead would be won at the hands of a woman. We learn in Judges 5, known as the Song of Deborah, that God sent a rainstorm that immobilized the iron chariots of the enemy army and allowed Israel to be victorious.

Deborah's Song Acknowledged the LORD as the Victor
Judges 5:4-5

4 LORD, when you set out from Seir,
when you marched out from Edom's fields, the land shook,
the sky poured down,
the clouds poured down water.
5 The mountains quaked
before the LORD, the one from Sinai,
before the LORD, the God of Israel. (CEB)

When the enemy's military leader, Sisera, realized his defeat was sure, he fled on foot to a camp that he thought was friendly territory.

Jael, the Other "Shero" in the Story
Judges 4:17-22

17 Meanwhile, Sisera had fled on foot to the tent of Jael, the wife of Heber
the Kenite, because there was peace between Hazor's King Jabin and the
family of Heber the Kenite. **18** Jael went out to meet Sisera and said to
him, "Come in, sir, come in here. Don't be afraid." So he went with her
into the tent, and she hid him under a blanket.

19 Sisera said to her, "Please give me a little water to drink. I'm
thirsty." So she opened a jug of milk, gave him a drink, and hid him
again. **20** Then he said to her, "Stand at the entrance to the tent. That way,
if someone comes and asks you, 'Is there a man here?' you can say, 'No.'"

21 But Jael, Heber's wife, picked up a tent stake and a hammer. While

Sisera was sound asleep from exhaustion, she tiptoed to him. She drove the stake through his head and down into the ground, and he died. **22** Just then, Barak arrived after chasing Sisera. Jael went out to meet him and said, "Come and I'll show you the man you're after." So he went in with her, and there was Sisera, lying dead, with the stake through his head. (CEB)

Sisera met his doom when a woman named Jael cunningly seduced him into her tent and then drove a tent peg through his head while he was sleeping. Victory was secured at the hands of Jael, fulfilling Deborah's prophecy as we read in Judges 4:9. The author of Judges had implied the victorious woman would be Deborah, yet the later verses and the Song of Deborah clarify that the woman was indeed Jael.

Judges 5:24-27, 31

24 May Jael be blessed above all women;
may the wife of Heber the Kenite
be blessed above all tent-dwelling women.
25 He asked for water, and she provided milk;
she presented him cream in a majestic bowl.
26 She reached out her hand for the stake,
her strong hand for the worker's hammer.
She struck Sisera;
she crushed his head;
she shattered and pierced his skull.
27 At her feet he sank, fell, and lay flat;
at her feet he sank, he fell;
where he sank, there he fell—dead. . . .
31 May all your enemies perish like this, LORD!
But may your allies be like the sun, rising in its strength.
And the land was peaceful for forty years. (CEB)

Deborah's song praised others for the help she received, especially Jael, in winning the victory. As a result of this shared responsibility for this military victory, the nation of Israel enjoyed the next 40 years in peace under Deborah's capable leadership.

The Message in Deborah's Voice

Women can be encouraged by Deborah's story. We don't know if Deborah had children, yet we can sense her maternal instincts of wanting to protect her family—her nation of Israel. God used Deborah's instincts to bring order, determination, and victory to her people. We also know that as a prophet, she spoke to the people for God. Sometimes, a woman's voice is the best vehicle for communicating God's truth and direction. Deborah's use of collaboration, usually seen as a more feminine skill than masculine, allowed more people to enjoy the victory, and kept her from taking the credit away from God, the ultimate protector. Let Deborah's voice remind you that your maternal instincts, your discernment skills, and your ability to work cooperatively with others are exactly the kinds of tools God has chosen through the ages to accomplish God's purposes. Take time to consider how God could use your gifts and abilities to bring God's victory to a situation at home, at the office, in the community, or in your church.

Biblical Truths Taught through the Story of Deborah

1. God chooses women to be both political and spiritual leaders of God's people.
2. God chooses women to govern nations and to be military strategists.
3. God chooses women as prophets through whom God speaks to the people.
4. God communicates directly to and through women.
5. God chooses women to lead and instruct both women and men.
6. God collaborates with good leaders who are careful to praise the work of others publicly and privately.
7. God blesses a leader who exhibits humility and gratitude.

Why the Voice of Deborah Matters . . .

To leaders: because Deborah's story is an example of what can happen when collaboration with God comes first, followed by collaboration with others to build a team, to accomplish far more than you could on your own.

To women: because Deborah's story provides evidence that God chooses women to be peacemakers and judges, to lead nations, to be military commanders, and to help bring God's victory in difficult times.

To men: because Deborah's story shows God sometimes chooses to speak the best leadership strategy through a woman.

Questions Raised by the Story of Deborah

Why was there only one female judge for the Israelites?

Who are other female leaders of nations and militaries throughout history from whom we could learn?

How could collaboration help us accomplish more on any project or in any group?

How are our current leaders in our nation, communities, and churches expressing humility, seeking collaboration, and publicly thanking others for their contributions?

Deborah's Key to Resilient Confidence

Deborah's collaboration was a hallmark of her leadership style and the key to her resilient confidence. Deborah's actions illustrate several practices that are valued today which can help you develop resilient confidence at home, church, work, and in your community:

1. Be prepared with knowledge and be quick to acknowledge your sources.

Confidence does *not* mean you already have all the answers. Confidence comes from fulfilling your responsibility of searching out reliable information and gathering pertinent research. It is *absolutely* necessary for you to give credit where credit is due for information and ideas. Being honest about the fact that you don't know everything and that others were the original sources for the information you are presenting are traits of authenticity and trustworthiness. Deborah knew when the Lord gave her instructions and she informed the people of that.

2. Demonstrate a willingness to do what you are asking others to do.

Confidence grows when you are a servant leader—one who is willing to get her hands dirty and work hard alongside others. After Deborah informed her military commander of God's instructions, he asked her to accompany him into battle and she said, "Yes." Deborah listened to the request of her subordinate and was willing to risk her own life for the lives of others. While your life's roles may not require such an extreme level of participation, you should expect to spend more time patiently explaining and demonstrating (multiple times and/or in multiple ways) how a task needs to be done, or giving personal examples of how you did a similar thing in the past.

3. Express your gratitude both in public and in private to anyone who helps you accomplish a task or achieve a goal.

While it is a good practice to mention people's names in a public expression of thanks, the art of the *handwritten* thank-you note on paper is quickly fading. You can bring it back and it will make you stand out as an appreciative leader. Chapter 5 of Judges is Deborah's thank-you note preserved for the ages. In the form of a song, this is one of the oldest poems in the Hebrew Bible, according to professor Susanne Scholz

(Scholz 2012, 118). In the poem, Deborah expresses praise for God's deliverance and gratitude for her military commander, for other groups who came to their aid, and to the woman, Jael, who was the one who personally defeated their enemy. Noticing the individual contributions of the people who help you will endear you to those people and to the ones who love them. If you are the person in a position of *leadership* who says thanks, your personal words have weight—they are important to the one who receives those words of appreciation. For some, a leader's praise is very empowering. Use any position of leadership to empower and encourage *others*.

These skills of collaboration will not only enhance your resilient confidence, but will also cause others to want to be part of your group because they know you care about them and will appreciate their efforts.

"She would sit . . . and the Israelites would come to her to settle disputes. She sent word to Barak, 'Hasn't the LORD, Israel's God, issued you a command?'"
—Judges 4:5, 6 (CEB)

9

Hannah's Story

ca. 1130 - 1050 BCE

God chose Hannah's voice to be the first . . .
- To use the term "messiah" in a prophetic way

Hannah's faith had grown deep and steadfast over the years in spite of the turmoil in her home. Her years of barrenness had brought much emotional pain and strife in the presence of the taunting Peninah, the haughty childbearing second wife of her husband, Elkanah. Even when he had tried to express his care and concern to Hannah in her low moments, it had only added to her grief of not having children. Yet, through it all, Hannah had held on to her faith, even though it seemed to dangle by a thread.

Finally, all that was in the past. Now the day had come for her to fulfill the vow she had made years ago when she had traveled with Elkanah and his other wife up to the tabernacle of the LORD in Shiloh. She remembered that day as if it were yesterday. For all of Elkanah's kindness, he still lacked an understanding of the deep longing in a woman's heart to bear a child. He had expected Hannah to see him as valuable as ten sons. She knew he just couldn't understand, so she had turned inward and upward instead. In her most desperate state, she had gone alone one day to the entrance of the tabernacle to pray to God to ask for a child. She knew God was the only one who could give her this deep desire of her heart. She had vowed to God that if she were given a son, she would dedicate him to the LORD's service all the days of his life.

She could chuckle to herself now, remembering how the old priest Eli accused her of being drunk just because she was weeping and praying silently while her lips were moving. She had experienced an inexpressible heartache that day. When she had defended her behavior to the priest Eli, he understood and blessed her with words of hope that the God of Israel would grant her petition, even though he did not know the nature of her request. Those words touched her deeply. She felt a new sense of expectation. When she got back to their temporary shelter in Shiloh, even Elkanah noticed the smile on her face and it seemed to make him glad. It also seemed to aggravate Peninah just a bit when her unkind remarks no longer seemed to bother Hannah.

When she returned home to Ramah from that trip to Shiloh, God answered her prayer and she became pregnant. Soon, she gave birth to a son and named him Samuel, meaning "I asked for him from the LORD." And tomorrow, almost five years from the day she made that vow, was the day she would be taking her four-year-old son Samuel back to Shiloh to live and work with Eli there in the tabernacle. She trusted that Eli and the women who served at the tabernacle would raise her son in the ways of the LORD. Hannah had begun to teach him his morning prayers and had demonstrated to the best of her ability the rhythms of a faith-filled, praying life dedicated to the laws of God. She had watched him grow to be a strong, loving child. He was helpful, obedient, and kind-hearted. Her mother's heart trusted that he would be a good servant of the LORD in the tabernacle and throughout his life.

In the midst of her packing for the journey, four-year-old Samuel came bounding into her room. "Is it time to ride the donkey yet, Mother?"

Hannah had been preparing the young boy with details of the new things he would see and experience on this trip instead of focusing on the fact that he would be living with Eli and not coming home with them. "Almost time, Samuel. We will leave before the sun comes up in the morning. Did you help your father fill the grain sack for the donkey?"

"Yes—Father said it would take us the whole day for us to get there!"

"That's right. But we will stop a few times along the way to let the donkey rest. Your father knows a pretty place where we can eat our midday meal and let you run around for awhile. I'm packing some of your favorite date cakes."

An excited Samuel smiled, wrapped his arms around his mother's legs for a brief moment, and then went skipping out of the room.

Hannah paused her work and looked up to heaven to whisper a prayer, "O LORD, you know how much I'm going to miss that boy. Help me stay strong to fulfill my vow to you." Then she carefully folded the small robe she had made for Samuel and placed it in his bag. She knew she was not the first mother to give up her child for the LORD's service, but it was *her* first child she was giving up. This was a different pain than the longing for a child. This was a pain of knowing she would miss Samuel tremendously, but she knew this was the best thing for him and would prepare him for the life God had for him. Not everyone had understood her decision, but it had changed Peninah's attitude toward Hannah. She treated Hannah with a bit more respect.

Hannah was also grateful for Elkanah's willingness to allow her to keep her vow. God's law provided for that and he was faithful to God's law, even though it meant letting his young son grow up in Shiloh. Hannah had often seen a tear well up in Elkanah's eye after playing with young Samuel or teaching him how to feed the animals or how to fish in the stream. She and Elkanah had to keep reminding themselves they were giving him up for a greater purpose.

In preparation for this time of dedicating Samuel to the LORD's service, she had asked Elkanah to write on a scroll the words of a prayer she had been composing in her heart. She wanted to recite it for Samuel when they took him to live at the tabernacle in Shiloh. She also wanted to leave a written version of it with Eli to give to Samuel when he grew old enough to read it for himself. She still did not fully understand some of the phrases in the prayer, but she knew they were from the LORD. Elkanah had asked her, "What did you mean when you said 'God will give strength to his King and exalt the power of his Anointed'? We don't have a king. Who were you talking about?"

Hannah had explained to Elkanah, "I don't know what that means, yet I know God placed those words in my heart. I am trusting our God to give Samuel an understanding of those details someday."

Elkanah was careful to write every word. Hannah was not able to read, yet she knew Samuel would learn to read from the priest Eli. She hoped this prayer would help Samuel understand how grateful to God she was and how much she trusted God to provide for the people who worshiped the one true God.

Hannah rolled up the scroll, kissed it, tied it with a beautiful ribbon she had embroidered, and then tucked it inside a fold of Samuel' s little robe. She went through her list of preparations in her mind once more. She had prepared the ephah of flour and the wineskin with new wine for the sacrifice and Elkanah had selected a fine three-year-old bull they would take with them, which was also required by law. Everything was in order. They would set out for the day's journey to Shiloh before sunup, anticipating the heartache of the trip back home, yet fully trusting in God's promises.

The Bible Speaks

Hannah's story is found in I Samuel 1-2

The experience of infertility is not uncommon in the Bible. The biblical term used is "barrenness" and, unfortunately, the belief in those days was that it was a punishment from God. When a wife was barren in Hannah's day, the husband would usually take another wife in order to have heirs. Those of us in the Western world today have a difficult time imagining such a situation, yet that was Hannah's painful reality.

Hannah Suffers with Barrenness
I Samuel 1:1-8

1 There was a certain man of Ramathaim, a Zuphite from the hill country
of Ephraim, whose name was Elkanah son of Jeroham son of Elihu son of
Tohu son of Zuph, an Ephraimite. **2** He had two wives; the name of the
one was Hannah, and the name of the other Peninnah. Peninnah had
children, but Hannah had no children.

3 Now this man used to go up year by year from his town to worship
and to sacrifice to the LORD of hosts at Shiloh, where the two sons of Eli,
Hophni and Phinehas, were priests of the LORD. **4** On the day when
Elkanah sacrificed, he would give portions to his wife Peninnah and to all
her sons and daughters; **5** but to Hannah he gave a double
portion, because he loved her, though the LORD had closed her
womb. **6** Her rival used to provoke her severely, to irritate her, because

the LORD had closed her womb. **7** So it went on year by year; as often as she went up to the house of the LORD, she used to provoke her. Therefore Hannah wept and would not eat. **8** Her husband Elkanah said to her, "Hannah, why do you weep? Why do you not eat? Why is your heart sad? Am I not more to you than ten sons?" (NRSV)

Hannah's deepest longing was to have a child. Since a woman's status in biblical times was determined by her ability to bear children, you can imagine how painful it was to be in a marriage where the second wife had already produced both sons and daughters for your husband. On one of their family's annual trips to worship God at the tabernacle at Shiloh, a heartbroken Hannah made her way to the tabernacle to pray.

Hannah Seeks God's Help through Prayer
I Samuel 1:9-20

9 After they had eaten and drunk at Shiloh, Hannah rose and presented herself before the LORD. Now Eli the priest was sitting on the seat beside the doorpost of the temple of the LORD. **10** She was deeply distressed and prayed to the LORD, and wept bitterly. **11** She made this vow: "O LORD of hosts, if only you will look on the misery of your servant, and remember me, and not forget your servant, but will give to your servant a male child, then I will set him before you as a nazirite until the day of his death. He shall drink neither wine nor intoxicants, and no razor shall touch his head."

12 As she continued praying before the LORD, Eli observed her mouth. **13** Hannah was praying silently; only her lips moved, but her voice was not heard; therefore Eli thought she was drunk. **14** So Eli said to her, "How long will you make a drunken spectacle of yourself? Put away your wine."

15 But Hannah answered, "No, my lord, I am a woman deeply troubled; I have drunk neither wine nor strong drink, but I have been pouring out my soul before the LORD. **16** Do not regard your servant as a worthless woman, for I have been speaking out of my great anxiety and vexation all this time."

17 Then Eli answered, "Go in peace; the God of Israel grant the petition you have made to him."

18 And she said, "Let your servant find favor in your sight." Then the woman went to her quarters, ate and drank with her husband, and her countenance was sad no longer.

19 They rose early in the morning and worshiped before the LORD;
then they went back to their house at Ramah. Elkanah knew his wife
Hannah, and the LORD remembered her. **20** In due time Hannah
conceived and bore a son. She named him Samuel, for she said, "I have
asked him of the LORD." (NRSV)

I am struck by Hannah's ability to voice her plight to the priest Eli. I wonder if her experience of being misunderstood at home by an irritating second wife and a well-meaning, yet clueless, husband had given her the fortitude to defend herself so boldly to Eli. Evidently, her plea was accepted by Eli and he blessed her and expressed his desire that God would grant her request, even though he did not know what that request was. I am sure Eli never imagined the impact this blessing would have on his own life and ministry. One day, Samuel—the answer to Hannah's request—would go to live with Eli in the Shiloh tabernacle and would eventually become Eli's successor. This passage is a good reminder of just how life-changing even one word of encouragement can be to a person in distress and, potentially, even to the one voicing the encouragement.

Hannah was faithful to the vow she made. Once again, those of us in today's world have a difficult time imagining sending your firstborn child away to serve in a religious institution because of your gratitude to God. Yet, that's exactly what Hannah did. Her prayer life must have been extraordinary.

Hannah Fulfills Her Vow to God
1 Samuel 1:21-28

21 The man Elkanah and all his household went up to offer to
the LORD the yearly sacrifice, and to pay his vow. **22** But Hannah did not
go up, for she said to her husband, "As soon as the child is weaned, I will

bring him, that he may appear in the presence of the LORD, and remain there forever; I will offer him as a nazirite for all time."

23 Her husband Elkanah said to her, "Do what seems best to you, wait until you have weaned him; only—may the LORD establish his word." So the woman remained and nursed her son, until she weaned him.

24 When she had weaned him, she took him up with her, along with a three-year-old bull, an ephah of flour, and a skin of wine. She brought
him to the house of the LORD at Shiloh; and the child was young. **25** Then
they slaughtered the bull, and they brought the child to Eli. **26** And she
said, "Oh, my lord! As you live, my lord, I am the woman who was
standing here in your presence, praying to the LORD. **27** For this child I
prayed; and the LORD has granted me the petition that I made to
him. **28** Therefore I have lent him to the LORD; as long as he lives, he is
given to the LORD. She left him there for the LORD." (NRSV)

While the Bible does not provide us with the details of a young Samuel's reaction to all of this, we do know that Samuel stayed with Eli and learned to hear God's voice. We are not sure how old Samuel was when he was weaned, yet we can estimate somewhere between the ages of 3 and 7. I have to believe that in his early years, while still living with his mother, he must have watched and listened to her as she prayed and remained faithful to the God who had blessed her with Samuel. I wonder what kind of bedtime stories his mother told him!

Hannah Prophesies a King and a Messiah for Israel through Her Prayer

The next chapter of 1 Samuel is where we find Hannah's prayer of thanksgiving for this child and it reveals how God blessed Hannah beyond her wildest dreams (see especially 1 Samuel 2:5 below). Since biblical scholars are not certain who wrote the book of 1 Samuel, it is interesting to ponder how this prophetic prayer came to be part of this book. Regardless of how it came to be, it is fascinating that **Hannah's voice was the first to use prophetically the term "messiah," which is translated "anointed"** in our English Bibles (see verse 10 below).

1 Samuel 2:1-10

1 Hannah prayed and said,
"My heart exults in the LORD;
my strength is exalted in my God.
My mouth derides my enemies,
because I rejoice in my victory.
2 "There is no Holy One like the LORD,
no one besides you;
there is no Rock like our God.
3 Talk no more so very proudly,
let not arrogance come from your mouth;
for the LORD is a God of knowledge,
and by him actions are weighed.
4 The bows of the mighty are broken,
but the feeble gird on strength.
5 Those who were full have hired themselves out for bread,
but those who were hungry are fat with spoil.
The barren has borne seven,
but she who has many children is forlorn.
6 The LORD kills and brings to life;
he brings down to Sheol and raises up.
7 The LORD makes poor and makes rich;
he brings low, he also exalts.
8 He raises up the poor from the dust;
he lifts the needy from the ash heap,
to make them sit with princes
and inherit a seat of honor.
For the pillars of the earth are the LORD's,
and on them he has set the world.
9 "He will guard the feet of his faithful ones,
but the wicked shall be cut off in darkness;
for not by might does one prevail.
10 The LORD! His adversaries shall be shattered;
the Most High will thunder in heaven.
The LORD will judge the ends of the earth;

he will give strength to his king,
and exalt the power of his anointed." (NRSV)

Note that verse 10 actually contains two prophecies: a "king" and the LORD's "anointed." This was prophetic not only for Israel to one day have a king, but it looked even farther into the future to Christ. According to the footnotes of *The Amplified Bible* for 1 Samuel 2:10, both the *Septuagint* (Greek translation of the Old Testament) and *The Latin Vulgate* translate the word "anointed" as "His Christ" (*The Amplified Bible* 1987, 253). When Hannah prayed this prayer, Israel did not yet have a king. The nation was still in the time of the judges. However, all the surrounding countries had kings and the Israelites complained enough and begged God enough for a king that God eventually allowed them to have one. Hannah's son, Samuel, would become Israel's last prophet/judge who would go on to be chosen by God to anoint Israel's first two kings. As stated previously, what a powerful prayer life Hannah demonstrated for her son and what far-reaching impact those prayers had!

This prayer would be immortalized by the Jews through the centuries. It would eventually influence Mary of Nazareth's "Magnificat" (see Luke 1) a thousand years later when she rejoiced over being chosen as the mother of that same prophesied Messiah!

God Blesses Hannah's Faithfulness

Later in the second chapter of 1 Samuel, we see another sweet picture of Hannah's faithfulness and God's blessing.

1 Samuel 2:18-21

18 Samuel was ministering before the LORD, a boy wearing a linen
ephod. **19** His mother used to make for him a little robe and take it to him
each year, when she went up with her husband to offer the yearly
sacrifice. **20** Then Eli would bless Elkanah and his wife, and say, "May
the LORD repay you with children by this woman for the gift that she
made to the LORD"; and then they would return to their home.

21 And the LORD took note of Hannah; she conceived and bore three sons and two daughters. And the boy Samuel grew up in the presence of the LORD. (NRSV)

Hannah became the mother of more children. What joy they must have brought her knowing she had waited on God's timing. Just imagine the joyful reunion it was each year when Hannah and Elkanah made their way to Shiloh for the yearly sacrifice and to see their growing son. I wonder if Hannah lived long enough to see the first fulfillment of her prophecy when Samuel anointed Saul as the first king of Israel.

For any of you who have watched your own children leave home for a long period of time for mission service, work, school, or a military assignment, you have a deeper understanding of Hannah's experience.

Hannah's prayer life undergirded her life and her family's life and influenced future generations. **Hannah's prayers are where we hear a woman's voice be the first one God chose to utter prophetically the term "anointed," looking to Christ in the next millennium.**

The Message in Hannah's Voice

If Hannah were with us today, here is what I imagine she would advise us regarding our impact on the next generation.

You have no way of knowing which ones in the younger generation God is preparing for a great service, yet you can trust that your prayers for the next generation of leaders will have long-lasting influence in their lives and in the lives of future generations! Consider these questions to prompt your ideas on how you can make a positive impact today on the generation of tomorrow:

1. What are some faith-filled, outlandish prayers you can voice for the next generation because of your belief in the power of God?
2. How can you be present among the younger generation where they can watch you demonstrate your commitment to God?
3. How does the way you talk about and to the younger generation communicate your confidence in God's activity in their lives?

4. What habit could you form that would encourage someone in the next generation?
5. How do your daily spiritual practices affect someone in the next generation?

You may know women today who are struggling with infertility as Hannah suffered with barrenness. You can be an encouragement to them as the priest Eli was to Hannah by supporting their prayers and their efforts to have a child. If it's not infertility, there are other women in your circle of influence who have deep longings that only God knows. Your one word of encouragement may be the first one someone has spoken to them in a long time. Teach them how to pray prayers of trust and expectation. As Hannah watched her young Samuel grow into a trustworthy man of God, her heart rejoiced in the ways God would lead him. As you pray for the girls and boys in your life, entrust them completely to God's care and leading and you'll be blessed. Let Hannah's voice remind you that your pain of unmet longings can be relieved through prayer for God's perfect timing and through your ability to continue to have expectant hope.

Biblical Truths Taught through the Story of Hannah:

1. God communicates directly to and through women.
2. God's plans for the future of God's people are sometimes best communicated through a woman's voice.
3. God expects the influence of a mother on her children to have far-reaching impact into future generations.
4. God sometimes chooses a time of barrenness to bring about a deeper understanding of the blessing that is to come. Barrenness may be infertility for some, but for others it could be unemployment, loneliness, divorce, the death of a spouse, or a failed business with no hope in sight. Those are difficult days in which God promises to be present.
5. God allows prayer to have long-lasting effects in any current situation and for generations to come.

Why the Voice of Hannah Matters . . .

To those with unfulfilled longings: because Hannah's story shows how desperation can help you become a person of deep faith in God, the only one who can fill your hungering needs.

To faithful pray-ers: because Hannah's story illustrates that God wants to hear your prayerful expressions of deepest sorrow and greatest joys and can use those expressions to prepare others for God's activity in their lives.

To mothers: because Hannah's story lets you see how demonstrating a faithful and fervent prayer life for your child will have a lasting impact beyond what you can imagine.

To those suffering with infertility: because Hannah's story shows God's timing is everything, and lets you remember that God uses both fertility and infertility for greater purposes. God will bring joy in the morning.

To those in difficult marriages: because Hannah's story shows how keeping your eyes on God's plan can help you endure the path before you with wisdom and grace.

Questions Raised by the Story of Hannah

Why does God allow infertility among those who seem best prepared to become parents?

How can we prepare our young children to hear and recognize God's voice calling them to service?

Why are women's voices suppressed in some churches when God often gives them such faith-filled prayers?

In what ways are we teaching the women in our churches to pray for their children?

What are we doing in our churches to equip parents to know how to demonstrate sacrificial service to God?

How do women's relationships within a family affect family dynamics?

Hannah's Key to Resilient Confidence

The story of Hannah shows us characteristics of someone living with expectant hope bathed in prayer, a trait of resilient confidence. I believe Hannah would say to us, "When we seek God through prayer as the source of our confidence, we can entrust to God's care the results of our acts of service." Hannah's example reveals **four habits of a hopeful heart bathed in prayer that can transform you into a woman who lives and leads with expectant hope.**

A hopeful heart bathed in prayer . . .

1. Makes plans for a hope only God can fulfill.
Hannah's vow to give her child back to God to serve God all his life shows how she believed in God's ability so much that she could make strategic decisions even before her prayer was answered. Do you trust God enough to make plans *before* you see God's answer, or do you wait—just in case God can't/doesn't come through? Which approach honors God?

2. Expresses God's peace with expectant hope on your face.
Hannah's faith in God's power showed in her attitude and actions. Scripture says that "her countenance was sad no longer." Have you considered what *your* face is telling others about your belief in God?

3. Remembers to thank and praise a faithful, strong, and active God.

Hannah's prayer in 1 Samuel 2 is full of words of gratitude for specific things God has done for her people, for the poor and weak, and for her personally. Hannah's prayer also expresses different attributes of her God who acts on behalf of people. Are you as careful to thank God as you are to write thank-you notes for acts of kindness you've experienced? How do you talk about God's activity in your personal life?

4. Entrusts the future to God's purpose and power.

In the last sentence of Hannah's prayer in 1 Samuel 2:10, two prophecies are expressed: that there will be a king in Israel's future and that there will be a Messiah. **Hannah's prayer is the first time in Scripture where the word translated "anointed" (which in Hebrew is "messiah") is used prophetically.** Is there a first-time message God is asking you to share with your audiences?

Practicing expectant hope through prayer will develop resilient confidence within you while also making an impact on future generations.

"Then Hannah prayed:
'My heart rejoices in the LORD.
My strength rises up in the LORD! . . .
May God give strength to his king
and raise high the strength of his anointed one.' . . .
The LORD paid attention to Hannah."
—1 Samuel 2:1a, 10b, 21a (CEB)

PART FIVE

God Chose Huldah

THE TIME OF ISRAEL'S MONARCHY AND DIVIDED KINGDOM

ca. 1100 - 600 BCE

Events that Shaped the World of Huldah

THE TIME OF ISRAEL'S MONARCHY AND DIVIDED KINGDOM
ca. 1100 - 600 BCE

The time of the Judges ended with the prophet Samuel. He was Hannah's long-awaited son whom she gave to the Lord's service (see the previous chapter). Samuel was still a young boy when God called him to become a prophet. God spoke through the boy Samuel to Eli about the doom of his wicked sons. Later, Samuel was chosen by God to anoint and prophesy over the first two kings of Israel.

Israel's Monarchy

First, with God's direction, Samuel anointed Saul to be king of Israel. This began the time of Israel's Monarchy, with the nation's people choosing to be ruled by a king as their neighboring nations were. Saul reigned around 1050-1010 BCE. As Saul's reign began to deteriorate, God led Samuel to anoint a young shepherd boy named David to be the next king. When he became older, David began his reign in 1010 BCE. He lived and ruled in his new capital of Jerusalem until his death in 970 BCE. Biblical stories from this time are recorded in 1 Kings and 1 Chronicles and much of King David's poetry can be read in Psalms.

Solomon, the son of King David and Bathsheba, succeeded his father and reigned from 970-931 BCE. Solomon was known as the wisest man in the world. Other nation's leaders came to pay him tribute, including the Queen of Sheba (possibly modern-day Ethiopia). Solomon's reign brought the greatest expansion to Israel's borders and to its wealth. With the financial help of the Phoenician king of Tyre, Solomon built the first Jewish Temple in Jerusalem. The innermost sanctuary of the Temple was called the Holy of Holies, which housed the Ark of the Covenant, a sacred chest reminding the Hebrews of God's presence among them.

Solomon's wisdom is recorded in the biblical books of Proverbs, Ecclesiastes, and Song of Solomon.

The Divided Kingdom

Upon Solomon's death in 931 BCE, his sons tore the kingdom apart. The kingdom split into the Northern Kingdom of Israel and the Southern Kingdom of Judah. This is known as the time of the Divided Kingdom and stories from this time are recorded in 2 Kings, 2 Chronicles, and the Major and Minor Prophets.

Over the next 200 years, a series of evil rulers in both kingdoms was punctuated briefly with a few good kings in the Southern Kingdom. Around 900 BCE, God began sending prophets, one after another, to help the people see the errors of their ways. This period began with the great prophet Elijah and his apprentice Elisha proclaiming God's truth to the tribes in the Northern Kingdom of Israel. Elijah prophesied from 875-848 BCE during the reign of the wicked King Ahab and Queen Jezebel. We read about some important lessons Elijah learned along the way in the books of 1 and 2 Kings. Elisha succeeded Elijah and prophesied from 848-797 BCE with many miraculous works recorded in 1 and 2 Kings. Other prophets would come and go to announce to the Israelites God's displeasure in their actions and to warn them of the coming doom. Jonah prophesied around 800-750 BCE in the Northern Kingdom and then God sent him to Nineveh, where he did not want to go. The first of the "writing prophets" was Amos, who was sent by God from the Southern Kingdom of Judah up to the Northern Kingdom of Israel, to help Israel understand how its prosperity had caused it to ignore the needs of the poor. Following Amos, God sent Hosea to warn the Israelites of the kingdom's plight if they did not repent.

Happenings in the Rest of the World - Assyria Rises to Power

While all of this was happening (between 1100 and 700 BCE) in the Divided Kingdoms of Israel of Judah, the rest of the world witnessed:

- Camel taming in Arabia, which allowed the establishment of desert trade routes

- The growth of urban societies in China
- The birth and development of Hinduism in India
- A woman reigning in the 9th century as an Egyptian high priest in Thebes
- The Phoenician princess Dido, according to legend, founding the city of Carthage in 814 BCE on the northern coast of Africa (in modern-day Tunisia), which would become a major trading port and metropolis
- The historical Queen Shammuramat (Semiramis) ruling in Babylon 811-806 BCE, while legends made her the founder of Babylon and a great military heroine
- The founding of Rome in 753 BCE
- In 738 BCE, the Arab ruler Queen Zabibi paying tribute to King Tiglath-pilesar III of Assyria, and Southern Arabia having a different female ruler, Queen Samsia, when Tiglath-pilesar III attacked Damascus in 732 BCE
- The first Olympic games being held in 776 BCE in honor of Apollo at Olympia
- The invention of the Greek alphabet
- The writing of the *Iliad* and the *Odyssey* into the forms we know today
- The use of bronze trumpets in Denmark
- Assyria capturing and destroying Babylon in 730 BCE

Focusing on the Bible's Story - The Exile of the Ten Tribes

God also sent prophets to the Southern Kingdom of Judah during this time. Isaiah prophesied from 740-698 BCE with a message of hope and repentance to both kings and ordinary people. Micah prophesied in Jerusalem during the same time (735-710 BCE) with a call for humble mercy and justice.

Then, late in the 8th century BCE, as a result of the Northern Kingdom of Israel's refusal to repent, God allowed the "Ten Tribes" of the Northern Kingdom to be captured and carried into exile to Assyria by the Assyrians in 722 BCE.

You would think this would have convinced the Southern Kingdom of Judah that the prophets' warnings were worthy of their attention. However, that was not the case. Judah had five kings between 735 and 641 BCE, only two of which were considered good, Hezekiah and Josiah, with two bad kings between them. God sent Nahum (prophesied 686-612 BCE) to the Southern Kingdom, shortly after the prophet Micah, to remind the Israelites of God's jealousy for them and also to warn Judah's Assyrian enemies of the coming destruction of their city of Ninevah.

Happenings in the Rest of the World - The Babylonians Regain Their Prominence

The 7th century BCE witnessed more wars, cultural developments, and significant events, such as:

- The development of horseshoes in Europe
- The use of the first coins in the country of Lydia (modern-day Turkey) and soon after, in Greece
- The Dorians supplanting the Mycenaeans in Greece
- Queen Naqi'a becoming regent of Assyria in 689 BCE while her husband, King Sennacherib, was at war. She had an impact on the country's building program and her influence continued into the next king's reign.
- The Greek woman poet Sappho, who flourished in the late 7th century, and was later considered one of the greatest poets of all time
- The Babylonians, in 612 BCE, destroying Assyria's capital, Ninevah, considered the greatest city in the world at the time (fulfilling Micah's prophecy)

Focusing on the Bible's Story - The Struggles of the Southern Kingdom of Judah

When good King Josiah started his reign of Judah around 641 BCE, he was only eight years old. His 31-year rule included restoring the Temple that had been allowed to deteriorate over the years. God's Law had not been followed by the previous two generations of kings; and the people of Judah had turned to the worship of Assyrian gods. Zephaniah (prophesied 640-621 BCE), Jeremiah (prophesied 626-584 BCE), and the woman prophet Huldah (prophesied around 621 BCE) were all contemporaries prophesying in Jerusalem trying to help the people return to God. Since most of the people refused to heed God's warnings, God's wrath would soon descend upon them just as it had on the Northern Kingdom of Israel.

Let's listen to the voice of Huldah, when God chose her to be first. . . .

11

Huldah's Story

ca. 700 - 600 BCE

God chose Huldah's voice to be the first . . .

- To authenticate and interpret a written document as the prophetic word of God, thus beginning the centuries-long process of scripture canonization

Huldah was startled by the knock on the door because it was so late in the evening. Her first thought was that her husband Shallum was being called back to work. He worked at the palace and was in charge of King Josiah's wardrobe. Sometimes, there was a need for a particular garment which the night shift servants couldn't locate and Shallum would have to return to the palace. He and Huldah were cleaning up the dishes from the evening meal and were discussing plans for Shallum's day off tomorrow, which may not come to pass if this was indeed an urgent call back to work.

"Who could that be at this hour?" Huldah asked as Shallum left the room and headed for the door at the front of the house.

Shallum opened the door, surprised to find the high priest Hilkiah and four other palace officials who worked in the king's service. A request for his return to work was usually delivered by a young servant from the palace. Shallum personally knew all five of the men, but had never seen them all together on the same errand and could not imagine the nature of their business. "Shalom, gentlemen. Please, come in." Shallum greeted them and motioned for them to enter. In his mind, he wondered, *What kind of errand would require the high priest, the king's personal servant, the king's private secretary and his son, and one of the king's guards?*

Hilkiah was carrying a large scroll while the other four men seemed to be there to guard Hilkiah and the scroll he held so carefully. "Good evening, Shallum. We apologize for the lateness of our visit, but we are here on the king's business," Hilkiah explained.

"How may I be of service to His Majesty?" Shallum quickly responded.

"Actually, Shallum, we are here to see your wife, Huldah."

With only a heavy wool curtain dividing the two rooms, Huldah could overhear the conversation. She quickly dropped the dish she was holding into the basin of water. She was still drying her hands as she pushed the curtain aside in the doorway and walked toward the group of men. "How may I serve His Majesty, gentlemen?" she asked as she approached them.

"Shalom, Huldah," Hilkiah greeted her with deep respect. "Thank you for seeing us at this late hour. As you know, the king has been having the Temple cleaned and restored. Earlier today, I found this scroll amongst the rubble. We think it might be one of the books of God's law that has been lost for so long. I showed it to Shaphan who, in his duty as the king's private secretary, took it to the king and read it to him. The king was very upset by the words he heard."

Hilkiah gently handed the fragile scroll to Huldah. Cradling the precious scroll in her arms, she walked across the room toward a long table she used for her studies. Shallum quickly moved her ink pot and stacks of scrolls to the far edge of the table to make room for the newly discovered, dusty, delicate artifact.

"Shallum, will you bring a couple of lamps, please?" she asked as she carefully laid the scroll on the table. Shallum placed the small oil lamps on two corners of the table as the group gathered around. Hilkiah untied the leather strap from around the scroll and helped Huldah unroll the scroll to see where the writing began.

Huldah felt as if she were looking at precious jewels. The words jumped off the scroll and into her heart. How she had longed to see with her own eyes these scrolls she had only heard about from the other prophets and priests in Jerusalem. She wondered, *Could this actually be one of the long lost books of God's Law for our people?* The possibility was thrilling, but she wanted to be cautious in her excitement.

Hilkiah continued, "After Shaphan read the scroll to His Majesty—oh, Huldah—well . . ."

Shaphan, the king's secretary, interrupted, breaking his silence from the back of the group and said with a trembling voice, "Huldah, the king tore his robe!"

Huldah and Shallum both gasped a little. They had never heard of King Josiah showing this sign of remorse. It had been several generations since anyone of noble stature had demonstrated this kind of grief. They now understood why there were so many of the king's closest advisors on this errand. This was a request of the most serious nature from the king.

"The king trusts you, Huldah. We suggested we could consult Jeremiah or Zephaniah, but he requested you, Huldah."

Shallum was beaming, yet trying to maintain a serious demeanor, as he thought to himself, *Finally, my wife is being given the chance to use her knowledge for a bigger purpose.*

Huldah graciously accepted the task. "What exactly was the king's request?" she asked, not wanting to assume any responsibility beyond his specific instructions.

Hilkiah answered with an authoritative tone, "Go, inquire of the LORD for me, for the people, and for all Judah, concerning the words of this book that has been found; for great is the wrath of the LORD that is kindled against us, because our ancestors did not obey the words of this book, to do according to all that is written concerning us."* Hilkiah resumed his normal voice, "Huldah, we need you to tell us if this scroll is authentic. We need your interpretation of these words to take back to the king. We have known you to be honest and trustworthy in your prophecies over the years and we know you will give the king an accurate understanding, regardless of the consequences."

Huldah glanced at Shallum. They both knew what "consequences" had been experienced by other prophets in the past with the wicked rulers; yet, they trusted King Josiah's heart. He had proven to be a man wanting to please God.

With a serious and humble tone, Huldah replied to the high priest Hilkiah, "I am honored to be given this opportunity," Huldah said with gratitude. "I will read it immediately and should be able to give you an answer in the morning."

"Thank you, Huldah. We will return tomorrow before midday. Good night, Shallum," Hilkiah spoke for the group as they walked toward the door. Turning back, Hilkiah held up his hand in a priestly manner and said, "May you hear a word from the God of Israel, Huldah."

"Yahweh is always faithful," Huldah responded as she said goodbye to the group.

Shallum closed the door and looked at his wife and smiled. He walked to the table where she was unrolling the scroll ever so slowly. Some of the edges were brittle from decay and she did not want to damage it further. She used a soft brush of fine horse hair to gently wipe away the layers of fine dust covering the hand lettering so carefully applied to the parchment.

"Can you tell what it is, Huldah?" he asked with eager curiosity.

"Well, if I am understanding this first section correctly, it is indeed one of the five books of Moses. I will need to read more before I can truly ascertain its authenticity. It looks like it will be a long night."

"How may I help?" asked a willing Shallum.

"Oh, Shallum, thank you, but I think this will be a lot of reading and praying. You go on to bed so at least one of us will enjoy your day off tomorrow."

"No, I'll stay up. I have a tailoring project of my own I can work on. Will I disturb you if I stay in this room with you?"

"I just need it quiet. I don't think you or your project will distract me." With that, Huldah returned to poring over the scroll, reading it aloud softly. Shallum left the room to retrieve his fabric and sewing basket.

As the night hours marched on, Huldah became more and more aware of what she was reading. She felt blessed to be able to actually see and touch and read this scroll for herself. It had been many years since such a scroll had been read by anyone in Judah. For several generations, not even the high priests had access to any of these scrolls. Their religious rituals were done from memory and had been passed down orally—and from what she was reading—not very accurately.

As she read the sections of the scroll that recalled her people's history, tears welled up in her eyes. She quickly caught them with the hem of her sleeve before they dropped onto the thin parchment. As the light of the small oil lamps dimmed, she realized she needed to refill them with olive oil. Periodically she would stop and read a section to Shallum who was amazed at what he was hearing. It was like a feeling of coming home, of something familiar, yet new and rather disturbing.

Huldah was now assured that this scroll was one of the books of Moses preserved for her people. Toward the end of the scroll's writing, she read where Moses commanded that this law should be read every seventh year to a gathering of all the people of Israel. She realized that had never happened in her lifetime. *Oh, how far we have strayed from the LORD our God!* she thought.

After a few more comparisons of passages in different sections of the scroll, she was confident of the message the LORD would have her tell the high priest to take to the king. As the sunrise peeked through the shutters, Huldah stood with her arms and face raised toward heaven and praised God for the understanding she had received in reading the scroll.

She knew the men would return for an answer before midday. Before she started writing her response, she decided she needed a bit of sleep. Shallum had finally gone to bed after finishing his tailoring project. She found him snoring gently in their bed. She tucked herself in next to him and closed her eyes.

~

The bustling carts of the spice merchants making their way to market awakened her not long after she had drifted to sleep. Shallum was getting ready for his day as she made her way to the water basin to wash her face. This was going to be a day she would remember forever: the day she was given the opportunity to prophesy for the king.

She ate some of yesterday's bread with a bit of honey and went straight to her work. She gently ran her fingers along the edge of the ancient scroll once more. She knew it was God's word for her people. She spread out a new parchment scroll in front of her and sharpened her quill pen. As she dipped it in the ink pot, she wondered what the consequences might be for herself. She began to write:

"Thus says the LORD, the God of Israel: Tell the man who sent you to me, Thus says the LORD, I will indeed bring disaster on this place and on its inhabitants—all the words of the book that the king of Judah has read. Because they have abandoned me and have made offerings to other gods, so that they have provoked me to anger with all the work of their hands, therefore my wrath will be kindled against this place, and it will not be quenched. But as to the king of Judah, who sent you to inquire of the LORD, thus shall you say to him, Thus says the LORD, the God of Israel: Regarding the words that you have heard, because your heart was penitent, and you humbled yourself before the LORD, when you heard how I spoke against this place, and against its inhabitants, that they should become a desolation and a curse, and because you have torn your clothes and wept before me, I also have heard you, says the LORD. Therefore, I will gather you to your ancestors, and you shall be gathered to your grave in peace; your eyes shall not see all the disaster that I will bring on this place."*

Over and over, she carefully re-read the words the LORD had given her. As she put down the quill pen one last time, Shallum entered the room. She asked him to read her response to the king. He was always a thoughtful reader of her documents. When he finished, he got up from the table and looked at his wife lovingly and said, "Huldah, I so admire how you demonstrate your faithfulness to the God of Israel. No matter what happens as a result of this prophecy, I know God will be with us. Even if this brings an end to us, you have been true to Almighty God."

Huldah hugged him and thanked him for always believing in her. She blotted her writing and as she rolled it up and tied it with a thin leather strap, the expected knock on the door came. Shallum greeted the five men once again and Huldah reported to them the good news that the scroll was authentic. It *was* one of the five books of Moses and they could trust its message. She then handed them her newly written scroll along with the precious, dusty, old one. They thanked her for her service and took her message back to the king.

The next day, preparations for a celebration began in the palace. Shallum was busy cleaning and preparing the king's best robes and polishing the crown he had chosen to wear for the occasion. Huldah took time that day to go visit the restoration work at the Temple. She wanted to be physically close to the Holy of Holies—or as close as she could get as a woman. She felt a new joy that day. Her king and her people would be turning back to God and she was the one God had chosen to interpret God's truth for the king. She wanted to seal in her memory all the details of this day.

*Quoted from 2 Kings 22 (NRSV).

The Bible Speaks

Huldah's story is found in 2 King 22-23 and 2 Chronicles 34-35

The above fictional account is a description of the movie that plays out in my head each time I read this wonderful Bible story from 2 Kings 22-23 and 2 Chronicles 34-35. I have discovered that most people I encounter in church—probably 99%—have never heard of Huldah. They might be familiar with the story of good King Josiah as I heard in my childhood Sunday School classes, yet Huldah was never mentioned. I remember the colorful Bible story picture that showed a faithful servant reading an unrolled scroll to a serious and attentive king, but there was never a picture of the woman prophet Huldah!

Huldah is described in Scripture as a prophet and the wife of Shallum, who was the keeper of King Josiah's wardrobe. Therefore, we can be sure she was familiar with the palace and the inner workings of the king's court. She lived in Jerusalem, the capital of the southern part of Palestine known as the land of Judah and this story took place around 621 BCE.

At this point in Judah's history, the Jewish Temple lay in ruins due to the wicked leadership, for almost 50 years, of the two previous kings. Then a very young Josiah became king—and he was a different kind of king. He wanted to please God as opposed to the wicked kings who ruled before him. At age 16, he ordered the tearing down of many of the altars to other gods which had been built around the country (see 2 Chron. 34:3-7). After that effort, in his eighteenth year as king, he had the Temple cleaned and restored. The rubble revealed some long lost treasures. Here are some excerpts from the 2 Kings account.

The Scroll is Found
2 Kings 22:8-13

8 The high priest Hilkiah said to Shaphan the secretary, "I have found the book of the law in the house of the LORD." When Hilkiah gave the book to Shaphan, he read it. **9** Then Shaphan the secretary came to the king, and reported to the king, "Your servants have emptied out the money that was found in the house, and have delivered it into the hand of the workers who have oversight of the house of the LORD." **10** Shaphan the secretary informed the king, "The priest Hilkiah has given me a book." Shaphan then read it aloud to the king.

11 When the king heard the words of the book of the law, he tore his clothes. **12** Then the king commanded the priest Hilkiah, Ahikam son of Shaphan, Achbor son of Micaiah, Shaphan the secretary, and the king's servant Asaiah, saying, **13** "Go, inquire of the LORD for me, for the people, and for all Judah, concerning the words of this book that has been found; for great is the wrath of the LORD that is kindled against us, because our ancestors did not obey the words of this book, to do according to all that is written concerning us." (NRSV)

Many scholars believe the scroll found was the book of Deuteronomy or the whole Torah. The next part of the story is what I discovered as an adult and realized—with great frustration—that the pivotal role played by the woman prophet Huldah was never mentioned in my childhood or youth Sunday School lessons. *Why?* I now ask myself.

Huldah Prophesies God's Truth
2 Kings 22:14-20

14 So the priest Hilkiah, Ahikam, Achbor, Shaphan, and Asaiah went to the prophetess Huldah the wife of Shallum son of Tikvah, son of Harhas, keeper of the wardrobe; she resided in Jerusalem in the Second Quarter, where they consulted her. **15** She declared to them, "Thus says the LORD, the God of Israel: Tell the man who sent you to me, **16** Thus says the LORD, I will indeed bring disaster on this place and on its inhabitants —all the words of the book that the king of Judah has read. **17** Because they have abandoned me and have made offerings to other gods, so that they have provoked me to anger with all the work of their hands, therefore my wrath will be kindled against this place, and it will not be quenched. **18** But as to the king of Judah, who sent you to inquire of the LORD, thus shall you say to him, Thus says the LORD, the God of Israel: Regarding the words that you have heard, **19** because your heart was penitent, and you humbled yourself before the LORD, when you heard how I spoke against this place, and against its inhabitants, that they should become a desolation and a curse, and because you have torn your clothes and wept before me, I also have heard you, says the LORD. **20** Therefore, I will gather you to your ancestors, and you shall be gathered to your grave in peace; your eyes shall not see all the disaster that I will bring on this place." They took the message back to the king. (NRSV)

This passage reveals **that Huldah was the first person in Scripture asked to verify the authenticity of a written document as the Word of God, thus beginning the centuries-long process of canonizing Scripture.** (Canonization is the process of determining which writings are authentic and should be included in the scriptural canon, which is the list of books accepted as Holy Scripture.) As professor Claudia Camp described Huldah's action, "Her validation of a text thus stands as the first recognizable act in the long process of canon formation" (Camp 2001, 96). Huldah's reverent, honest, and thorough interpretation of the scroll caused a king to repent and to lead a whole nation's return to God.

The King's Covenant
2 Kings 23:1-3

1 Then the king directed that all the elders of Judah and Jerusalem should be gathered to him. **2** The king went up to the house of the LORD, and with him went all the people of Judah, all the inhabitants of Jerusalem, the priests, the prophets, and all the people, both small and great; he read in their hearing all the words of the book of the covenant that had been found in the house of the LORD. **3** The king stood by the pillar and made a covenant before the LORD, to follow the LORD, keeping his commandments, his decrees, and his statutes, with all his heart and all his soul, to perform the words of this covenant that were written in this book. All the people joined in the covenant. (NRSV)

The story of Huldah has been one of my favorite tools to introduce the spiritual truths taught by the stories of biblical women. Huldah's ability to discern whether a written document contained God's Truth is an inspiration to anyone who has a love for God's Word. Helping others discover God's Word and the hope it provides for our everyday lives is one of my greatest joys.

The Message in Huldah's Voice

This story makes me wonder what our churches and world would be like if more women throughout the centuries had been encouraged to become biblical interpreters, seminary professors, preachers, prophets, and writers of biblical studies. Would we be a more repentant people? Would we have a deeper and more complete understanding of God's Word?

Huldah's prophetic wisdom changed a nation when she was willing to communicate faithfully, honestly, and authoritatively with the knowledge she had! Huldah must have been known for her knowledge of ancient texts, which means she had learned to read and had studied and/or memorized them carefully. She was also respected by the religious leaders and they knew she could be trusted with a request from the king. When the high priest took her message back to the king, several things could have happened. The king could have simply ignored the prophecy. He could have had the prophet and/or the messenger killed for bringing bad news. Or, he could have chosen to make the necessary changes that would align his people with God's laws once again. He chose to follow Huldah's guidance. Now that Huldah is no longer hidden from you, how will you use her story to inspire others—especially women—to share their biblical wisdom with men and women? Let Huldah's voice remind you that sometimes God will choose a woman's voice to interpret God's message for God's people, and it could be yours.

Biblical Truths Taught through the Story of Huldah

1. God appointed women prophets who were respected and consulted by the high priest and by at least one king in biblical days.
2. God chose a woman prophet instead of the more well-known men prophets (Jeremiah, Habakkuk, and possibly Zephaniah and Nahum) to be the one to interpret God's written word for a king, who then led his country to repent and turn back to God.
3. God gave Huldah a message of truth, which she was courageous enough to tell, even if it would disappoint the king.
4. God chose Huldah to be the first person we read about in Scripture who was called upon to authenticate a written document as the word of God—thus beginning the centuries-long process of canonizing Scripture.
5. God communicates truth through women to both women and men.
6. God chooses women to teach, influence, guide, and direct men and their decisions.
7. God affirms a woman's study of God's word.
8. God chooses women's voices to speak the truth of God's Word, even when that truth is not good news.
9. God, who is the same yesterday, today, and forever, ensured this story was preserved through the ages for us to see the amazing influence a woman can have when she knows God's Word.
10. God sometimes appoints a woman to deliver an important message that can have national consequences.

Why the Voice of Huldah Matters . . .

To women: because Huldah's story confirms that God approves of women studying Scripture, teaching Scripture, interpreting Scripture, and of women being consulted by men for scriptural wisdom.

To men: because Huldah's story gives you the freedom to consult women for their knowledge and guidance on spiritual and leadership matters.

To Bible teachers: because Huldah's story reminds you how life-changing your teaching can be for your students and how vital it is that you spend time discerning the truth before you teach your students.

To leaders: because Huldah's story shows that good leaders realize they don't know everything and they must consult with others who can help them understand the issues of the day.

To national leaders: because Huldah's story illustrates the value of having both women and men on any team making decisions that will affect a whole country.

Questions Raised by the Story of Huldah

How different would our biblical history be if Huldah had *not* given an accurate interpretation?

Why have women often been denied the opportunity to study Scripture —or any other subject—on the same level as men?

How often are female theologians, preachers, teachers, and writers quoted by the leadership of your church?

What do we need to do as individuals to be known for our knowledge of God's Word and our ability to interpret it for others?

How is your church encouraging and equipping girls and women to pursue theological and/or seminary education to become Bible teachers and interpreters?

Huldah's Keys to Resilient Confidence

I believe Huldah would tell us her keys to resilient confidence were the diligent study of God's Word and the willingness to communicate with bold and righteous intent.

Discernment through study

Huldah's ability to communicate a difficult truth to the king was based on her complete trust in the truth of God's Word. She had obviously studied it enough to be able to tell a false document from a true one. If you are fully committed to becoming the woman God has called and created you to be, then a desire to study God's word will be one of your diligent pursuits. This is the most effective way to develop the skill of spiritual discernment. Your discernment skills will certainly add fuel to your ability to function with resilient confidence.

Communicating with bold and righteous intent

Huldah's expression of this kind of confidence also demonstrated some helpful guidelines for the times we, as women, are trying to communicate with men. Huldah's seemingly unwavering ability to communicate directly with men in power is a skill we can all develop and it will also greatly contribute to our development of resilient confidence. Communicating with men leaders can be challenging for a woman, especially if you are more accustomed to working only with women. Research has shown that women and men really do have different styles of communication (see linguistics professor Deborah Tannen's books on male/female communication). Yet, the precedents set by many biblical women—who lived in a very patriarchal culture—can empower you to overcome your communication challenges.

Five keys for communicating with men leaders:

1. Be prepared.

Huldah was faithful to use her knowledge wisely. She had been diligent in studying God's word.

Nothing can substitute for the preparation time required of you to lead, to communicate, or to inspire others.

2. Be accurate and truthful.

In a day when it was not unusual to "kill the messenger," Huldah still interpreted the prophecy's message of coming destruction.

Your honest—yet compassionate—communication will get a lot more accomplished than sugar-coating bad news.

3. Know the reliability of your source.

Huldah knew the prophecy was from God. According to the biblical record, **Huldah was the first person ever to authenticate and interpret a written document as God's Word.** This also indicates that she was the first person to begin the centuries-long process of canonizing Scripture (Camp 2001, 96).

The reliability of your sources can make or break you.

4. Answer the questions they ask directly and succinctly.

Huldah was concise and did not give extra details.

Show your respect of others by listening carefully to ***their*** *specific questions and by answering* ***only*** *those questions. Wait for a request to provide extra details. Men usually greatly appreciate this.*

5. See the purpose in your message beyond your need for recognition.

Even though Huldah fades into the background of this story, the biblical record lets us know that it was *her interpretation* that persuaded the king to institute national reforms that turned the nation of Judah back to God. The fact that her name and prophetic communication were preserved in Scripture is an honor no leader today will ever have.

Your individual contributions may be overlooked, but if a grander purpose that brings God glory is fulfilled, then what is important is accomplished.

Resilient confidence will be developed in anyone who studies God's Word diligently and is faithful to communicate with bold and righteous intent.

"She replied, 'This is what the LORD, Israel's God, says:
Tell this to the man who sent you to me . . .'"
—2 Kings 22:15 (CEB)

PART SIX

God Chose Elizabeth, Mary, and Anna

THE TIME OF THE JEWISH EXILE AND

THE 400 YEARS OF SILENCE

ca. 600 - 6 BCE

Events that Shaped the World of Elizabeth, Mary, and Anna

THE TIME OF THE JEWISH EXILE AND
THE 400 YEARS OF SILENCE
ca. 600 - 6 BCE

About 13 years after Huldah's prophecy of Judah's coming doom, King Josiah was killed in battle in 609 BCE and the Kingdom of Judah endured four more bad kings over the next 23 years. During that time, prophets continued to speak for God to the inhabitants of the Southern Kingdom of Judah, including Jeremiah, Zephaniah, and Nahum, warning them over and over about the judgment that was to descend upon them. The Israelites in Judah wouldn't listen.

The Israelites in Exile (600 - 500 BCE)

The Southern Kingdom of Judah was captured in 586 BCE by the Babylonians, the dominant world power of the time, and most of the Israelites were taken into exile. This is known as the Babylonian exile or captivity. From that point on, the Ark of the Covenant, which had been kept in the Temple, was lost. While the Israelites were in exile in Babylon, the prophet Ezekiel spoke for God there. God sent even more prophets to the people in exile including Obadiah, and Joel.

Happenings in the Rest of the World - Highlights of the 6th Century BCE (500s)

In other parts of the world during the 6th century, history tells us:

- The earliest known female lawyer won a case against her brother-in-law in Babylon. Babylon was a prosperous territory ruled by Nebuchadnezzar who built for his queen the famous Hanging Gardens (which may or may not be historical), which became known as the Second Wonder of the World.

- Other religions and philosophies developed including the founding of Buddhism in India, the beginning of Confucianism in China, and the flourishing of philosopher and mathematician Pythagoras in Greece (you may remember his name from geometry class).
- China issued its first codes of law and saw the birth of philosopher Lao-Tzu (ca 604-531 BCE), the founder of Taoism.
- The Greeks built their first stone temple for the goddess Artemis and developed black-figure painted pottery.

Focusing on the Bible's Story

The next world power to rule over the Jews in exile was the Persians whose King Cyrus conquered the Babylonians in 539 BCE. The biblical stories from that era include the ones about Daniel and his friends, Meshach, Shadrach, and Abednego, and of the cunning Queen Esther.

The Israelites Return to Jerusalem (538 - 400 BCE)

Toward the end of the 6th century BCE, the first group of Israelite exiles returned to Jerusalem in 538 BCE under the Israelite leader Zerubbabel. This was a result of the benevolent policies of Persia's King Cyrus who allowed the displaced people in his kingdom to return to their homelands and to reestablish their religious practices (see the Bible's book of Ezra, chapters 1-6).

Over the next century, two other leaders emerged to lead more Israelites back to Jerusalem from exile. Ezra led the second group back to Jerusalem in 458 BCE (see Ezra 7-10). Nehemiah led the last group back to Jerusalem in 444 BCE (see Nehemiah 1-13). Ezra and Nehemiah governed the people and led them to rebuild the walls and city of Jerusalem and to restore Solomon's Temple. During this time, God provided prophets for the Israelites, whose prophecies are preserved in our Bible's books of Haggai, Zechariah, and Malachi. These prophets spoke to the people as they were trying to re-establish their religious practices in Jerusalem.

Scholars think that Malachi's prophecies promising a forerunner to a messiah ended by 400 BCE.

Happenings in the Rest of the World - Highlights of the 5th Century BCE (400s)

While Jerusalem was being rebuilt in the 5th century:

- Athens developed democratic ideals and the Parthenon was reconstructed and dedicated to the goddess Athena.
- Around 450 BCE, the Celts conquered the British Isles.
- The Greek writer Herodotus, the "father of history," wrote his History by being the first to collect materials systematically and test their accuracy.
- In the Mediterranean, Sparta won the 27-year Peleponnesian Wars against Athens.
- The Olmecs' city of La Venta in Central America was abandoned by 400 BCE and the group died out, but their way of life influenced future cultures, such as the Mayan.

The 400 Years of Silence (400 - 6 BCE)

By the end of the 5th century BCE (around 400 BCE), the Hebrew Bible's first five books were canonized, meaning they were verified as authentic teachings. These five books are known to the Jews as the *Torah,* or God's law, and include Genesis, Exodus, Leviticus, Numbers, and Deuteronomy. They are also known as the Pentateuch and the Five Books of Moses. The biblical record indicates that the woman prophet Huldah was the first person to start the canonization process (around 620 BCE) when she authenticated the book of the law found in the Temple's rubble (see 2 Kings 22 and 2 Chronicles 34). It is thought that the scroll was probably the book of Deuteronomy. From the time of the canonization of the *Torah* around 400 BCE, it would take another 300 years (till around 100 BCE) to determine which other writings would comprise the Hebrew Scriptures (also known as the Old Testament to Christians).

Around 400 BCE, after the last prophetic word from Malachi, God became silent for the next 400 years providing no new prophets or prophecies for the Israelites. This time is known as the Period of Silence. Four centuries is a long time to wait. If a generation is considered 40 years, that means 10 generations had come and gone in those 400 years. I don't know about you, but I know nothing about my great-grandparents except some of their names. Even with all the DNA testing and ancestry research accessible to us today, we might be able to trace our direct lineage back through 400 years, but it is still difficult and feels very far removed. However, for many of the Jews of the first century, at the time of the events of the New Testament, their family histories had been carefully kept and passed down through the generations for more than 2,000 years. Through storytelling and written records kept in the Temple in Jerusalem, Jewish families were able to trace their roots back to the original Twelve Tribes.

Can you imagine holding on to a promise that was made to your grandfather with nine "greats" in front of his name? Yet that is the amount of time that passed between the conclusion of the events written about in the Old Testament ending with Malachi's prophecy of a forerunner to the Messiah (see Mal. 4:5-6) and the beginning of the events of the New Testament (see Luke 1).

What happened during those 400 years known as the "years of silence"? We can't fully understand why God waited 400 years. After all, the Bible tells us that 1,000 years is like one day to God (see Ps. 90:4). And while that is poetic language talking about something we can't actually measure, we get the idea that God's ability to see, know, and experience all eternity is infinitely more expansive than our ability to tell time on a clock and a calendar, which only work on this planet called Earth. Even though we don't know God's reasons for waiting, we do know that God's timing is perfect. The Apostle Paul phrased it, "When the fullness of time had come, God sent his Son, born of a woman" (Gal. 4:4, NRSV).

Even though we can't know God's reasons for waiting, we can look at history and see what happened during those four centuries and get a better picture of the world into which Jesus was born and a greater understanding of the events that shaped life for women in New Testament times. Remember, the events of the Old Testament happened over a period of thousands of years, while the historical events recorded in the New Testament happened over a period of only about 100 years. And because the New Testament events happened more recently, we know much more about those times than we do about the ancient times of the Old Testament.

Happenings in the Rest of the World - Highlights of the 4th Century BCE (300s)

During the 400 years of silence, with no new prophetic word from God, many events occurred that would shape the world into which Jesus would be born:

- In Greece, the 4th century BCE was the time of Socrates, Plato, and Aristotle, the great philosophers. It was Aristotle's negative view of women that would provide the still-lingering rationale for women's second-class status throughout the West. However, Plato's *Republic* recommended equal training for men and women including gymnastics, music, wrestling, and the arts of war.
- By mid century, China's ruler Shang Yang was using totalitarianism to govern.
- In what we know as modern-day Turkey, the famous Temple of Artemis was being rebuilt in Ephesus and, in Caria, the great tomb of governor Mausolus was built and would become known as one of the Seven Wonders of the Ancient World.
- On the other side of the world in Central America, the Mayans were building stone cities and understood astronomy well enough to develop an accurate calendar.
- In North America, the Hopewell people were building huge earth mounds in different shapes and trading with other tribes from the Great Lakes to the Gulf of Mexico.
- In Africa (specifically, modern-day Nigeria), the Nok people were thriving and skilled in making iron tools and becoming expert farmers.
- The last third of the 4th century BCE was dominated by Alexander the Great (son of Philip II of Macedon and student of Aristotle) and his rise to power when he conquered the Persian Empire. He began efforts to spread Greek, or Hellenistic, culture throughout

the world. Hellenistic culture would continue to expand for the next 300 years and reach from Greece to Egypt, through the Middle East, and extend all the way to India in the East. He founded Alexandria-in-Egypt which became the largest city in the Greek world by the mid 3rd century. Alexandria was the Hellenistic world's leading cultural center with the ancient world's largest library and where Euclid started his School of Geometry. One of the Seven Wonders of the Ancient World, the Lighthouse, was constructed in Alexandria. Hellenistic culture also included the development of modern medicine and the establishment of the Hippocratic Oath. When Alexander the Great died in 323 BCE, his vast kingdom was divided between his general Ptolemy, who obtained Egypt (and established the family of rulers through which Cleopatra would come); and his general Seleucus, who established the Seleucid Empire over much of the Near East, including Palestine.

Happenings in the Rest of the World - Highlights of the 3rd Century BCE (200s)

Hellenistic culture swept across the world. As the center of Hellenistic Judaism, the city of Alexandria in northern Egypt was where the Hebrew Scriptures were translated into Greek around 275 BCE, and called the *Septuagint* (the Latin word for 70), based on the legend that about 70 scholars translated it in about 70 days. This was the version of the Old Testament used by Greek-speaking Jews during New Testament times and would have been known to Jesus and the apostle Paul. The abbreviation LXX used for it today is the Roman numeral for 70.

In other parts of the Hellenistic world, another of the Seven Wonders of the Ancient World, the 110-foot tall Colossus of Rhodes statue, was erected on the Greek island of Rhodes, but was destroyed by an earthquake by the end of the century. In Greece, the pottery and vase painting showed women as tumblers, playing stringed instruments, and attending and serving at banquets. Hellenistic scientific knowledge was growing with Eratosthenes' measurement of the circumference of the

Earth to within 10% of the correct value and Archimedes' establishment of the basic laws of mechanics.

In parts of the world outside of Greek influence, the following events took place:

- The country of Nubia, covering part of modern-day Egypt and Sudan, had its first ruling queen.
- Among many people groups surrounding the Jews, the worship of goddesses was still prevalent, such as the goddess of the hearth, Vesta, whose priestesses in Rome, the Vestal Virgins, maintained the fire that was never allowed to go out.
- In China, women's political roles decreased but some people believed women had ties to the supernatural allowing them behind-the-scenes political and social powers. While parts of the Great Wall of China had been built as early as the 7th century BCE, sections were unified in the 3rd century BCE and the wall would continue to expand for many centuries. By the end of this century, China had its first emperor; the Han dynasty was established; and the cruel ruler Shih-Huangdi was buried with an underground terra-cotta army of more than 6,000 life-sized statues of soldiers.
- Ancestors of today's Japanese people moved from Korea to Japan and established agricultural communities.
- In India, the Maurya Empire reached its peak.

Happenings in the Rest of the World - Highlights of the 2nd Century BCE (100s)

While Hellenistic art was developing, such as sculptor Pythokritos' *Winged Victory of Samothrace* and Alexandros of Antioch's *Venus de Milo,* other parts of the world witnessed these events:

- China was manufacturing paper and Chinese women were working mainly in the household instead of the public square.
- Roman women marched on the Senate to have a law repealed which forbade them to wear jewels, purple, or gold embroidery, or to drive in carriages.
- People in Central America began building the city of Teotihuacan in 100 BCE, grew into the world's sixth largest city by 500 CE.

Focusing on the Jewish People's Story

In Judea, the ruling Hellenistic Seleucids tried to destroy all copies of the *Torah*, banned circumcision, sacrificed a pig on the altar, and erected idols in the Temple itself, thus sparking the Maccabean Revolt of the Jews against the Seleucids in 167 BCE. The revolt was led by Mattathias and his five sons: Judas (Maccabeus), Jonathan, Simon, John, and Eleazar. The battle waged for 24 years and resulted in the independence of Judea in 142 BCE. It was during this battle against the Seleucids that the miracle of the menorah occurred. There was only enough sacred oil to last for one day in the Temple's lampstand, yet it lasted for 8 days. This is what the Jewish holiday Hanukkah (or Festival of Lights or Feast of Dedication) commemorates each year. Once the Maccabees (later known as the Hasmoneans) won Judea's independence, their reign would last till 63 BCE, almost 80 years.

Happenings in the Rest of the World - At the End of the 2nd Century BCE

While Judea existed as an independent state, the Romans were expanding their territories. By mid century, the Romans annexed Greece and destroyed Carthage and Corinth, and became the new dominant world power. By the end of this century:

- The Hebrew Scriptures canon was finalized
- China had expanded its borders even more
- The library at Alexandria had grown to 490,000 volumes.

Focusing on the Jewish People's Story

The century before the birth of Christ was filled with wars and political intrigue, which had a direct impact on Palestine. At the beginning of the 1st century BCE, Judea was an independent state still ruled by the Hasmonean dynasty, including the Queen Salome Alexandra, who ruled piously and peacefully for nine years encouraging the education of all Jewish children. By the end of the century, however, Palestine would be ruled by Rome through a puppet king.

Happenings in the Rest of the World - Highlights of the 1st Century BCE (100 - 1 BCE)

During this century, Julius Caesar would conquer the Celts in Gaul and would rise to power in the Roman Republic only to be assassinated by senators who thought he had too much ruling authority. Caesar had an affair with Cleopatra of Egypt, who ruled from 51-31 BCE. She would be the last of the Ptolemy rulers in Egypt. In 40 BCE, Caesar's successors appointed an ambitious and cunning man named Herod as the king of Judea as the Parthians marched into Jerusalem and conquered it. Caesar's successor, Mark Antony, and Cleopatra would also have an affair and after Antony's defeat at Actium in 31 BCE, both he and Cleopatra committed suicide.

In the arts in this century, glass-blowing developed and flourished throughout the Roman world and Virgil, the great Roman poet, wrote his epic the *Aeneid*.

While Rome was dominating the Mediterranean world, here are some highlights of happenings in the rest of the world:

- World population reached 200-250 million by 1 BCE, having doubled over the course of the previous 1,000 years.
- The Trans-Asian Silk Road, which increased trade dramatically, was established between China and Western Europe.
- Buddhism was a major religion in India and numerous monuments were being built there in honor of the Buddha.
- The Bantu peoples of west Africa were spreading their farming skills as they migrated to central Africa on their way to their final destination of Lake Victoria by the end of the century.
- The country of Sri Lanka had a ruthless woman ruler, Queen Anula, from 47-42 BCE (until her son succeeded her). She is said to have poisoned numerous husbands and consorts.
- In the country of Meroe, Egypt's southern neighbor, Queen Amanishakete's rule lasted from 41-12 BCE. She was known for her building program and for bringing her country prosperity, widespread trade, and iron working. Her rule was followed by the joint rule of Queen Amanitere and King Natakamani from 12 BCE-12 CE. They oversaw Meroe's greatest building program.

Focusing on the Bible's Story

Back in Palestine, Herod was able to take Jerusalem back for Rome in 37 BCE and began his oppressive reign over Judea. Herod was a cunning ruler politically, aligning himself with the Roman powers that would give him the advantage in the affairs of the state and help him maintain peace. Octavian, Julius Caesar's adopted son, became the first emperor of Rome in 27 BCE, taking the name Caesar Augustus. He is mentioned in the gospel of Luke as the one who called for the census of the entire Roman world. Augustus was emperor until 14 CE, throughout Jesus' childhood.

Herod became known as Herod the Great. He put Judea on the map with his amazing construction projects including Caesarea Maritima on the Mediterranean coast, the Masada fortress near the Dead Sea, and the world's largest platform with the refurbished Jewish Temple sitting atop it in Jerusalem, to name a few. His megalomania was matched only by his insanity and paranoia which caused him to have his own family members executed. Judea was just one territory in the land known as Palestine and its major city was Jerusalem. Herod's reign expanded to encompass the area of Idumea (his own homeland to the south of Judea) and Perea on the east side of the Jordan River, as well as territories north of Judea, including Samaria, Galilee, and Traconitis.

This was the world in which Elizabeth, Mary of Nazareth, and the prophet Anna would come of age. Their people were still waiting for the 1000-year-old promise of a Messiah to be fulfilled. Their people had not heard a new prophetic word from their God, Adonai, for 400 years. Herod had been on the throne for more than 30 years and the Jewish people were desperate for some relief from the occupation of Roman forces in their homeland. When would God's silence be broken to bring a glimpse of hope?

Let's listen to the voices of Elizabeth, Mary, and Anna, when God chose them to be first. . . .

13

Elizabeth's Story

ca. 6 BCE

God chose Elizabeth's voice to be the first . . .

- To break the 400 years of silence with a new prophetic word from God

- Human to confirm to Mary that she was pregnant with the Messiah

Elizabeth's mind was racing with thoughts of all that needed to be done before her baby was born. She was frustrated with all she had let accumulate over the past six months in this small room. Yet, as she looked around, the memories of her quiet days spent in this room during those first five months of her pregnancy brought a warmth to her heart and a smile to her lips.

Zechariah was busy in his stone mason workshop, but not on baby things. *Well, that is not exactly true,* Elizabeth reminded herself. After all, he had taken on those extra projects from his best clients to be able to save a bit more money for the baby's needs. He and Elizabeth had both accepted the fact that in their advanced age, they probably would not live to see their son grow into adulthood. They were trying to prepare for an uncertain economic future under the rule of the heavy-handed King Herod. They had come to see that Herod's taxation policies were as benevolent as his killing sprees.

All that future planning was not getting the small room cleaned out for their young guest who should be arriving in a day or two. In preparation for their baby's birth, Zechariah had finally persuaded a reluctant Elizabeth to invite her great niece Mary to come stay for awhile to help with the delivery of the baby. Mary, even though she was only 14, had helped her own mother through two difficult births and Zechariah was confident she would not only be helpful with the birth, but would be some welcome company for Elizabeth. They did not want to bring undue attention to this birth, so they did not inform Mary's parents of

Elizabeth's pregnancy. They just sent their servant, Mordecai, up north to Nazareth to get Mary with a word of explanation for her parents that Mary's help was needed for a few months. Knowing how difficult it would be to have Mary gone from that household for so long, Elizabeth and Zechariah had also sent along some money to cover their taxes for several months and gifts of grain, dried fish, and fabric for Mary's mother to sew and sell.

Elizabeth let out a quiet chuckle as she remembered the day six months ago when Zechariah arrived home from his twice-yearly Temple duty not able to speak. He was completely mute. She had never seen anyone write so fast on a clay tablet or gesture so dramatically as Zechariah had that day. While on duty in the Temple, Zechariah had been visited by the angel Gabriel. Zechariah's startled interaction with Gabriel resulted in the temporary loss of his voice. At least the angel had promised it would be temporary. So they waited as expectantly for the return of Zechariah's voice as they did for the child Gabriel announced would be born in answer to their prayers. In the meantime, Elizabeth had grown accustomed to Zechariah's note-writing. Of course, their forty-plus years of marriage had taught them to finish each other's sentences. Elizabeth did have to admit that an actual back-and-forth conversation with Mary would be a nice addition to her days. Elizabeth knew all these memories would be the seedbed someday for bedtime stories for their young son.

Mary's trip from Nazareth would take several days. Now those days were quickly passing and the room was still a mess. The faster the days passed, the bigger Elizabeth's swollen feet became. Elizabeth struggled to take a deep breath before she bent over to fill yet another basket of unfinished sewing projects piled up on the bed. After the baby was weaned, this would become the baby's room. Elizabeth would still let out a sigh of contented joy every time she thought about the fact that she, a 60-year-old woman was about to have her first baby!

As the cool afternoon air turned brisker with the setting of the sun, Elizabeth approached the window to close the shutter. She looked out and noticed the silhouette of a girlish figure making her way quickly down the slippery hillside path on the western horizon and hoped she would make it into warm shelter soon. The pillowy purple clouds against the orange sky caught Elizabeth's attention and reminded her of that night six months ago when Zechariah arrived home from Jerusalem. That thought led her to realize that it was time for supper. She dropped the basket on the bed and made her way—carefully on painful feet—to Zechariah's workshop across the courtyard. As she and Zechariah reentered the courtyard, the sunset was just magnificent and they stood in quiet wonder remembering all that their God Adonai had done for them.

Suddenly, their silent moment was interrupted by their servant Mehira as she ran up to them and exclaimed, "She's here! She's here! Your niece from Nazareth has arrived!"

Elizabeth gave Zechariah a surprised and somewhat frustrated look and said, "But you said they would not arrive until late tomorrow at the earliest." Zechariah shrugged his shoulders looking as stunned as she was. It was times like these when she really missed his voice! By now Mary was through the gate and entering the courtyard. As soon as Elizabeth saw her young figure and bright smile, she opened her arms and wanted to run to greet her, but her heavy feet would not carry her as fast as she desired. Zechariah took her arm to offer support and assistance as they moved more determinedly toward Mary. The pebbles on the ground beneath them were a little more obvious to Elizabeth's swollen feet.

Mary's youthful arms were extended as she rushed toward Elizabeth. She threw her arms around Elizabeth with a strong embrace. Elizabeth stepped back to look into her bright, young face. Elizabeth's tears of joy flowed freely. This seemed to happen more frequently these days.

All of a sudden, after Mary's loving and familiar greeting, Elizabeth felt a strange sensation—a deep, tightening pressure—not painful—just unexpected and startling. She strengthened her grasp of Mary's arm with one hand while she clutched at her belly with her other hand. Zechariah looked alarmed and stood like a pillar. Elizabeth felt the baby move in her womb with great strength, as if he could leap right out of her. And then, as quickly as it had tightened, it released and she was filled with a tingling warmth flowing all through her like she had never felt before. It was as if someone had suddenly wrapped her in a huge cloak that had been warmed by a fire. Mary held Elizabeth's arm more securely and then reached over to touch Elizabeth's hand resting on her belly. Elizabeth looked back into Mary's young smiling face and saw something new--a *woman's* sense of knowing. Elizabeth felt a deep assurance that here was one who would understand this miracle she was carrying.

Elizabeth gasped and smiled with a joy welling up from deep within. She loosened her grip on Mary's arm, took Mary's face in both her hands and kissed her on both cheeks. Elizabeth could no longer contain her joy, and with an exuberant voice Elizabeth exclaimed, "On what a blessed woman you are, Mary! I am so grateful you have come."

Mary smiled and said, "I was so excited to get here, I made Mordecai let me run the rest of the way when he stopped at the blacksmith's on the edge of town to repair something on the wagon." Mary embraced Elizabeth again and whispered in her ear so that only Elizabeth would hear her, "I know you are six months pregnant, Aunt Elizabeth. Our God, Adonai, sent an angel to tell me!"

Elizabeth pulled away and looked deep within Mary's shining eyes reflecting the glow coming from the lamplit window. Mary's face was assured of the truth she spoke. They both stood there almost breathless—as if time simply stopped for them to emblazon this moment in their memories.

Zechariah could be patient no longer. He got their attention and with some dramatic hand motions made sure Elizabeth explained to Mary why he was not talking. In the midst of Elizabeth's cursory explanation, Mordecai entered the courtyard and asked in a somber tone to speak to Zechariah, motioning toward the shelter for the animals. Zechariah frowned as if worried and then quickly gave Elizabeth a reassuring glance as he departed and left her alone with Mary.

Elizabeth took Mary by the arm and they headed into the house filled with the warmth of a family's love. "Oh, Mary, we have so much to talk about!" They made their way to the seating near the fire. Mary helped her ease down onto the bench covered with cushions and then Mary sat on the cushion next to her.

"When did you know you were with child?" Mary asked curiously.

"Oh, Mary, where to start?" Elizabeth put her hand to her head. Her thoughts were coming so quickly. "Let me think for a moment. . . . Wait, you must be exhausted. Oh, let me look at you! It has been two Passover holidays since we have seen you or your mother. And you have a new baby brother since we saw you last. Why, you are absolutely glowing!" Elizabeth admired Mary's youthful beauty and envied her ease of movement. "You know, we did not expect Mordecai to be able to return with you until tomorrow or the next day. How did you get here so quickly?"

Mary started to answer but Elizabeth was so excited to see Mary, she just kept asking questions and never gave her a chance to answer. Then, in a flash of recognition, Elizabeth said, "Oh, that must have been you I saw coming down the path earlier." Suddenly that feeling of consuming warmth came over Elizabeth's body again. Distracted by the sensation, she sat still a moment. Then, she looked back into Mary's dark eyes and reached out to caress Mary's tender face. Mary took Elizabeth's hand and gently redirected it to her own belly. With great amazement, Elizabeth gasped. A thousand thoughts suddenly filled Elizabeth's mind. Some were frightful thoughts and then an immediate, calming sense of peace arrested any fears. Speaking just above a whisper, Elizabeth said with a determined tone, "And blessed is the fruit of *your* womb." Mary smiled and nodded.

Elizabeth was not sure what to think. *If Mary is pregnant and not yet married to Joseph, what will happen?!* That thought disappeared as Elizabeth was filled with a new sense of awe—a feeling of a wondrous presence. Speechless, Elizabeth glanced back and forth from Mary's belly to her big midnight eyes. Then with a profound assurance, Elizabeth suddenly realized just who was sitting before her. "Oh, Mary, why am I so blessed?"

"What do you mean?" a surprised Mary asked.

Almost breathlessly, Elizabeth said with great reverence, "I mean . . . why am I so honored to have the *mother* of my *Lord* come to visit *me*?" Elizabeth lowered her head as a gesture of sincere humility since she was unable to get on her knees.

With a combination of worry and absolute glee, Mary asked, "How did you *know*? How did you *know*?" Tears sat on her raven black eyelashes. "I have not told anyone!" she stated matter-of-factly as if trying to convince herself more than Elizabeth. "How *did* you know?" was all she could say until they were both calm enough to start a conversation.

Elizabeth stroked her cheek and they leaned in close, forehead to forehead, as if ready to share a secret; which indeed they were—a secret they both now knew.

"Oh, my sweet child. Somehow, in my spirit, our God, Adonai, let me know just then that you, too, are with child—the child who will be *the Anointed One—our Messiah!* I thought I was sending for you so you could help me birth *my* baby . . . but apparently, Adonai has other plans as well."

The Bible Speaks

Elizabeth's story is found in Luke 1

The Jewish people had been able to maintain their religious observances, albeit, off and on, and had maintained their identity as God's chosen people for more than two *thousand* years by the time our story of Elizabeth begins. Their multi-millennia history included stories of God's deliverance from famine, slavery, exile, wicked kings, oppressive foreign rulers, and wars. Their prophets of old had told them that someday God would send a savior for their people. However, the last prophet to make such a promise was Malachi and he had come and gone four centuries ago!

The only biblical account we have about Elizabeth is found in Luke's gospel, which is known for its details and portrayal of women in the life of Jesus. In Luke 1:5, Luke sets the stage by telling us that Elizabeth lived during the time of Herod, king of Judea. For those original hearers and readers of this gospel, that one phrase would probably have sent groans through the audience.

At this point in history, Herod had reigned in Judea for more than 30 years as a paranoid, ruthless, oppressive ruler who functioned under the authority of Rome. The oppressive atmosphere in Judea was a daily reminder to the Jews of their desire for a savior who would deliver them from this torturous Roman domination.

Because Palestine was on the eastern border of the Great Sea, the Mediterranean, it was a major thoroughfare for merchants from the West and East getting their wares to Palestine's seaports to be transported to faraway destinations. This meant that many different cultures and people passed through Jerusalem. Not everyone in the city or territory was Jewish, yet the Jews were very influential politically and Herod worked hard to keep them under control.

Palestine in the 1st century BCE was known for King Herod's extravagant building projects which had brought international fame to the area. While Herod's wealth increased, so did his mental instability. His household and kingdom lived in constant fear of his next reaction to some of his paranoid beliefs. He was known to call for executions on a whim—whether family members, certain political factions that disagreed with him, or religious leaders who got in the way of his total control.

Herod rebuilt the Jewish Temple to appease the Jewish population and it was considered an architectural marvel in its day. He had forced 1,000 priests into manual labor for the reconstruction project and it was completed in record time. He was also known for his many wives, 10 or 11 altogether, 9 of whom could have been living in the palace at the same time.

Herod was not Jewish by birth, but was from the territory of Idumea in southern Palestine where his father, Antipater, had ruled. The Jews had conquered the area when Herod was a boy and had forced the population to convert to Judaism. Needless to say, that certainly did not cause him to want to be a faithful, God-fearing Jew, but he managed to use religion to his advantage whenever he needed to.

Zechariah and Elizabeth
Luke 1:5-7

5 During the rule of King Herod of Judea there was a priest named
Zechariah who belonged to the priestly division of Abijah. His wife
Elizabeth was a descendant of Aaron. **6** They were both righteous before
God, blameless in their observance of all the Lord's commandments and
regulations. **7** They had no children because Elizabeth was unable to
become pregnant and they both were very old. (CEB)

Elizabeth was the devout wife of a Jewish priest. She was from the prestigious tribe of Levi from which Aaron and his siblings, Miriam and Moses, came. Aaron had been the first high priest for the Jews. Elizabeth grew up in a priestly family and was therefore well-suited and qualified to marry a priest. She lived according to the Jewish laws which would have been distinctly different from the dominant pagan Roman culture of the time. However, Elizabeth's role was not related to Zechariah's priestly duties. Zechariah would have had Temple duty a few weeks each year, not a weekly or daily responsibility we see our modern-day pastors and priests fulfill. Zechariah would have had another job as well, though we don't know what that was.

For women in that time, bearing children was almost the only means of status a woman could claim. Since women were mostly dependent on men for their livelihood, they needed to have sons who could care for them when they became widowed. Not having sons and only having daughters was an unwelcome situation, but not having any children at all was viewed as a curse from God. Elizabeth's story was one of heart-wrenching infertility, known as barrenness then. Elizabeth had endured the misunderstanding and shame from ignorant people her whole married life and was now past childbearing years. Yet, the author of the gospel of Luke was careful to record that Elizabeth and her husband were righteous people. In spite of their ages, she and her husband, Zechariah, had continued to pray for a son.

Zechariah was one of 1,000 Jewish priests living throughout Judea in the time of King Herod's ruthless rule. He may very well have been conscripted by Herod to help with the building of the Second Temple. In the story in Luke, we see Zechariah being chosen by lot (a sacred way, ordained by God at that time, of throwing the dice) to be the one who would tend the incense on one of his assigned days to serve at the Temple. Considering how many priests worked at the Temple at any given time, this was probably a once-in-a-lifetime honor. And on this momentous occasion, Zechariah was about to have a life-changing encounter with an angel.

The Angel Gabriel Appears to Zechariah; Elizabeth's Miraculous Pregnancy
Luke 1:8-25

8 One day Zechariah was serving as a priest before God because his
priestly division was on duty. **9** Following the customs of priestly service,
he was chosen by lottery to go into the Lord's sanctuary and burn
incense. **10** All the people who gathered to worship were praying outside
during this hour of incense offering. **11** An angel from the Lord appeared
to him, standing to the right of the altar of incense. **12** When Zechariah
saw the angel, he was startled and overcome with fear.

13 The angel said, "Don't be afraid, Zechariah. Your prayers have been
heard. Your wife Elizabeth will give birth to your son and you must name
him John. **14** He will be a joy and delight to you, and many people will
rejoice at his birth, **15** for he will be great in the Lord's eyes. He must not
drink wine and liquor. He will be filled with the Holy Spirit even before
his birth. **16** He will bring many Israelites back to the Lord their
God. **17** He will go forth before the Lord, equipped with the spirit and
power of Elijah. He will turn the hearts of fathers[a] back to their
children, and he will turn the disobedient to righteous patterns of
thinking. He will make ready a people prepared for the Lord."

18 Zechariah said to the angel, "How can I be sure of this? My wife
and I are very old."

19 The angel replied, "I am Gabriel. I stand in God's presence. I was
sent to speak to you and to bring this good news to you. **20** Know this:
What I have spoken will come true at the proper time. But because you
didn't believe, you will remain silent, unable to speak until the day when
these things happen."

21 Meanwhile, the people were waiting for Zechariah, and they wondered why he was in the sanctuary for such a long time. **22** When he came out, he was unable to speak to them. They realized he had seen a vision in the temple, for he gestured to them and couldn't speak. **23** When he completed the days of his priestly service, he returned home. **24** Afterward, his wife Elizabeth became pregnant. She kept to herself for five months, saying, **25** "This is the Lord's doing. He has shown his favor to me by removing my disgrace among other people." (CEB)

The time represented by the distance between verses 23 and 24 leaves much to the imagination! How on earth did Zechariah explain to Elizabeth what had happened to him in the Temple without being able to speak?! I choose to assume Elizabeth knew how to read and Zechariah wrote his story on a clay tablet accompanied by dramatic hand gestures and some acting ability. And the word "afterward" in verse 24 is filled with meaning. Other translations say, "after these days" or simply, "after this." I'm just saying those "days" must have been a time of wonderful romance for this much older couple to get pregnant. It may have been miraculous, but it still happened the human way as compared to Mary's virgin birth.

Verse 24 also reveals that Elizabeth "kept to herself for five months" or as other translations say, "went into seclusion" (NASB, NIV) or "hid herself" (KJV, NKJV). This was not a common practice at that time, and it is unclear what this could mean. My thought is that she wanted to relish each moment of this miracle in her life, such as stated in *The Message*: "went off by herself for five months, relishing her pregnancy." Or maybe she wanted to prevent herself from exclaiming it to everyone she saw and only increasing their doubts of her integrity. After all, Elizabeth was past childbearing years. Was she 50? 60? Maybe she had some supernatural motivation to have as much solitude as possible to prepare her for all that was to come. The Scripture gives no indication at this point that she knew Mary would be coming to see her or that she was about to be related to the Messiah!

In verse 25, Elizabeth expresses heartfelt praise and gratitude to God for bringing this miracle of pregnancy into her life and for removing the "disgrace" she had suffered all those years—maybe 40-50 years—from the taunts, whispers and misguided advice from neighbors, family, and friends. All her waiting was for a much bigger purpose than she could have ever imagined! Elizabeth's faithfulness, even in the midst of false accusations and suspicions, and her obvious attitude of gratitude, made her a well-suited parent for a uniquely gifted son. These traits also made her a wise and trustworthy companion for a much younger Mary, the soon-to-be mother of Jesus.

The next passage reveals the intersection of the lives of John the Baptist and Jesus through their mothers (not their fathers!) and the busy itinerary of God's messenger, the angel Gabriel.

The Angel Gabriel Reveals Elizabeth's Pregnancy to Mary
Luke 1:26-28, 35-38
26 When Elizabeth was six months pregnant, God sent the angel Gabriel to Nazareth, a city in Galilee, **27** to a virgin who was engaged to a man named Joseph, a descendant of David's house. The virgin's name was Mary. **28** When the angel came to her, he said, "Rejoice, favored one! The Lord is with you!" . . . **35** "The Holy Spirit will come over you and the power of the Most High will overshadow you. Therefore, the one who is to be born will be holy. He will be called God's Son. **36** Look, even in her old age, your relative Elizabeth has conceived a son. This woman who was labeled 'unable to conceive' is now six months pregnant. **37** Nothing is impossible for God."

38 Then Mary said, "I am the Lord's servant. Let it be with me just as you have said." Then the angel left her. (CEB)

The angel Gabriel has had two errands in the first chapter of Luke and they were for the purpose of delivering miraculous birth announcements. After 400 years of silence with no new prophetic word from God to the Jewish people, the news that will break that silence is about birthing babies. What does that say about the tremendous respect our God has for an act only women can perform? To think, God worked through the willingness of an older woman past childbearing years to bring into the world the one who would prepare the way for the Messiah. Then, God also worked through a young, betrothed—yet still unwed—teenager to birth the Messiah! What great value God has placed on women's bodies and the process of conception and childbirth!

Mary Visits Elizabeth
Luke 1:39

39 Mary got up and hurried to a city in the Judean highlands. (CEB)

Hurrying or going with haste to a city 90 miles away across dry, rugged, hilly terrain was a challenge for anyone in biblical times. Tradition has claimed the small town of Ein Karem—still there today—as Elizabeth's city in the Judean hill country. Ein Karem was about 5 miles west of the bustling, multi-cultural metropolis of Jerusalem. This small village was lush and green and its hills and valleys were a bit steeper than the plateaus and hillsides of Jerusalem. Jewish girls at that time were betrothed as early as 12 or 13 years of age, so Mary may have been about 14 years old. She certainly would not have been able to travel alone that distance. A 90-mile walk in those days would have taken 4-5 days. More than likely, she would have traveled in a caravan of family or trusted friends, so the length of the trip could have been a bit shorter or a bit longer. We are not sure how she got to Elizabeth's, but we know it was not just around the corner and down the block!

The phrase "got up and hurried" or as other translations have said, "went with haste," allows us to imagine that Mary wanted to be with Elizabeth more than anyone at this time. We can assume that Elizabeth had provided a warm and welcoming home for Mary on previous visits and Mary knew she would be received by her now. The fact that Elizabeth and Mary were the only two people in the world at that time who were experiencing miraculous pregnancies is evidence that God wanted them to be together in a place where no explaining or persuading would be needed. They would find the perfect support in each other's company. For me, this short story is filled with inspiring messages about the high value God places on women's relationships and about mentoring.

Elizabeth Breaks the Silence
Luke 1:40-45

40 She [Mary] entered Zechariah's home and greeted Elizabeth. **41** When Elizabeth heard Mary's greeting, the child leaped in her womb, and Elizabeth was filled with the Holy Spirit. **42** With a loud voice she blurted out, "God has blessed you above all women, and he has blessed the child you carry. **43** Why do I have this honor, that the mother of my Lord should come to me? **44** As soon as I heard your greeting, the baby in my womb jumped for joy. **45** Happy is she who believed that the Lord would fulfill the promises he made to her." (CEB)

Because of the greeting Elizabeth expressed when Mary arrived, we know Elizabeth was thrilled to see her. Yet we can also detect in Elizabeth an attitude of reverent awe and admiration for this much younger mother-to-be. Personally, I think *that* is almost miraculous! Elizabeth could have been jealous and frustrated that God chose this young, unwed teenager to be the mother of the Messiah over her and her lifetime of faithfulness. But instead, we don't get just a sense of love and joy in this greeting, we get to hear **Elizabeth as the *first* human voice in Scripture to confirm the imminent birth of the Messiah to Mary and as the first person to rejoice with her about this news!** According to the biblical narrative, no other person talked with Mary about the coming Christ child before she went to see Elizabeth. So, **when God chose a person to break 400 years of silence with a prophecy declaring the coming of the Christ child, God chose Elizabeth to speak it.** What a blessing it must have been to Mary to hear her dearly loved Elizabeth say those words and to discover there was someone who would believe her stories of her encounter with the angel!

Three Busy Months
Luke 1:56

56 Mary stayed with Elizabeth about three months, and then returned to her home. (CEB)

This verse gives us a clue of just how hospitable Elizabeth was. Remember, Elizabeth was much older and six months pregnant with her own miracle baby when she welcomed an unwed, pregnant teenager into her home! Mary's pregnancy could have been blamed on adultery, and she could have received the death penalty. What a risk-taker and what an open heart on Elizabeth's part! Notice, Mary didn't come for a weekend. She stayed for three months. The Bible is not clear whether Mary was present for John's birth, but I would like to think she was.

Can you imagine the late-night conversations? I can just see Elizabeth helping Mary get through those first morning sickness months. I can hear Mary telling Elizabeth more about the angel Gabriel since Zechariah had been struck mute after he saw the same angel. I can smell good things in the oven as Elizabeth and Mary shared lots of laughter and fun around the table while working on sewing projects in preparation for the births of their firstborn sons.

Elizabeth's story is often overshadowed by the Christmas story and yet she plays a significant role in the preparation of Mary as the mother of the Messiah. Because Elizabeth had stayed faithful all those years in the midst of false accusations, she had learned how to endure social ridicule and maintain an attitude of gratitude. She was not only a well-suited parent for her uniquely gifted son John, but she was the older and wiser confidant for a much younger and vulnerable Mary. Elizabeth knew she and Zechariah were innocent before God in spite of *not* having a baby. God used this to help her to believe and encourage Mary who was innocent before God in spite of *having* a baby!

The Message in Elizabeth's Voice

We learn as much from Elizabeth's example as we do from her words. I have never been pregnant, but I have been around enough pregnant women to know that the last few months can be especially exhausting. Yet, Elizabeth opened both her home and her life to this young woman. That's what mentoring is: no particular agenda, just being there. I like how *The Message* expresses Matthew 5:16, "Keep open house; be generous with your lives. By opening up to others, you'll prompt people to open up with God, this generous Father in heaven." Here are some of the characteristics I see Elizabeth demonstrating as the perfect mentor for Mary:

1. She was a faithful woman who lived out her beliefs.
2. She was the only other woman experiencing a miraculous pregnancy at that time.
3. She had struggled and prayed through a personal issue for many years. Her issue was barrenness and the accompanying shame that came with it in biblical days.
4. She was hospitable and provided a welcoming place for Mary.
5. She respected Mary for the role God had chosen for her.
6. She was sensitive to the Holy Spirit's activity in her own life and in Mary's life.
7. She spoke boldly when necessary.

However, mentoring would go in both directions. Mary had experienced things that would help Elizabeth: talking with the same angel as Zechariah and having scriptural insights (see Luke 1:46-55). God understands a woman's need to be with other women to share deeply personal feelings and experiences. No one else in the world could have understood what they were going through as they could for each other. Women's relationships with other women are very important to God. God made sure that Elizabeth and Mary would have each other as mentors for their miraculous pregnancies. The biblical account of their visit gives us a beautiful example of an older woman respecting and valuing the younger woman.

Elizabeth's voice would be the first human voice to confirm Mary's pregnancy with the long-awaited Messiah and in so doing be the first human voice to break the 400 years of silence with a new prophetic word from God!

How to Bless Younger Women

Let Elizabeth's voice remind you that your voice can bless younger women. Here are five ways we can speak blessings into the next generation:

1. Demonstrate how you apply God's word to your life.

Actions speak louder than words. However, it is still important to talk about specific Scriptures and how they have ministered to you at different times in your life.

2. Be welcoming and fully present whenever you meet with a younger woman.

Silence your cell phone and remove it from sight. Remove any other distractions that take your attention away from her. This demonstrates respect and love. You want her to *want* to be with you.

3. Be genuinely encouraging.

Acknowledge all the good things you see going on in her life or in her abilities. Be specific in identifying specific gifts, skills, and talents that you see God using in her life. Help her to see her value in being the unique gift she is to the world. Remember, you are not encouraging her to become like *your* generation, you are encouraging her to be the best of *her* generation.

4. Talk about deeply spiritual things.

Make it easy for her to express questions and doubts about her faith so you can study and discern the answers together. When it is appropriate, confess to her the doubts you have worked through over the years. Be sure to acknowledge your lack of expertise and your desire to learn alongside her.

5. Be careful that you listen more than you speak.
Invite her to share her story and her questions by asking open-ended questions. When she shares personal information, keep that information strictly confidential to build trust. Give advice *only* when asked.

Biblical Truths Taught through the Story of Elizabeth

1. God fills women with the Holy Spirit.
2. God communicates directly to and through women.
3. God chooses women's voices to break the silence with announcements of God's presence and prophecies.
4. God values women's relationships with each other and wants those relationships to be uplifting, encouraging, and supportive, regardless of differences in age or social status.
5. God has placed such high value on women's bodies that God chose to work through them to usher in the perfect plan of salvation with the birth of Elizabeth's and Mary's sons.
6. God chooses women to announce God's activity in the world.

Why the Voice of Elizabeth Matters . . .

To ministers' wives: because Elizabeth's story reveals how sometimes the message your spouse gets from God may be best communicated through your voice and actions.

To women who long for a child: because Elizabeth's story reminds you God knows your greatest pains and deepest desires and has a purpose for all of them beyond your wildest imagination.

To husbands of hurting wives: because Elizabeth's story says your wife's pain may need the encouragement and support she can get only by spending time with other women.

To women with younger women in your lives: because Elizabeth's story reminds you God has placed you uniquely in their path to be role models, encouragers, and places of warm hospitality, and also to glean wisdom *from* them and their experiences.

Questions Raised by the Story of Elizabeth

Why do we not hear the story about Elizabeth's role in Mary's life more often at Christmas?

Why is it not emphasized in our churches that when God was ready to break the silence of 400 years, God chose to use a woman's voice to announce God's activity, which related to experiences unique to women —pregnancy and childbirth?

Who is someone younger than you who needs a mentor?

How could God use some of the pain of your past to bring comfort and faith to someone else in a similar situation?

How could you invest your time in the younger generation of women at work, in your neighborhood, in your church, or even in your extended family?

If you are a women's ministry leader, what are some ways you can mentor younger women?

Which young woman in your circle of influence needs a word of affirmation from you?

What can you do to affirm the calling from God another woman thinks she is hearing?

What are some areas of knowledge and experience you are lacking and who is a younger woman who could enlighten you?

What are some ways the Spirit could use you to speak into a younger woman's dreams?

How might God use your voice to encourage the next generation as they prepare to lead and influence others?

Elizabeth's Keys to Resilient Confidence

I believe Elizabeth would say that expectant faithfulness and open-hearted hospitality were her keys to resilient confidence. Her lifetime of faithfulness in spite of the deep anguish of infertility is shown by the description that she was "righteous before God" and that she and Zechariah had continued to pray for a son. These expectant habits—along with the pain—taught her valuable lessons which she was prepared to share with the younger generation. And she made room in her life to welcome a younger woman from whom she was willing to learn as well. Elizabeth's example provides six traits you can adopt in your role as a mentor or look for in a potential mentor.

As an open-hearted, hospitable mentor:

1. You look with admiration at what God is doing in the life of your mentee.

Elizabeth was not jealous of the role of a younger Mary in God's kingdom. *Your* words of encouragement are what your mentee needs to hear.

2. You allow your mentee to take up "space" in your world for a period of time.

Just imagine: the elderly, mother-to-be Elizabeth opened her home and her heart during the last three months of her pregnancy to the unwed, pregnant, teenaged Mary during her first trimester with all the morning sickness and mood swings that accompany it. What generosity and love! This demonstrates how important women's relationships are to God. Even in the midst of her own major life changes, Elizabeth made time and provided a place for a young woman in need of her unique knowledge and experience. You have experienced God's grace in a unique way which may be the inspiration your mentee needs.

3. You are consciously aware of God's activity in your mentee's life and express joyful exuberance in that activity.

Elizabeth was supernaturally made aware of God's purpose for Mary and expressed heartfelt joy in that purpose. As a matter of fact, according to the biblical record, **Elizabeth's voice was the first human voice to confirm the coming birth of the Messiah to Mary.** (Note: it wasn't Joseph or any other man who provided verbal confirmation.) Through the Holy Spirit, you can sense how God is working in your mentee's life.

4. You express your thoughts with humility.

Elizabeth's humble acknowledgement of Mary's role indicated her delight in simply getting to be a part of it. Whether you are responding to your mentee's questions or offering helpful observations, you must demonstrate your own teachability and your need to continue to learn as well. You can be deliberate in finding ways that your mentee can teach you something.

5. Take time to listen to the heart cry of your mentee.

Since Elizabeth was the first person to confirm Mary's miraculous pregnancy, maybe that was Mary's first opportunity to speak of it aloud. Can you imagine the joyful release that was? God may use you to be the first safe place your mentee will have to share a deep concern or joy.

6. Realize that as you fulfill your mentor role, God is doing a new thing in your own life as well.

Elizabeth was aware of God's activity in her own life and in connection with her relationship with Mary. God is allowing the people and experiences in our lives to help mold us into the people we were created to be.

Living out these traits as a mentor will contribute to the development of your resilient confidence.

"With a loud voice she blurted out, . . . 'Happy is she who believed that the Lord would fulfill the promises he made to her.'"
—Luke 1:42a, 45 (CEB)

14

Mary's Story

ca. 20 BCE - 70 CE

God chose Mary's voice to be the first . . .

- To discuss with the angel Gabriel the news that the Messiah was about to be born and that his name would be Jesus

- To rejoice with Elizabeth about both their pregnancies

- To sing a song of prophetic praise after 400 years of prophetic silence from God

- To request a miracle from Jesus

Mary couldn't remember the last time she and John had laughed so long and hard. Their dinner guests, Silas and Luke, had regaled them with the stories of their adventures to foreign lands and people. She couldn't believe it had been more than 30 years since her son Jesus had ascended to his Heavenly Father or that she had been with her "adopted" son John that long. And it had been almost that long since she had first met these two committed missionaries. She was delighted they had come to spend a few days with her and John in their new home in Jerusalem.

Mary was glad to be settling back into life in the bustling city of Jerusalem after a busy few years. She did not really believe things would calm down, but at least Jerusalem was a bit more familiar territory. Helping John start several churches in Asia had been exciting—and exhausting—work. This place made life feel a bit more restful. They were planning to stay here until God called them elsewhere.

At each of the churches where John and Mary served over the years, she had become known as "Mother Mary" to the young families in those communities. She was a grandmother to everyone. Her date cakes were everyone's favorites and her seamstress work had helped provide for her and John's needs as well as give her some special opportunities to get to know the young mothers in the neighborhoods. The children loved to hear Mary tell stories of when Jesus was born and of his growing up learning to be a fine carpenter from his earthly father Joseph. Since Mary lived so far away from her own grandchildren, she treasured any chance to pour out her grandmotherly love on the children in the different churches they served.

Sensing the late hour, Mary finally spoke up, "Now, John, I'm sure our guests would like to get some rest. We can visit more tomorrow."

The weary travelers were grateful for the home-cooked meal and the clean beds. John took the hint and started to lead Silas and Luke to their rooms where fresh linens, some of Mary's handiwork, awaited them. As they headed to their rooms, Luke made a special request of Mary, "Mother Mary, I have decided to write an account of your son's ministry. I know John Mark has written one. I am privileged to have a copy. But I want to start at the beginning. I want to tell the story that you tell. Would you allow me to interview you during our few days here together?"

"Why, Luke, I am so glad you want to write about Jesus," replied a beaming mother. "I am sure that will be a big help to the churches." Her eyes were distant for a moment. "It is so hard to believe that he's been gone for more than 30 years. But I don't know that my part of the story is so important. The focus needs to be on Jesus and his power and the grace and mercy he offers all of us."

"I totally agree, Mother Mary, but I want to write for a Gentile audience," explained Luke. "They need to see Jesus as a real man—not just another god to add to their list. And then I think they can begin to see him as the Only God who can relate to them and their human struggles. I think the story of his birth is vitally important! And I know you can talk about details that no one else knows, if you're willing."

"Well, Luke, I will be happy to help any way I can. We can start fresh tomorrow after you've had a good rest. I may talk your ear off, though." Mary's whole face was smiling as she began to remember the details of that night so long ago.

~

The next morning, a sleepy Luke came out of his room with a quill, ink pot, and papyrus sheets in hand to find a busy Mother Mary already working on a sewing project. "Good morning, Luke. I trust you slept well," welcomed a cheery Mary.

"Oh, I have never slept on such fine linens. Where did you find such fabric?"

"I usually weave my own, Luke, but that fabric was a gift from a merchant in Philadelphia when John was pastoring the church there. I only sewed the pieces together to make the bed linens and embroidered the edges. They are soft, are they not?"

Luke nodded as he took a bite of the warm, freshly baked bread on the table. "Are you ready to start our interview, Mother Mary?"

"I believe so. I'm not sure how much this 80-year-old mind can offer, but I'll do my best."

"So, start at the beginning, please, with how you met Joseph, what it was like to meet the angel Gabriel, and how people reacted to your news of being with child."

"Those are all sweet memories indeed, Luke. Well, most of them. But, I don't think you have enough ink or papyrus to tell everything that happened in that year Joseph and I were preparing to be married! I'll tell you all the details on another visit. For now, I'll tell you about meeting the archangel Gabriel. Oh, now let me think . . . where to start?" Looking into the distance as if reading her own ponderings, Mary began to think out loud, "Well, you need to know about my Great Aunt Elizabeth and Great Uncle Zechariah, too . . . They are an important part of this story. Let's see . . . No, I think I'll start with Gabriel's visit and then tell you about Elizabeth. You can sort it out in your writing later."

Luke's quill was poised to jot down notes.

"It was just after the Festival of Lights and Mother and I had put away the special candles we saved for that special celebration each year. I went outside early one morning to gather wool for my mother. In the courtyard, at the corner of the house, Father had built a big waterproof crate to store the lamb's wool Mother used to make her fine threads and fabric. With my arms full of soft, fluffy wool, I suddenly noticed a warm glow all around me. I also noticed that there was a wonderful aroma in the air—like cinnamon and fresh baked bread, but even better. As I turned around, away from the crate, I saw the most amazing circle of bright colors. And it sparkled like when the sun touches the ripples in the sea."

Luke couldn't write fast enough, so he gave up. He decided just to sit back and listen; he would write it down later.

An animated Mary continued, "I wasn't sure what I was seeing. I dropped the wool and rubbed my eyes. When I looked again there was a dazzling white creature—or man—or something, standing in front of me."

"Were you frightened?"

"Of course! But I was so stunned by the beauty I was seeing, I couldn't speak."

"What did you do?"

"I fell to my knees first and put my face in hands. Then this creature—this angel—gently touched my shoulders and lifted my head. He knelt down in front of me and smiled and seemed so happy to see me. His first words were, 'Rejoice, favored one. The Lord is with you.' I wondered who he thought I could be. I didn't consider myself 'favored.' I was really confused."

Luke interrupted, "What did he sound like?"

"Oh, it was a gentle voice, yet deep and . . . confident . . . determined. He wasn't loud, but he was very clear and direct. It was as if he was looking deep within me. I will never forget that feeling. Of course, Jesus gave me that feeling, too, even when he was a child—like the time we found him in the Temple teaching the elders, but that's another story."

"How I wish I had met him while he was here walking among us," said a wistful Luke. They were both silent for a moment caught up in the memories. "So what else did he say? . . . Try to remember the exact words," Luke pleaded.

"He could tell I was frightened, so the next thing he said was, 'Don't be afraid, Mary. God is honoring you.' I was amazed he knew my name. I was still speechless. I'm sure he could see the bewilderment on my face. So, he started over and told me he was Gabriel and that God had sent him to me. He was very careful in what he said next, speaking calmly and with great assurance in the truth of the words."

Luke interrupted, "That must have been amazing. What did he say next?"

Mary continued, "He was so kind and gentle with me. Then he said, 'God has a surprise for you! You will conceive and give birth to a son, and you will name him Jesus. He will be great and he will be called the Son of the Highest. The Lord God will give him the throne of David his father. He will rule over Jacob's house forever, and there will be no end to his kingdom.' I'm not sure what the expression on my face was by that time. It was so much to take in. But I do remember realizing that I wasn't married yet, so how was I supposed to conceive this baby? When I could finally gather my thoughts, I asked in a whisper, 'How can I have a baby? I am a virgin.'"

"How did Gabriel explain that?" Luke's physician mind was fully engaged.

"Well, he said these words—with a big smile—but they didn't really make sense until later, 'The Holy Spirit will come over you and the power of the Most High will overshadow you. Therefore, the one who is to be born will be holy. He will be called God's Son.'"

"When do you think you started to understand what he was saying?"

"I'm not sure. I do remember having this feeling of warmth flow over me. He must have sensed I needed some sort of sign that this could really happen, so then he told me some other news that was just as amazing. For him—a messenger from God—it was just a fact, so he did not announce it with the same excitement as I would have. He said, 'You need to know that your relative Elizabeth, even in her old age, has also conceived a son. The one who everyone thought was barren, is now six months pregnant. As you can see, nothing is impossible with God.' His words were music to my ears. Oh, how long our family had prayed for Elizabeth and Zechariah. I was certainly convinced by now and said to him, 'I am the Lord's servant. Let it be with me just as you have said.'"

"Oh, Mary, what a story! May I include that in my writing?"

"If you think it will help, Luke."

"So you're saying that the angel came to you first, not to Joseph?"

"That's right. You know, sometimes our God chooses women to be the first ones to speak or receive messages from God; and then we must tell the men."

"Oh, I'm well aware of that! I've learned the story of Judge Deborah—the first judge of Israel who spoke for God as a prophet. And the story of Huldah—the woman prophet who was the first to verify a written document as God's law. And I know Paul certainly relied on women as faithful proclaimers of the gospel. He even asked our deacon friend, Phoebe, to deliver his letter to the church in Rome and I'm sure she was the first to read it to the folks there. And the church in Philippi wouldn't exist without their leader, Lydia, whom Paul led to the Lord. Yes, you women are the backbone of most of the churches we've visited over the years."

"You have learned our history well, Luke!" Mary was smiling with pride at this Gentile Christian.

"Well, being with Paul all those years, I had a very good tutor!"

They laughed and Mary responded, "Yes, I'm sure you learned more than you ever thought you'd need to know!"

"Okay, back to your story . . . What did you do? What did Gabriel do? Did you tell your parents? Or Joseph?"

Mary continued, "Surprisingly, the angel disappeared just as quickly and quietly as he had arrived. I'm sure I sat there rather stunned for a moment. Of course, I knew that if I started showing I was pregnant before Joseph and I were married, it would cause great hardship for my family. I also was fully aware of the penalty for adultery and I knew that's what this pregnancy would look like to Joseph and anyone else. So, I decided I wouldn't tell anyone and I would figure out a way to get to my Aunt Elizabeth's house as soon as I could. She and Zechariah lived in the village of Ein Karem not too far from Jerusalem. I knew she would understand and she could protect me till I figured out how to tell Joseph."

"But Ein Karem is a five-day journey from Nazareth! How did you get there?"

"Well, that was another small miracle. That very same day, Mordecai arrived at our house in Nazareth with his wagon. Mordecai was Elizabeth and Zechariah's steward. As soon as I heard his voice, I knew God was at work in all the details."

"So why had he come—and just at that time?"

"He came with a letter and gifts for my parents asking them to let me come stay in Ein Karem for three months. My parents loved Zechariah and Elizabeth and were happy to let me go. And they were so grateful for the gifts Mordecai brought from them from Elizabeth and Zechariah. My absence from home would mean I couldn't help my mother with the sewing jobs she had; and I couldn't help my father with the olive oil business, so my being away would hurt their wages. It also meant I would be away from my soon-to-be husband, Joseph, whom I would miss terribly. Yet, I was convinced God had prepared all this in advance. I smiled on the inside and got ready in a hurry to return to Ein Karem with Mordecai."

"So were your parents excited to hear about Elizabeth's pregnancy?"

"As a matter of fact, Mordecai didn't mention it, and the letter didn't mention it. So, neither did I! But I couldn't wait to see my Aunt Elizabeth and to talk to her about all this."

"So did you and Mordecai talk about it on your way back to Ein Karem?" Luke asked.

"No, he was the quiet type anyway. He never said a word about it on the trip. And I certainly did not tell him my news. That would have put him in a difficult position. It actually made it even more special to be able to surprise Aunt Elizabeth with the fact that I already knew about her pregnancy before I arrived. And then . . . Oh, then, her reaction to my news!"

"What happened? Was she upset? Was she scared?"

"She was surprised, of course, but God made it clear to her that my baby was from God and that he was going to be our long-awaited Messiah. Her words to me were the first words *any* person had spoken about my pregnancy. They were such sweet, affirming, and humble words and they gave me permission to finally express my utter joy in what God was doing through me. That is a moment I will never forget."

Note: In the story above, quotations from Scripture, such as the angel's words to Mary, used phrasing from the *Common English Bible* and from *The Message*.

The Bible Speaks

Mary's story is found in Matthew 1-2; 12:46-50; 13:54-58; Mark 3:31-35; 6:3-4; Luke 1-2; 8:19-21; 11:27-28; John 2:1-12; 6:42; 19:25-27; Acts 1:14; Romans 1:3; Galatians 4:4

We are so familiar with the biblical account of Jesus' birth that it is easy to overlook the details of Mary's life when we read it. The many paintings, Christmas pageants, live Nativities, and children's storybooks about the events have been etched into our minds making it difficult to separate biblical details from fictional scenes. The two gospel accounts (Matthew and Luke) that mention the birth of Christ do not place events in perfect chronological order, also confusing the issue. While Matthew's gospel is placed before Luke's gospel in our New Testaments, some of the events surrounding Jesus' birth in Luke's gospel happened before the events presented in Matthew's gospel.

Since Luke's gospel was written more for a Gentile audience, the connection of Jesus' birth to ancient prophecies was not emphasized as much as it was in Matthew's gospel, written for a Jewish audience. Luke's gospel starts with birth announcements in story form and Matthew's gospel starts with a long genealogy showing Jesus' fulfillment of prophecies about the Messiah coming through the line of Judah and King David.

According to Luke's gospel, **Mary was the first person to know of the coming birth of Jesus** and the biblical account indicates she did not speak about it to anyone—not even Joseph—until she got to Elizabeth's house.

Gabriel Visits Mary of Nazareth
Luke 1:26-38

26 When Elizabeth was six months pregnant, God sent the angel Gabriel
to Nazareth, a city in Galilee, **27** to a virgin who was engaged to a man
named Joseph, a descendant of David's house. The virgin's name was
Mary. **28** When the angel came to her, he said, "Rejoice, favored one! The
Lord is with you!" **29** She was confused by these words and wondered

what kind of greeting this might be. **30** The angel said, "Don't be afraid,
Mary. God is honoring you. **31** Look! You will conceive and give birth to a
son, and you will name him Jesus. **32** He will be great and he will be
called the Son of the Most High. The Lord God will give him the throne
of David his father. **33** He will rule over Jacob's house forever, and there
will be no end to his kingdom."

34 Then Mary said to the angel, "How will this happen since I haven't
had sexual relations with a man?"

35 The angel replied, "The Holy Spirit will come over you and the
power of the Most High will overshadow you. Therefore, the one who is
to be born will be holy. He will be called God's Son. **36** Look, even in her
old age, your relative Elizabeth has conceived a son. This woman who
was labeled 'unable to conceive' is now six months pregnant. **37** Nothing
is impossible for God."

38 Then Mary said, "I am the Lord's servant. Let it be with me just as
you have said." Then the angel left her. (CEB)

Gabriel, the angel, has been busy. First, he went to Jerusalem to visit Zechariah and tell him about the coming birth of his and Elizabeth's long-awaited son (see the previous chapter in this book). Zechariah and Elizabeth were not informed at that time about the coming birth of Jesus. Then, six months later, Gabriel went to Nazareth to visit Mary to tell her she had been chosen to be the mother of God's son. We may be tempted to assume that these prophetic messages delivered to humans by angels would be uttered first by prominent Jewish men. However, according to the biblical account, the first person in the gospels to voice a prophetic word—after 400 years of silence from God—was Elizabeth when she was the first person to confirm Mary's miraculous pregnancy. That encounter was also described in the previous chapter.

Mary Visits Elizabeth
Luke 1:39-45

39 Mary got up and hurried to a city in the Judean highlands. **40** She
entered Zechariah's home and greeted Elizabeth. **41** When Elizabeth
heard Mary's greeting, the child leaped in her womb, and Elizabeth was

filled with the Holy Spirit. **42** With a loud voice she blurted out, "God has blessed you above all women, and he has blessed the child you carry. **43** Why do I have this honor, that the mother of my Lord should come to me? **44** As soon as I heard your greeting, the baby in my womb jumped for joy. **45** Happy is she who believed that the Lord would fulfill the promises he made to her." (CEB)

Can you imagine the relief, the joy, and the amazement of that moment for Mary? We don't know if Mary ever knew of Joseph's plans for a divorce before the baby was born, but it is certainly likely. As a matter of fact, she would have easily assumed she could be facing the death penalty for adultery. The distance between these two extreme emotions of fear for her life and joyful celebration was immeasurable. Yet, in an instant, Mary may have experienced the change from terror to peaceful joy. Elizabeth's words of prophecy and encouragement allowed Mary to finally and fully express her deepest praise to the God who had put all this in motion. This moment in time has been immortalized through countless paintings, stained glass windows, and sculptures entitled "The Visitation."

Mary's Pregnancy Fulfills Prophecy

Matthew's gospel for his Jewish audience helped them make the connections between messianic prophecies from the Hebrew Scriptures and Jesus. Matthew was careful to quote the prophets from the Hebrew Scriptures throughout his gospel account of Jesus, such as the passage from Isaiah 7:14 quoted in Matthew 1:23. Matthew's gospel gives us the story of the angel's visit to Joseph to confirm Mary's miraculous pregnancy.

We don't know at what point in Mary's pregnancy Joseph got this news. The passage certainly implies that he, at first, believed the pregnancy was the result of adultery since he was ready to call off the betrothal (engagement) with Mary. To do so, Jewish law would have required a divorce in those days.

Matthew 1:16, 18-25
16 Jacob was the father of Joseph, the husband of Mary—of whom Jesus
was born, who is called the Christ. . . .

18 This is how the birth of Jesus Christ took place. When Mary his
mother was engaged to Joseph, before they were married, she became
pregnant by the Holy Spirit. **19** Joseph her husband was a righteous man.
Because he didn't want to humiliate her, he decided to call off their
engagement quietly. **20** As he was thinking about this, an angel from the
Lord appeared to him in a dream and said, "Joseph son of David, don't
be afraid to take Mary as your wife, because the child she carries was
conceived by the Holy Spirit. **21** She will give birth to a son, and you will
call him Jesus, because he will save his people from their sins." **22** Now
all of this took place so that what the Lord had spoken through the
prophet would be fulfilled:

23 *Look! A virgin will become pregnant and give birth to a son,*
And they will call him, Emmanuel. (*Emmanuel* means "God with us.")

24 When Joseph woke up, he did just as an angel from God
commanded and took Mary as his wife. **25** But he didn't have sexual
relations with her until she gave birth to a son. Joseph called him Jesus.
(CEB)

The quote of Isaiah 7:14 in Matthew 1:23 makes me wonder if the Jewish people expected a virgin birth for their Messiah. Were Mary and Joseph comforted by their knowledge that such a prophecy was being fulfilled, or would they have even known enough to connect that Isaiah passage to their situation? We can't really answer those questions.

Mary Sings a Hymn of Praise to God

The next passage in Luke, which is placed after Mary's arrival at Elizabeth's, is known as "The Magnificat" in Latin because the first word in the Greek text and Latin translation which Mary spoke was "magnify." We cannot pinpoint the moment when Mary uttered this hymn of praise, yet its placement in Scripture seems to imply that she voiced it to Elizabeth before Elizabeth's son, John, was born. **Therefore, this passage**

shows Mary as the first person to sing a song of praise and prophecy in the New Testament events at the end of 400 years of prophetic silence.

Luke 1:46-55

46 Mary said, "With all my heart I glorify the Lord!
47 In the depths of who I am I rejoice in God my savior.
48 He has looked with favor on the low status of his servant.
Look! From now on, everyone will consider me highly favored
49 because the mighty one has done great things for me. Holy is his name.
50 He shows mercy to everyone,
from one generation to the next,
who honors him as God.
51 He has shown strength with his arm.
He has scattered those with arrogant thoughts and proud inclinations.
52 He has pulled the powerful down from their thrones
and lifted up the lowly.
53 He has filled the hungry with good things
and sent the rich away empty-handed.
54 He has come to the aid of his servant Israel,
remembering his mercy, **55** just as he promised to our ancestors,
to Abraham and to Abraham's descendants forever." (CEB)

This song of praise seems to be modeled after Hannah's prophetic prayer recorded for us in 1 Samuel 2:1-10. This could indicate Mary was very familiar with Hannah's prayer as it had been passed down through the ages in the stories of the Jewish people. **It is interesting that it was Hannah's voice who first used the term "messiah" in a prophetic way** (see 1 Sam. 2:10 and chapter 4 in this book) **and it was two women's voices—Elizabeth's and Mary's—who would be the first humans to acknowledge the fulfillment of that prophesied Messiah.** And, consider this: the first praise and worship leader in the Bible was Miriam, Moses' sister (see Exodus 15 and chapter 3 in this book), and the first song of praise offered in the New Testament was sung by Mary (whose name would have been Miriam in Hebrew). The last sentence of Mary's song of praise (Luke 1:54-55) acknowledges that Jesus would be the final fulfillment of God's promise to Abraham.

A Three-Month House Guest

The next verse in Luke's gospel provides a glimpse of the hospitality of Elizabeth and the closeness of Mary's relationship with her. While the Bible does not state it specifically, I choose to believe that Mary stayed through the time for the birth of John and was a big help to Elizabeth and Zechariah.

Luke 1:56

56 Mary stayed with Elizabeth about three months, and then returned to her home. (CEB)

While we don't know exactly how Mary got back home to Nazareth 90 miles away after spending three months with Elizabeth, we do know she was going to make that trek again in about six months when she would travel with Joseph to Bethlehem for the census. The most familiar Christmas passage in Luke 2 paints a picture in our minds of the events surrounding the actual birth of Jesus in the overcrowded little town of Bethlehem.

Mary Gives Birth to Jesus

Luke 2:1-7

1 In those days Caesar Augustus declared that everyone throughout the
empire should be enrolled in the tax lists. **2** This first enrollment occurred
when Quirinius governed Syria. **3** Everyone went to their own cities to be
enrolled. **4** Since Joseph belonged to David's house and family line, he
went up from the city of Nazareth in Galilee to David's city, called
Bethlehem, in Judea. **5** He went to be enrolled together with Mary, who
was promised to him in marriage and who was pregnant. **6** While they
were there, the time came for Mary to have her baby. **7** She gave birth to
her firstborn child, a son, wrapped him snugly, and laid him in a manger,
because there was no place for them in the guestroom. (CEB)

One of the details seldom mentioned in the retelling of this story is that according to Luke 2:5, Joseph and Mary weren't married yet when Jesus was born. That could simply be an indication that she was still a virgin and not that they hadn't yet fulfilled their year of betrothal. I wonder what kind of wedding they had.

While Matthew gave us the stories of the angel visiting Joseph, the Wise Men, Herod's massacre of the babies, and the Holy Family's flight into Egypt, Luke's gospel provided the Nativity scene with the shepherds and the angels, and a few glimpses of Jesus' infancy and childhood.

Mary, the First to Request a Miracle from Jesus

Overall, the gospel accounts and Acts provide many scenes with Mary, the mother of Jesus. The only other one I want to emphasize here is when the biblical account shows that **Mary was the first person in Scripture to ask Jesus to act on behalf of someone else, which resulted in his first miracle, the turning of water into the best wine at a wedding celebration.** Since John's gospel does not include an account of the birth of Christ, this is actually the first mention of Jesus' mother in the gospel of John. For some reason, thought, John never uses Mary's name anywhere in his gospel.

John 2:1-5

1 On the third day there was a wedding in Cana of Galilee. Jesus' mother
was there, and **2** Jesus and his disciples were also invited to the
celebration. **3** When the wine ran out, Jesus' mother said to him, "They
don't have any wine."

4 Jesus replied, "Woman, what does that have to do with me? My time hasn't come yet."

5 His mother told the servants, "Do whatever he tells you." (CEB)

The exchange between Jesus and his mother sounds a little harsh to our modern ears. I'm sure Jesus was not being disrespectful, but the use of the language there makes it seem so when he called his mother, "Woman." At that time, calling someone "Man" or "Woman" was a common form of address. Mary, in this situation, was sensitive to the social embarrassment about to be experienced by the newlyweds and their families due to running out of wine. And, even though Jesus seemed to be saying he was not ready to make himself and his miraculous powers known, Mary is convinced that he will do the right thing and expressed her unwavering faith to the servants. Even in her statement to the servants, we hear Mary's complete trust in God's power just as we heard in her statement of surrender to God's plan for her when Gabriel announced she was to be the mother of God's Son.

John 2:6-11

6 Nearby were six stone water jars used for the Jewish cleansing ritual,
each able to hold about twenty or thirty gallons.

7 Jesus said to the servants, "Fill the jars with water," and they filled
them to the brim. **8** Then he told them, "Now draw some from them and
take it to the headwaiter," and they did. **9** The headwaiter tasted the
water that had become wine. He didn't know where it came from, though
the servants who had drawn the water knew.

The headwaiter called the groom **10** and said, "Everyone serves the
good wine first. They bring out the second-rate wine only when the
guests are drinking freely. You kept the good wine until now." **11** This
was the first miraculous sign that Jesus did in Cana of Galilee. He
revealed his glory, and his disciples believed in him. (CEB)

Mary's faith was rewarded when Jesus decided to help. Could this imply that Mary had a strong influence over Jesus? Or could this be an indication that a mother's sensitivities were simply more in tune to the needs at hand than was her human son? We tend to forget that Jesus laid aside some of his divine power and rights in order to have the full human experience. This may have simply been a time when his humanness was more at work than his divine nature, until his mother made the request and he realized this was an appropriate time and place to reveal his heavenly glory. Wouldn't you have like to have been at that party?

Mary Travels with Jesus and His Disciples
John 2:12
12 After this, Jesus and his mother, his brothers, and his disciples went down to Capernaum and stayed there for a few days. (CEB)

Apparently, Mary traveled some with Jesus and the disciples. Since there is no other mention of Jesus' earthly father, Joseph, after the birth accounts, most scholars assume that he had died by the time Jesus started his ministry. The Bible does indicate Mary had more children after Jesus. Matthew, Mark, and Luke all mention Jesus' siblings, some by name. Capernaum would then become Jesus' base for his ministry. We don't know if Mary lived there as well, but we do know she and many other women would follow Jesus from Galilee to Jerusalem when he would be crucified several years later.

Mary's image in our minds is usually centered on scenes of the Nativity of our Lord or of Christ's crucifixion. However, Mary was a human mother who lived through extraordinary circumstances. She allowed God to work through her in miraculous ways. Yet, she also suffered great grief, may have been widowed at a young age, reared other children, and participated in Jesus' earthly ministry and the ministry of his disciples. Tradition tells us that the apostle John became the leader of the Jerusalem church, and may have traveled through Asia Minor helping churches, so it is possible that his adopted mother, Mary, worked and traveled with him. When you consider all Mary experienced in her lifetime, she is an example of great spiritual fortitude to which we can all aspire.

The Message in Mary's Voice

The first words we hear Mary speak in the New Testament are a question to the angel Gabriel (Luke 1:34). Then we have a statement of complete surrender to God's will for her (Luke 1:38). Her next words are her song of praise for God's glory and thanks for the fulfilling of God's promise (Luke 1:46-55). In the Christmas story of Luke 2, Mary doesn't say a word, but she "treasured all these words and pondered them in her heart" (Luke 2:19, NRSV).

Later in Luke 2, when Jesus is presented in the Temple and prophesied over by Simeon and the prophet Anna, she takes it all in, but we have no recorded words of hers. Then, we get a sound bite of true "mother-speak" when she scolds a twelve-year-old Jesus for lingering in the Temple too long, "Child, why have you treated us like this? Look, your father and I have been searching for you in great anxiety" (Luke 2:48 NRSV). I believe this one question allows all of us to relate to her on a completely human level.

It is interesting to me that the spoken words recorded in Mary's voice only total 182 in Luke, as explained by author Lindsay Hardin Freeman in her book *Bible Women: All Their Words and Why They Matter* (Freeman 2015, 399). The additional 9 words she spoke in the New Testament are in the gospel of John when she requested Jesus' help at the wedding in John 2:3, 5 (Freeman 2015, 399). The gospels of Matthew and Mark provided no words of hers. We never heard her speak at the cross, or the tomb, or even later in the upper room on the day of Pentecost, yet Scripture indicates she was present at each of those places. So, while her voice may not be prominent throughout the gospels, the message delivered by her words, "Here am I, the servant of the Lord," is that whenever we, as sinful humans, make ourselves wholly available to God's design for us, we will be participants in God's eternal plan of salvation and restoration.

Mary's story reveals God's choice to work through the physical body of a woman to birth the Truth. Young women—and young men—need to know how valuable their bodies are to the one who created them and need to be helped to understand how to protect them and cherish them for God's purposes. Mary and Joseph's story can help us communicate that. Let Mary's voice remind you that praising God in total surrender to God's plan for you will always be the best use of your voice.

Biblical Truths Taught through the Story of Mary

1. God chose to work through the physical body of a woman to bring the Source of salvation into the world, affirming the value of women's bodies and the birthing process, from the moment of conception to a baby's first breath and first meals.
2. God chooses women to have a deep understanding of spiritual things and gives them the ability to communicate them.
3. God values women's relationships with each other and wants those relationships to be uplifting, encouraging, and supportive, regardless of differences in age or social status.
4. God communicates directly to and through women.
5. God chooses women to bring God's hope, peace, and divine surprises to a situation.
6. God fills women's hearts and voices with songs of praise and prophecy.
7. God blesses lifelong faithfulness and a willingness to be fully available to God's plan.

Why the Voice of Mary Matters . . .

To young women: because Mary's story shows God is willing to communicate directly to teenage girls about your purpose in life.

To unmarried women: because Mary's story reveals God has a purpose in your singleness beyond what you can see, so protect your virginity until God provides a husband.

To unwed mothers-to-be: because Mary's story reminds you God has a special purpose for both you and your baby that only God can bring to pass.

To any follower of Christ: because Mary's story illustrates that anything less than complete surrender to God's will is no surrender at all, and yet, surrender is all that is required to become an active participant in God's plan.

To anyone who feels misunderstood: because Mary's story shows how God can provide someone who will listen and understand, even if it's not the person closest to you (emotionally or geographically).

To women of all ages: because Mary's story says God has wonderful purposes in store for women's relationships that will bring encouragement, hope, celebration, and understanding.

To mothers: because Mary's story lets you see how sometimes God chooses a mother's voice to direct their children in unique ways.

To men: because Mary's story shows one of your callings is to protect and honor a woman's body and purpose just as God does. It also provides evidence that God chooses women to do things men are unable to do, such as birth babies, and God sometimes calls women to specific tasks without the need for a man's approval.

To husbands: because Mary's story exemplifies how sometimes God will first communicate truths to your wife and you can trust that.

To spouses of women in ministry: because Mary's story illustrates that sometimes God's purpose for you is to be behind the scenes in support of your wife's calling.

Questions Raised by the Story of Mary

Why did God choose to tell Mary first of the coming birth of the Messiah and not Joseph, the king, or the high priest, or to use some other method of proclamation?

Why did God let Joseph get to the point of wanting a divorce before revealing the truth about Mary's pregnancy?

At what point did Joseph and Mary's betrothal actually become a marriage? In other words, how did betrothal then compare to engagement today? Did Mary and Joseph get to have the week-long wedding celebration common in those days?

Tradition tells us Mary's parents were Anna and Joachin. How do you think they reacted to the news that Mary was pregnant?

Why was it important for Jesus to be born of a virgin? Were the Jews expecting a virgin birth for their Messiah?

How did Mary travel from Nazareth to the Judean hill country?

How were Elizabeth and Mary actually related?

How can our churches encourage more mentoring among younger and older women?

How can Mary's example of surrender (and virginity) be used as a model for discipleship for boys as well as girls?

Was Mary involved in the birth of John?

Was Elizabeth involved in the birth of Jesus?

How can we adopt the habit of pondering things in our hearts to deepen our relationships with family, friends, and God?

How can God use our sensitivities to the needs around us to bring about God's surprises and blessings into the lives of others?

When do you think Mary first discovered Jesus' miracle-making abilities?

Mary's Key to Resilient Confidence

When you think of Mary, the mother of Jesus, what is the first image that comes to mind? During Advent, we see beautiful paintings of Mary cradling her newborn son at the manger. During Easter, sculptures remind us of Mary cradling her crucified Savior at the cross. Those images try to capture the love between a mother and son, yet they cannot express the inner strengths that prepared Mary to be the servant leader who would cradle the Expectant Love for the world.

When God chose Mary, the angel Gabriel was sent to have a conversation with a poor, young teenage girl in a small, backwater town. **According to the biblical text, Mary was the first person God informed about the coming birth of the Messiah and the first to sing a song of prophetic praise after 400 years of prophetic silence.** God did not make the first announcement to Joseph, to the King, to the High Priest, or to any other person. God communicated the plan first to the one who would fulfill it—a very young woman. God chose Mary specifically, and I believe it was partly because of the inner strengths she must have demonstrated, or ones that God knew she would develop.

Mary's strength in surrender is a key to resilient confidence for us today. Scripture reveals when Mary surrendered to God's will for her, she demonstrated her strengths in being, doing, and going, which we can still emulate today as God's servant leaders.

Servant leaders develop . . .

1. Strength in BEING

"Here am I, the servant of the Lord; let it be with me according to your word" (Luke 1:38 NRSV). Mary knew who she was in relation to the God who was asking her to yield her plans, her reputation, and maybe even her life to this new role as the mother of Jesus.

Who is God asking you to BE?

You can choose to become a human *being* by taking time to develop yourself from the inside out—get to know WHO you are and look only to Jesus for your affirmation. Mary's example of focusing on who GOD is in her song of praise teaches you how to keep things in perspective. Twice we're told that Mary "treasured" things in her heart (Luke 2:19 and 51). To me, that says she knew how to be quiet and contemplative and really consider how the activity swirling around her was affecting her and the people she loved. I think she learned early how to hear the still, small voice that calls us to trust and simply BE.

2. Strength in DOING

"The Mighty One has done great things for me" (Luke 1:49 NRSV). Her song of praise lists all that *God's* power has accomplished, and the poetry is modeled after Hannah's prayer in 1 Samuel 2. Mary understands that she is *not* the source of her accomplishments and blessings - God, alone, is the source!

What is God asking you to DO?

While Mary's song of praise focuses on God's activity in the lives of people, she was able to sing about it as a result of her acceptance of the task God had asked her to DO. Learning to discern what God's task is for you comes through prayer, fasting, meditation, worship, and Scripture study. These are the prelude for DOING something that will bring God glory. There are no shortcuts!

3. Strength in GOING

"Mary set out and went with haste to a Judean town in the hill country" (Luke 1:39 NRSV). That was the first of at least six treks we watch this young woman make in the first two chapters of Luke alone! When Mary said, "Yes," to God's purpose and plan, it included a willingness to GO whenever and wherever God called.

Where is God asking you to GO?

God never promised you would stay in one place or that you would put down roots that would never be transplanted. God promised to be with you and never forsake you (Heb. 13:5). A servant leader who is yielded completely to God's service may indeed be asked to change locations--your office, your home, your vocation, or your country. And when you GO in joyful obedience, you will discover, "Blessed is she who believed that there would be a fulfillment of what was spoken to her by the Lord" (Luke 1:45 NRSV).

Which of these three areas is most challenging for you? For me: it's the BEING. The practice of simply BEING in God's presence, learning to still my mind and my activity long enough to hear God's voice requires much more discipline than most other things in my life. Stillness is not valued in our culture. We have to choose to be still and remove ourselves from the noise in the world and even in our own minds. Mary's ability to surrender and ponder reveal inner strengths that can change our world and the world around us.

As you become stronger in being, doing, and going according to God's call on your life, you will develop your own resilient confidence.

"Then Mary said, 'I am the Lord's servant. Let it be with me just as you have said....
He has come to the aid of his servant Israel,
remembering his mercy, just as he promised to our ancestors,
to Abraham and to Abraham's descendants forever.'"
—Luke 1:38, 54-55 (CEB)

15

Anna's Story

ca. 6 CE

God chose Anna's voice to be the first . . .
- *Eye-witness proclamation by a prophet that the Messiah had been born*

Anna's aging bones were reminding her of her advanced years on this brisk spring morning. After her daily ritual bath at the Temple, required by all who wanted to enter the Temple courts to worship, she ascended the steps toward the Court of Women. She caught herself grinning and almost giddy with some unusual sense of anticipation. She wondered what had stirred her soul on this particular morning.

While thinking through the past few days and considering what lay ahead for this new day, she settled into her favorite spot on the bench that was bathed in the morning sunlight in the corner of the Temple court. The wisps of sunbeams floated in between the tall marble columns surrounding the large platform on which the glistening white Temple stood.

From this vantage point, she watched hurried priests go by and people delivering their sacrificial offerings to the priests at the next gate. She had noticed the elderly Simeon was out early this fine morning. She had not seen him for a few days. He was always a welcome sight. He was a faithful old soul that could make her laugh and one of the few who could reminisce with her about the days before the rule of the wicked King Herod. As she passed the time, she especially loved to see young Jewish families showing their children the splendor of the Temple. She remembered with bittersweetness her brief married life. It had ended more than six decades earlier when her husband died unexpectedly. Ever since then, she had spent more time in the Temple courts than in her home.

The rhythm of her days was comforting, but never boring. She had long established a habit of fasting several days a week and her prayers were frequent and fervent. She had been a comfort to many by helping people understand God's activity in their lives and how God's grace and mercy was with them always. This and her daily presence at the Temple had established her reputation as a respected prophet and she was sought out for her wisdom. She could share God's truth with great conviction because she was now in her 80s! God had been so merciful to her as a widow all these years, providing for her, and giving her such a life of peace and joy in spite of the oppressive culture King Herod had wrought on her people, the Jews. She would bring her mending projects with her about once a week. Usually on market day, she would gather with other women friends in a tucked-away corner on the expansive porch where they could spend an afternoon visiting and sharing the latest news from their families.

Resting her head against the cool stone wall behind her bench, she closed her eyes and took in all the sounds: the laughter of some nearby children, the heated discussions between teachers of the law, and the clinking of the coins being dropped in the offering urns. Then she caught the sweet sound of an infant cooing along with some turtledoves. She opened her eyes and saw a young couple with a babe in arms approaching the elderly and wise Simeon who seemed overjoyed to see this couple. Anna wondered if they were friends of his.

Simeon had been around the Temple almost as long as Anna, but not quite as often. Anna watched as a very young mother, still looking a little tired, gently placed her infant into the waiting arms of Simeon. The father put down the small cage he was carrying that held the two turtledoves for their sacrifice of thanksgiving for this firstborn son. He stood close to Simeon in a protective posture. Anna stood from her bench to move in a little closer and leaned on the marble column nearest the scene in front of her. Simeon was obviously enraptured by the child. Anna hadn't seen Simeon smile like that in ages. Then, quite unlike Simeon's normal behavior of softspoken stillness, he raised the infant above his head and danced around in sheer delight. The couple stood there mesmerized at the old man's confidence in handling their tiny infant. The father was poised ready to catch the infant dangling in midair.

As a gleeful Simeon lowered the child from overhead, the new father breathed a sigh of relief. Then a ray of sunshine crept over the glistening Temple roof and sunbeams danced around the baby's face. Anna gasped and for a moment she couldn't breathe. She felt that familiar warmth when Adonai, the God of Israel, would give her a word of prophecy. But this time, she was aware of something unique. God's presence was tangible, palpable. She knew she was in the physical presence of God Almighty. She could stand still no longer. She rushed to Simeon's side to get a closer look at the baby. Simeon held the baby so Anna could see his tiny face and introduced her to the new parents, Joseph and Mary from Nazareth. Anna exchanged happy smiles with the couple as she put a supportive arm around the young mother. She marveled at the youth of the mother and the questioning face of a more mature father. Anna looked back into the joyous face of Simeon and they nodded to one another in full recognition of this baby's identity. "He's here," they whispered to each other in utter amazement.

Anna and the young family watched Simeon raise his face toward heaven and exclaim, "Now, Master, let your servant go in peace according to your word, because my eyes have seen your salvation. You prepared this salvation in the presence of all peoples. It's a light for revelation to the Gentiles and a glory for your people Israel."*

Anna glanced back and forth between the radiant face of Simeon and the somewhat startled faces of the baby's parents. She now fully understood that unexpected stirring in her soul earlier that morning.

Simeon gently returned the squirming infant to his father's arms and then gave a firm, congratulatory squeeze to the new father's shoulders. As he raised his face toward the heavens once more, he gently placed his hands on Mary's and Joseph's shoulders and spoke a blessing over the young family. As he lowered his eyes, they met the warm, midnight eyes of the young mother and he spoke softly yet decisively to her saying, "This boy is assigned to be the cause of the falling and rising of many in Israel."* Then he looked seriously at Joseph and spoke a word of warning, "And to be a sign that generates opposition so that the inner thoughts of many will be revealed."* Simeon paused, closed his eyes as if listening to someone. When his eyes opened, his demeanor changed and Anna watched a tear stream down the weathered face of Simeon. He swallowed, took a deep breath as if he was being compelled to voice these final words to the young, new mother before him, "And a sword will pierce your innermost being, too."* Mary put her hand to her mouth and her knees buckled. Anna's arm steadied Mary as the concerned father held tightly to the baby.

After a moment for Mary's composure, Anna asked her permission to hold the infant. Mary nodded. As Joseph handed the baby to Anna, he proudly said, "His name is Jesus." Anna brought the infant close and drank in the sweet aroma of fresh baby skin. She caressed his head of soft black baby hair and gazed into his eyes squinting in the sunlight. She uncovered his hands and feet and let his new little fingers wrap around a finger on her aged hand. That unusual feeling of anticipation came upon her again but more intensely as if a warm cloak was enveloping her. She knew Adonai was confirming in her heart the message she should proclaim. Her voice lifted to the heavens and she praised Adonai for the answered prayer she was holding in her arms. She knew full well that this tiny infant would grow into the One who would redeem Israel. After a few moments of sheer delight in the presence of this infant and his parents, she gently laid a whimpering Jesus in his mother's arms. Joseph picked up the cage with the turtledoves and they said their goodbyes. A few steps away, Mary paused and turned to see these two aged people once more as if to seal this memory in her mind. She smiled and held Jesus so they could see his face peeking out from the swaddling clothes once more and then walked quickly and carefully to catch up to Joseph.

Anna stood there with Simeon quietly, trying to memorize every detail of the moment. After a few exchanges of awed wonder at the blessing they had just experienced, it was time for Simeon to join the men gathering in the Temple's inner court to worship. Anna stayed behind because women were not allowed past the Court of Women.

As a prophet, Anna knew the task ahead of her: to proclaim to all who would listen that the long-awaited redemption of Israel was at hand—the Messiah had been born! She made her way to a group of women gathering for a time of prayer and told them what she had just experienced. The reactions were mixed. The hardness of some hearts would not allow Anna's words of truth to penetrate. For others, Anna's joy told them all they needed to know. Finally, their God was about to fulfill the Promise of the ages.

*Quoted from phrases in Luke 2 (CEB)

The Bible Speaks

Anna's story is found in Luke 2

Jerusalem was a bustling crossroads in Palestine during Jesus' lifetime. While the Jews may have been the majority population, the pagan Romans had certainly made their presence known as the occupying rulers. The Greek language and culture had been influencing the city and its residents for centuries. Jerusalem was a big city compared to the small village of Nazareth where Mary and Joseph lived. They must have stayed in or around Bethlehem for at least 40 days after the birth of Jesus since they were there in Jerusalem for Mary's time of purification, or ritual cleansing. To be considered purified, a Jewish woman would enter a *mikveh* bath and immerse herself completely after her monthly period and after childbirth. Since Bethlehem was just a few miles from Jerusalem as compared to the 90-mile journey from Nazareth, it made much more sense, especially for a poor couple, to stay in Bethlehem than to journey home and back again.

On the day that Mary and Joseph brought their son to the Temple, Jerusalem may have still been pretty crowded with people who had traveled there to register for the census. The many confused travelers trying to figure out which alleyway would get them to their destination had no idea who the tiny baby was who just passed them. Can you imagine the anxiousness of a teenage mother and a new father trying to navigate their way through the streets that day? Mary and Joseph are about to be surprised by two people *expecting* their arrival.

The Prophet Anna's Encounter with the Infant Jesus
Luke 2:21-38

21 When eight days had passed, Jesus' parents circumcised him and gave
him the name Jesus. This was the name given to him by the angel before
he was conceived. **22** When the time came for their ritual cleansing, in
accordance with the Law from Moses, they brought Jesus up to Jerusalem
to present him to the Lord. (**23** It's written in the Law of the Lord, "Every
firstborn male will be dedicated to the Lord.") **24** They offered a sacrifice
in keeping with what's stated in the Law of the Lord, *A pair of turtledoves
or two young pigeons.*

25 A man named Simeon was in Jerusalem. He was righteous and
devout. He eagerly anticipated the restoration of Israel, and the Holy
Spirit rested on him. **26** The Holy Spirit revealed to him that he wouldn't
die before he had seen the Lord's Christ. **27** Led by the Spirit, he went
into the temple area. Meanwhile, Jesus' parents brought the child to the
temple so that they could do what was customary under the
Law. **28** Simeon took Jesus in his arms and praised God. He said,
29 "Now, master, let your servant go in peace according to your word,
30 because my eyes have seen your salvation. **31** You prepared this
salvation in the presence of all peoples. **32** It's a light for revelation to the
Gentiles and a glory for your people Israel."

33 His father and mother were amazed by what was said about
him. **34** Simeon blessed them and said to Mary his mother, "This boy is
assigned to be the cause of the falling and rising of many in Israel and to
be a sign that generates opposition **35** so that the inner thoughts of many
will be revealed. And a sword will pierce your innermost being too."

36 There was also a prophet, Anna the daughter of Phanuel, who
belonged to the tribe of Asher. She was very old. After she married, she
lived with her husband for seven years. **37** She was now an 84-year-old
widow. She never left the temple area but worshipped God with fasting
and prayer night and day. **38** She approached at that very moment and
began to praise God and to speak about Jesus to everyone who was
looking forward to the redemption of Jerusalem. (CEB)

The Bible tells us Anna was a prophet and a widow. I would think that since the gospel writer was sure to include her title of prophet, she must have had a positive and respected reputation. And the fact that she was an elderly widow faithful to Temple worship indicates her devotion to her God and to her faith. At that time, widows were often left destitute if they had no sons to care for them. The Bible gives us no indication of Anna's economic condition, so I am assuming that she was well cared for and had the freedom to spend her days at the Temple for prophesying and worshiping—instead of needing to spend her time begging. Since the gospel writer did not acquire the details of this story firsthand, we can be sure that Anna's part in this birth account of our Savior was memorable and significant enough to be recorded for all eternity. According to the biblical record, Anna was the first named prophet (male or female) in Scripture who actually *saw* the Christ child and then went about telling others about him. **God chose a *woman's* voice to be the first eye-witness proclamation by a *prophet* of the Messiah's birth**.

We don't know much about Anna, but the details that are provided reveal an interesting background of her people. The gospel of Luke seems to try to authenticate people's names and history by giving their lineage. Anna's father, Phanuel, is named and we know nothing else about him except that he was descended from the Israelite tribe of Asher. Asher's name meant "happy" and he was born to Jacob through his wife Leah's maid, Zilpah. Anna's name is actually the Greek version of the Hebrew name Hannah. Isn't it interesting that the first person to use the term "messiah" prophetically in the Hebrew Scriptures was a woman with the same name, but different version of the name, as the first prophet to see the Christ child and proclaim his birth in the New Testament?

When you look at a map of ancient Israel and the locations of the allotments of land given to the different tribes, Asher's land is located farther north than any other tribe. They were next to the mighty Phoenicians who dominated the coast. According to the biblical record, Asher was blessed by his father Jacob to produce rich crops and to provide delicacies for kings (see Gen. 49:20), yet his tribe never produced a king or even a mighty warrior. The tribe of Asher is even chastised in Deborah's song in Judges 5 because that tribe did not come to the aid of its brothers during the battle against the Canaanites. So, I wonder why this gospel writer wanted to be sure we knew Anna was from the tribe of Asher. My suggestion is that the writer wanted to make it clear that a person's background has no bearing on the purpose or message God has for any individual with whom God chooses to have a relationship.

Anna was married for seven years and then lived as a widow for a very long time, indicating that she had never remarried. So, we know she was single. We are not informed about any children, yet the Scripture does not indicate that she was destitute. The Bible also lets us know that she was at least in her 80s when she saw the Christ child.

The picture Luke's gospel paints for us of Anna's encounter with Mary and Joseph and their infant son Jesus allows us to enter into that sacred instant of recognition when Anna witnessed the fulfillment of the promise of God. This singular moment in time reminds us that even brief encounters with the holy are worth the wait.

The Message in Anna's Voice

Even though we have only a few verses telling us about Anna and how she responded to the Christ child, those few verses actually speak volumes about her influence and leadership. **According to the biblical record, Anna was the first *prophet* to proclaim to others that their long-awaited redemption had arrived.** We do not know how the people received her message. We do not know if they thought she meant this child would grow up to rescue them from Rome in a military fashion. We don't even have the exact words she spoke. All we know is that she responded to her encounter with Jesus with praise and then fulfilled her prophetic purpose by telling others about God's activity in their time. Let Anna's voice remind you that whenever we respond to God with praise, there will be a message we can share with others.

Biblical Truths Taught through the Story of Anna

1. God chooses women to announce God's activity in the world.
2. God chooses women prophets to proclaim God's message of redemption.
3. God affirms and blesses a single woman's commitment to faithful, religious service.
4. God chooses women of all ages to be the communicators of God's hope.
5. God sometimes chooses a woman's voice as the best voice to announce that God is with us!
6. God blesses faithful women worshipers with firsthand knowledge and experience of God's activity in the world.

Why the Voice of Anna Matters . . .

To elderly women: because Anna's story proves age does not determine your usefulness to the kingdom or the need for your message.

To faithful church workers: because Anna's story shows no matter how long you serve or wait for God to act, there *will* come a moment of God's revelation.

To widows and single women: because Anna's story illustrates the absence of a husband does not excuse you or prevent you from continued faithful service in a worshiping community.

To communicators of God's truths: because Anna's story shows there is no more powerful testimony than firsthand knowledge and experience of God's activity in the world.

To those who announce/celebrate a baby's birth: because Anna's story reminds you each newborn child is a proclamation to the world of God's hope, peace, and purpose.

To those eager to hear a message of peace and hope: because Anna's story reminds you the elderly people around you may be the best source for such a message.

Questions Raised by the Story of Anna

Why has the church remembered Simeon's song of benediction but has not created a more memorable picture of Anna's experience with the Christ child?

Why don't we have the words Anna used to praise God or to announce Jesus' birth?

Why do some churches deny women the opportunity to speak or proclaim God's truth in their pulpits?

Who are the elderly women who faithfully serve in your church? What message might they be ready to share? What truths have they witnessed that could inform your church about God's faithfulness?

How is your ability to communicate God's truths affected by your level of church involvement, faithful worship participation, fasting, and praying?

How do you determine who your waiting audience is and what they need to hear?

Anna's Keys to Resilient Confidence

I believe Anna would tell us that her keys to resilient confidence were faithful participation in a worshipping community and *purposeful* communication of truths experienced in the presence of God. Anna's story reminds us that a word of good news wraps peace around a longing heart.

During Advent, we celebrate the arrival of the Prince of Peace—the long-awaited Messiah—and we are reminded how Jesus was born into a world that was anything but peaceful. Yet, even then, there were faithful people still waiting expectantly for God to change things.

When God was ready for the people who were hoping for the liberation of Jerusalem to hear of the birth of their long-awaited Messiah, **God chose a woman's voice to be the first to proclaim that message.** The careful writing of Luke's gospel indicates that **Anna was the first *prophet* to see the Christ child and then tell an eager audience that their expectant peace had arrived.**

God continues to choose women's voices to communicate important messages. Whether you are announcing the next meeting, leading a Bible study or training session, preaching or teaching, asking for volunteers, making a formal presentation, giving a report to your boss, or telling a story to your grandchildren, you need to have a purpose for communicating your message.

The prophet Anna is described by Luke as one who "never left the temple area, worshiping night and day with her fasting and prayers. At the very time Simeon was praying, she showed up, broke into an anthem of praise to God, and talked about the child to all who were waiting expectantly for the freeing of Jerusalem" (Luke 2:37b-38 MSG). In two sentences, the **prophet Anna's actions confirm some applicable practices.**

Four practices of a purposeful communicator:

1. Participate faithfully in a worshiping community.

Anna's constant presence at the Temple allowed her the privilege of seeing God at work firsthand. Her response to the sight of baby Jesus was to praise God. Establishing an unwavering habit of committed church involvement will provide a faith foundation like no other. Anna's habits of worship, fasting, and prayer are still the habits that will give you the awareness and discernment of God's activity around and through you. *Your spiritual authenticity as a communicator of God's truths depends on your committed involvement.*

2. Know your audience.

Anna spread her message to those who shared her expectant attitude. A purposeful communicator studies her audience *before* she speaks or writes to them to understand whether she needs to be persuasive and practical or encouraging and empathic. *Compassion as a communicator depends on knowing your audience.*

3. Use trustworthy sources.

Anna had firsthand experience with the content of her message, was sensitive to God's Spirit, and had probably witnessed Simeon's prophecy as well. A purposeful communicator is diligent in using reliable sources. Just because something is in print doesn't make it true or accurate. Research any information you use back to its original source whenever possible. *Integrity as a communicator depends on using trustworthy sources.*

4. Communicate a message your audience is both longing and needing to hear.

Anna communicated a message of peace to people who were living in a land occupied by their enemies and whose faith practices were tolerated, at best, by the ruling government. Freedom, deliverance, redemption, and liberation were their deepest desires. A purposeful communicator finds a way to make her message resonate within the spirits of her listeners or readers. *Having people who want to listen to you depends on telling them something they want and need to hear.*

Effective communicators know that *how* you communicate a message is often as important—if not more so—than the content of the message. Being faithful in participating fully in worship, in taking the time to know your audience, in researching your sources, and in being committed to sharing a relevant message will help you communicate with purpose and be important keys to developing your resilient confidence.

"She approached at that very moment and began
to praise God and to speak about Jesus
to everyone who was looking forward to the redemption of Jerusalem."
—Luke 2:38 (CEB)

PART SEVEN

God Chose the Samaritan Woman, Martha, and Mary Magdalene

THE TIME OF CHRIST'S EARTHLY MINISTRY

ca. 6 BCE - 30 CE

Events that Shaped the World of the Samaritan Woman, Martha, and Mary Magdalene

THE TIME OF CHRIST'S EARTHLY MINISTRY
ca. 6 BCE - 30 CE

Jesus lived during the time known as Pax Romana, the Latin term for "Roman Peace," which was ushered in by the 41-year reign of Octavian, who took the title Caesar Augustus and declared himself the first emperor of the Roman Empire. Augustus reigned from 27 BCE to 14 CE and this sense of Pax Romana lasted through the reign of Marcus Aurelius (161-180 CE). This period of relative peace in the Roman world extended throughout the Mediterranean, North Africa, and over to Persia. All the rulers of Palestine during this time were subservient to Rome. It was this sense of peace and prosperity among the Roman elite that allowed for the construction of the many Roman roadways that made travel and trade so much easier, and would literally pave the way for the gospel to advance in the years to come.

Who ruled Palestine during Jesus' lifetime?

Scholars have placed Jesus' birth about two years before the death of Herod the Great, who died in 4 BCE, placing Jesus' birth around 6 BCE. It is the gospel of Matthew that gave us the accounts of the visit of the wise men from the East and the angel's instructions to Joseph to take Mary and the infant Jesus to Egypt to escape the cruelty of Herod. Matthew's gospel also indicated that it was an angel who informed Joseph that Herod was dead and that he could take his family back to Israel.

The cause of Herod the Great's death has been speculated but never really determined. The last few years of Herod's life were characterized by extreme behaviors of cruelty toward his own family members and toward anyone who would defy him. Needless to say, everyone lived in fear of him. He would just as likely have religious leaders killed as he would criminals. He usually maintained some level of adherence to Jewish religious holidays and to laws that forbade any human or animal images to be displayed in the Temple, but toward the end of his life, he had a golden eagle installed above the Temple gate. Two Pharisees persuaded some youths to tear down the eagle and, as a result, Herod ordered all the perpetrators burned alive. The gospel of Matthew attributes to Herod the slaughter of the infant boys in and around Bethlehem at the time of Jesus' birth. Such an atrocity would certainly fit Herod's mental condition at the time.

After Herod's death, and based on his will, Palestine's territories were divided among three of Herod's sons. His son Archelaus inherited Judea, Idumea, and Samaria making him an ethnarch ("national ruler" in Rome's eyes). He was as cruel as his father. When both Jews and Samaritans complained about his brutality in his tenth year as ruler, Emperor Augustus banished him to Gaul in 6 CE. After Archelaus' exile, Judea was governed by Roman prefects as a Roman province from 6-41 CE, including Pontius Pilate from 26/27-36/37 CE. These prefects were the Roman rulers in Judea throughout Jesus' lifetime. However, there is also evidence that the Herodian family members continued to exercise significant political power as part of the Jerusalem aristocracy.

Herod's son, Antipas, was a full younger brother to Archelaus and he became the tetrarch ("ruler of a quarter" of the kingdom) over Galilee and Perea at Herod's death in 4 BCE. After Archelaus' departure in 6 CE from Judea, Antipas assumed the dynastic title "Herod," which is how we know him in the gospels of Matthew, Mark, and Luke during Jesus' public ministry. He ruled rather peacefully for 43 years. He founded the city of Tiberius on the Sea of Galilee in honor of Emperor Tiberius, who reigned 14-37 CE. Antipas was the ruler responsible for the death of John the Baptist (see Matt. 14; Mark 6; Luke 3). In Luke 13:31-32, Jesus was warned that Antipas wanted to kill him and Jesus called him a "fox." In Luke 23:6-12, Antipas is placed at Jesus' trial. According to history, Antipas and his unlawful wife Herodias were exiled to Gaul in 39 CE.

In 4 BCE, Herod's son Philip, who was the half-brother to Archelaus and Antipas, became the tetrarch over the predominantly Gentile lands of

Iturea, Panias, Gaulanitis, Batanea, Trachonitis, and Auranitis. He reigned for 37 years and was considered generally successful. He was mentioned briefly in Luke 3:1 at the beginning of John the Baptist's ministry.

Those were the political leaders in Palestine, who ruled under the authority of Rome, during the time of Christ's earthly ministry. The Romans taxed their subjects heavily, yet even Herod the Great had been known to reduce taxes on occasion and to provide food in times of famine. Unfortunately, those moments of benevolence did not outweigh his fits of rage and cruelty. His sons learned their father's tactics well, although some of Herod's sons were remembered with more kindness than others.

Happenings in the Rest of the World

Throughout most of Christ's life on earth, Augustus ruled the Roman Empire and Herod's three sons governed the different areas in Palestine. Here are some of the historical highlights from other parts of the world during that time:

- By 2 CE, China's population had grown to more than 57 million people; and between 9 and 23 CE, China went through two rulers and the reinstatement of the Han Dynasty. Wang Zhengjun, empress of China during the Han Dynasty, became very involved in government affairs and even became the de facto ruler of the empire for some of the time from 48 BCE until 13 CE, influencing all her male relatives who became government leaders and successive emperors.
- The Trung sisters in Vietnam organized a revolution against the Chinese and became co-queens of an independent Vietnam from 30-42 CE; they are still venerated as heroes in Vietnam.
- In North America, the Basketmaker phase of the Pueblo culture flourished in the American Southwest. Eastern and Central prairie peoples were raising crops and shaping pottery. The Old Bering Sea culture had been thriving in the western Arctic since 500 BCE. The Adena culture in the Ohio River Valley was carving fine stone pipes which were placed with their dead in burial

mounds. The Norton tradition had developed along the Alaskan shore of the Bering Strait since 1000 BCE and would continue well into the 9th century CE.

The Greco-Roman World for Women During the Time of Christ

New Testament professor Lynn Cohick wrote *Women in the World of the Earliest Christians* in which she painted a picture of the lifestyles of all classes of women in the Roman Empire around the time of Christ. She described Emperor Augustus' wife, known as Empress Livia, who apparently had great influence as a political advisor to both Augustus and her son Tiberius, who would succeed Augustus as Emperor of Rome. She lived until 29 CE, which would have been during most of Jesus' lifetime on earth. She was a wealthy benefactor of many. She helped to raise senators' children, some of whom would grow up to hold important political positions. She paid for important building projects. She was an example to other wealthy women who followed her practices of giving their money to improve their cities architecturally, economically, and culturally. Her husband, Caesar Augustus, even willed to her the title *mater matria,* mother of the country, but this honor had to wait until after the death of her son Tiberius. Her grandson had her deified posthumously as Diva Julia and Julia Augusta. A cult celebrating her grew up in the Roman Empire. She was even named as a beneficiary in the wills of Herod the Great and his sister indicating her far-reaching influence. While she was not mentioned in Scripture, Philo, the Hellenistic Jewish historian of the 1st century CE, wrote about Empress Livia giving many golden articles and other costly items to the Jerusalem Temple, even though she was not Jewish. Her influence was benevolent in so many ways, yet she was also considered meddlesome by her son and the politicians of the day. (Cohick 2009, 291-294)

Other wealthy women have been noted throughout the Roman Empire as benefactors of the arts, of trade guilds, and of municipal building projects. Surely, women throughout the Roman world, including the Jewish women we read about in Scripture, would have been aware of the very public activities of these women. Greco-Roman society of Jesus' day afforded more autonomy to women than we may typically imagine, according to more recent research and excavations of ancient sites. Women were known to be shopkeepers, weavers, and business owners. Cohick stated that Philo, the historian, provided evidence of women philosophers who lived an ascetic and celibate lifestyle near Alexandria, Egypt, during the 1st century CE (Cohick 2009, 249). This would indicate that some women, at least, were highly educated. Some common virtues applauded by both the Greco-Roman society and Jewish society were faithfulness in marriage (on the woman's part) and motherhood (Cohick 2009, 241).

Marriage in the Greco-Roman world at the time of Christ had gone through some legal changes over the past century and Emperor Augustus also made some changes. One of the problems of Augustus' day was a declining birthrate among Roman citizens. Therefore, some of the changes encouraged more marriages and births (Cohick 2009, 76). Some of the changes in the Roman laws were probably influenced by the Greek culture, Hellenism, and may have even filtered into Jewish society. For example, new laws allowed the dowry to be returned to the woman if her husband divorced her instead of staying with the husband's family. Another thing we as Westerners must remember is that marriage in the 1st century was more motivated by the need for family and societal stability, moving up the social or political ladder, and for providing heirs than it was motivated by love or passion. This is not to imply that loving marriages did not exist. It is just a reminder that our, especially Western, idea of marriage today and the reality of marriage during Jesus' lifetime on earth are two different things.

While there were some wealthy Jews in the world, especially in Alexandria, Egypt, and among the religious leaders in Palestine, most of the Jewish population lived modestly or even in peasant conditions. Based on the fact that Jesus' parents offered two turtledoves (Luke 2:24) for their sacrifice of thanksgiving for the birth of their son, we know that Jesus' family was poor. Most women were busy rearing children, if they survived their pregnancy and if the child survived. Infant mortality was high and pregnancy was always risky. Among the Greco-Roman population, infant exposure (abandoning an unwanted infant out in the elements to die) was common, but it was not allowed among the Jews. However, we also know from Scripture that women were prophets, business owners, home owners and managers, tailors and weavers, tentmakers, teachers, servants, prostitutes, and professional mourners. We know from historical writings that some women were well educated, courtesans, and philanthropists, as well as influential in the Roman political world (though informally).

What would Jesus' ministry bring to women? How did an encounter with Jesus change the lives of the women he knew?

Let's listen to the voices of the Samaritan Woman, Martha, and Mary Magdalene, when God chose them to be first. . . .

17

The Samaritan Woman's Story

ca. 25 - 30 CE

God chose the Samaritan Woman's voice to be the first . . .

- To have the longest recorded theological conversation with Jesus

- To evangelize a non-Jewish community

Photini* approached her modest home on the edge of the village of Sychar. The man she lived with, Alexander, was in the courtyard tending his animal stable. He saw Photini was empty-handed so he asked in a disgusted tone, "Where's the water? You've been gone way too long, woman!"

Photini was so affected by the conversation she had just experienced with a man—a rabbi—at the well, she did not even notice the tone in Alexander's voice. "Come, Alexander, come quickly! You must meet this rabbi I was talking to at the well!"

"Is this another one of your tales, woman? You—YOU—were talking to a rabbi?!?!" He chuckled as he shook his head.

Photini took his arm and looked pleadingly into his eyes. He had never before seen her like this. She was genuinely smiling.

"Please, Alexander, he's waiting. He asked me to bring you to meet him!"

"I'm busy, woman!" Alexander just kept sweeping the stable shaking his head.

"I'm going to tell the neighbors. I'll come back by here on my way back to the well." As she rushed toward the gate, she called back to Alexander, "He knows all about you . . . about us . . . about my past. He told me everything I had ever done. But it was like he understood. He wasn't condemning. Could it be that this is the Messiah?" She was almost breathless now. As she closed the gate behind her, she called back toward Alexander, "He's a prophet, Alexander! And he has Living Water!"

What is she talking about . . . Living water?!?! Alexander was somewhat intrigued now.

She ran next door to her neighbor Helena and walked confidently through the gate. Helena saw her from the window and thought someone must be hurt. She met her at the door before Photini could even knock. "What is it, Photini? Is Alexander hurt?"

"No, no, nothing like that, Helena! I'm coming to invite you and your family to join me to go see this man I met at Jacob's Well. Helena, he knew everything about me, yet he offered me Living Water!"

"What do you mean 'living water'?" a confused Helena asked.

"He can explain it much better. He explains everything better. He's a rabbi! We talked about where we should worship God and how we should worship God and . . . well, just all kinds of things. He is certainly a prophet. He said he is the Messiah! Oh, Helena, what if it's true?!?!"

"I must see this for myself. I'll gather the children and we'll head to the well."

Photini hurried out of her neighbor's gate and ran to the market. She approached the spice merchant where several women were gathered. She usually avoided a group of women because she always felt they were looking down on her, but today—today was different. She had news she wanted everyone to hear. "Good afternoon, ladies. I am sorry to interrupt, but I have just met a man out at Jacob's Well who said he is the Messiah. Come see. He's waiting to meet with us." The women were skeptical. Then Photini mustered the courage to say, "He even knew about my five husbands! He's definitely a prophet! Could he be the Messiah?!" The women looked at each other in utter disbelief. They couldn't belive that Photini would say such a thing in public—and with a smile on her face. Now they *were* curious. They agreed they would join her to go see this man. "Why don't you go home and invite your families first," Photini suggested and then she was off to find more women in the market.

There were four women waiting for the fishmonger to unload another batch of fish. "Ladies, I know you're busy shopping, but I have just met a man out at Jacob's Well who is a prophet. He even said he is the Messiah! He's waiting to meet with more people. Bring your friends and families!"

The women were startled, and while they were discussing whether to go, the fishmonger left his stall and followed Photini.

Photini continued her trek through the market inviting anyone who would listen. A large group began to form and rumors started spreading throughout the village.

As Alexander finished cleaning the stable, he could hear a crowd of people approaching the path near his house. The conversation was lively and they sounded as if they were in a hurry. Suddenly, Photini opened the gate and called out, "Alexander, everyone is coming. Please, please come with us!"

Then he heard his friend Eleon yell from the other side of the courtyard wall, "Come on, Alexander! The whole town is going out to see this man your woman has told us about. She even thinks he's the Messiah!" Then Eleon stepped just inside the gate, "You don't want to miss this, my friend!" Convinced, Alexander dropped his shovel and rushed toward the gate to join his friend.

In the meantime, back at the well, Jesus' disciples had not been able to convince Jesus to eat the food they had brought him. He said to them, "I have food to eat that you don't know about." He was smiling and acting very joyful and as if he was anticipating something or hiding a surprise.

They began whispering among themselves wondering what he meant. One of them asked, "Could someone have brought him food?" To them, he seemed distracted by what had just happened. They certainly were. They were astonished and shocked to have found him talking to a Samaritan woman when they returned from the village with food, but no one had the courage to ask him about it.

Jesus' excitement wouldn't let him sit still. He kept looking back toward the village as if he was expecting something or someone. Seeing the disciples' concern, he tried to explain, "My food is to do what the one who sent me wants and to bring his work to completion." The looks on the disciples' faces showed they were still confused. He knew they would soon understand, so he let them wonder for a bit.

Back in the village, Photini was now leading a growing crowd which was gaining attention and stirring up quite a commotion. As they crested the hill where they could catch the first sight of Jacob's Well in the distance, Photini said, "There he is, with his followers from Galilee."

The crowd began to murmur with questions as to why a group of Jewish Galileans would come to their Samaritan town at all, let alone a rabbi who actually wanted to meet their townsfolk. Their curiosity increased.

As soon as Jesus could see the crowd approaching, he began to grin from ear to ear. His disciples didn't quite know what to expect from this crowd, which far outnumbered them. Jesus' face indicated this was a good thing. He said to his disciples, "Don't you have a saying, 'Four more months and then the harvest'? Well, what I say to you is: open your eyes and look at the fields." Facing the crowd still a ways off with his arms outstretched, he continued, "They're already ripe for harvest!"

The disciples then realized he was talking about the people, not the wheat fields!

Then Jesus reminded them, "The one who reaps receives his wages and gathers fruit for eternal life so that the reaper and the sower may be glad together—for in this matter, the proverb, 'One sows and another reaps,' holds true. I sent you to reap what you haven't worked for." Then Jesus looked toward the crowd approaching and acted like it was his long lost family coming home.

With Photini out in front of the crowd, Jesus stepped forward and held his hands out to her. Looking back at his disciples, he said, "Others have done the hard labor, and now you are benefiting from their work."

Photini looked into Jesus' smiling eyes and then turned to face her villagers. After the quick walk up the hill, she was almost breathless, but was able to say with great pride, "I want you all to know my friend Jesus."

The people began to sit down so they could hear Jesus speak. Photini asked him to tell them about the Living Water and their discussion about worship. So that's where Jesus began. Jesus also let Photini tell her story about their conversation. Then some of the villagers started commenting on how courageous Photini had been to come and tell them that she had believed in Jesus as soon as he had told her all the things she had done. They were so impressed by her bold public confession that they had to come meet this man she talked about.

As dusk approached, the people persuaded Jesus and his disciples to stay with them for a few days to teach them more. He was delighted with the invitation and the people were honored to have him and his disciples. It seemed each home wanted a disciple as a guest, so the disciples were divided up amongst the villagers. After the first night, other villagers insisted that the disciples should stay in other peoples' home the next night. A fresh joy and newfound excitement overtook that village for several days as new friendships were formed. The wall of hatred between Jews and Samaritans had begun to be chipped away.

On the morning after two nights in this city of Sychar, Jesus and the disciples made ready to depart. Tears of joy were shed and warm hugs were shared. As the townsfolk accompanied Jesus and the disciples to the edge of town, Photini and Alexander were on either side of Jesus. Jesus had been their guest both nights and Alexander just couldn't stop asking questions. Photini didn't know he could talk that much! As Jesus turned to say his final goodbye, one of the city leaders quieted the crowd and asked to speak: "Photini, I think I can speak for everyone here when I say, we no longer believe because of what you said, for we have heard for ourselves and know that this one is truly the Savior of the world."

*Photini is the name given to the Samaritan Woman at the Well in the Eastern Orthodox Church's tradition. For a more detailed description from the Orthodox perspective, see http://ww1.antiochian.org/st-photini-samaritan-woman.

The Bible Speaks

The Samaritan Woman's story is found in John 4

I want to re-introduce you to a familiar character: the Woman at the Well from Samaria we read about in John 4. She is a character with whom most church-goers are at least familiar. Unfortunately, we were not given her name in the biblical account. She had several obstacles working against her—even today, in our willingness to hear her story. Things we've been taught over the years may have given us an inaccurate picture of her and her circumstances. Let's take a fresh look at the Scriptures describing this encounter Jesus chose to have with a Samaritan woman.

Jesus Chooses to Go through Samaria
John 4:1-7

1 Jesus learned that the Pharisees had heard that he was making more disciples and baptizing more than John (**2** although Jesus' disciples were baptizing, not Jesus himself). **3** Therefore, he left Judea and went back to Galilee.

4 Jesus had to go through Samaria. **5** He came to a Samaritan city called Sychar, which was near the land Jacob had given to his son Joseph. **6** Jacob's well was there. Jesus was tired from his journey, so he sat down at the well. It was about noon.

7 A Samaritan woman came to the well to draw water. Jesus said to her, "Give me some water to drink." (CEB)

I am always intrigued by verse 4: "Jesus had to go through Samaria." Jews in that day tended to go around Samaria—even though it was the shorter route between north and south—because of the mutual disdain between the Jews and Samaritans. This hatred dated back to the time of the return of the southern tribes from exile in Babylon, which had occurred 500-600 years earlier. During the exile, some Jews had remained in Palestine while most were taken to Babylon. Foreigners—the Samaritans—had been brought in to settle there by the conquering armies. As time went on, the remaining Jews began to intermarry with the Samaritans around whom they lived. When the exiled Jews returned to Palestine, they looked down on the Samaritans. The Samaritans had actually started worshiping the God of the Israelites, but had their own methods and place of worship that the Jews didn't like. I'm sure any of us who have endured church debates over the preferred styles of worship music can relate. So, this simple verse is letting us know that Jesus made a conscious choice and had a purpose for going through Samaria that day.

Then, in verse 6 we get a glimpse of Jesus' humanity: he was tired, so he sat down. If even Jesus could get tired, that explains a lot about our own physical limitations.

The Scriptures mention that it was noon when this scene transpired. This means the woman was coming to the well in the middle of the day. This seems to imply there was some reason for her not to come in the earlier, cooler part of the day. We can only make assumptions about that. The assumption I've been taught through the years was that she was ashamed to come to the well with the other women earlier in the day. We really don't know that. The Scripture simply tells us the time of day when this meeting occurred.

The details of this scene John painted for us would have caused an audible gasp among his original readers. For starters, Jewish men did not speak to women in public, let alone a Samaritan woman, and they, especially, didn't initiate a whole conversation. And yet, that was exactly what Jesus did. Be sure to notice where the disciples were at this point.

The Conversation Begins
John 4:8-9

8 His disciples had gone into the city to buy him some food.

9 The Samaritan woman asked, "Why do you, a Jewish man, ask for something to drink from me, a Samaritan woman?" (Jews and Samaritans didn't associate with each other.) (CEB)

While verses 6-7 show us Jesus' humanity, I believe verse 9 reveals his divinity. Considering the fact that Jesus was the Creator of the universe, and of the woman in front of him, and of the very water in that well, he still proceeded to ask *her* for help when he asked for a cup of water. Her surprised response must have delighted Jesus. His one request of her showed both his humility and foreknowledge of the life-changing conversation that was to follow. **So while the disciples were out shopping, Jesus was engaged in his longest, sustained theological conversation with anyone, recorded in Scripture.** Let's see how the conversation unfolded.

Jesus' Longest Theological Conversation in Scripture
John 4:10-18

10 Jesus responded, "If you recognized God's gift and who is saying to you, 'Give me some water to drink,' you would be asking him and he would give you living water."

11 The woman said to him, "Sir, you don't have a bucket and the well
is deep. Where would you get this living water? **12** You aren't greater
than our father Jacob, are you? He gave this well to us, and he drank from it himself, as did his sons and his livestock."

13 Jesus answered, "Everyone who drinks this water will be thirsty
again, **14** but whoever drinks from the water that I will give will never be thirsty again. The water that I give will become in those who drink it a spring of water that bubbles up into eternal life."

15 The woman said to him, "Sir, give me this water, so that I will never be thirsty and will never need to come here to draw water!"

16 Jesus said to her, "Go, get your husband, and come back here."

17 The woman replied, "I don't have a husband."

"You are right to say, 'I don't have a husband,'" Jesus
answered. **18** "You've had five husbands, and the man you are with now isn't your husband. You've spoken the truth." (CEB)

Many of us have been taught that the Samaritan woman was promiscuous since Christ revealed that he knew she had had five husbands before her current situation of living with a man who was not her husband. Yet, there is no biblical evidence for promiscuity. There are a variety of reasons why that could have been her situation, such as levirate marriage where the brother of her deceased husband is responsible to take the widow as his wife and to give her children in her husband's name. There could have been illnesses or wars or accidents that killed previous husbands. Or they could have abandoned her or divorced her. And if you read Jesus' statement carefully, it is simply a declaration of her background and current living situation, not a condemnation of immorality. There is also a commendation from Jesus that acknowledges her confession. This statement validates the woman and her testimony, an act by a man which was typically unheard of in that day.

The next part of the conversation has also been misinterpreted many times. I have heard male preachers say that because she asked a question unrelated to Jesus' statement about her marital status she must have been changing the subject to distract Jesus from her sinful behavior. We don't know that. A careful reading of the text shows a woman beginning to understand who sits before her and her opportunity to ask Jesus, a prophet and learned rabbi, about one of the main things that separated Jews and Samaritans of that time: the proper location for worship. Since the gospel writer who recorded this story was not an eyewitness to the conversation, he must have gotten the details from Jesus or the woman or from stories passed down through the years. Therefore, our interpretations of this conversation are just that, interpretations, which could be mistaken.

Jesus First Identifies Himself as the Messiah to the Samaritan Woman
John 4:19-26

19 The woman said, "Sir, I see that you are a prophet. **20** Our ancestors worshipped on this mountain, but you and your people say that it is necessary to worship in Jerusalem."

21 Jesus said to her, "Believe me, woman, the time is coming when you and your people will worship the Father neither on this mountain nor in Jerusalem. **22** You and your people worship what you don't know; we worship what we know because salvation is from the Jews. **23** But the time is coming—and is here!—when true worshippers will worship in spirit and truth. The Father looks for those who worship him this way. **24** God is spirit, and it is necessary to worship God in spirit and truth."

25 The woman said, "I know that the Messiah is coming, the one who is called the Christ. When he comes, he will teach everything to us."

26 Jesus said to her, "I Am—the one who speaks with you." (CEB)

The Samaritan woman had some theological questions and took advantage of the opportunity to talk to a Jewish rabbi about her concerns. She was curious. She was a thinker. She already had faith that the

Messiah would come. And then, what appears to be a reward for her thirst for knowledge, **Jesus gave his only pronouncement in Scripture of his messiahship to her, a non-Jewish woman with a questionable past.**

The Samaritan Woman Evangelizes Her Town
John 4:27-38

27 Just then, Jesus' disciples arrived and were shocked that he was talking with a woman. But no one asked, "What do you want?" or "Why are you talking with her?" **28** The woman put down her water jar and went into the city. She said to the people, **29** "Come and see a man who has told me everything I've done! Could this man be the Christ?" **30** They left the city and were on their way to see Jesus.

31 In the meantime the disciples spoke to Jesus, saying, "Rabbi, eat."

32 Jesus said to them, "I have food to eat that you don't know about."

33 The disciples asked each other, "Has someone brought him food?"

34 Jesus said to them, "I am fed by doing the will of the one who sent me and by completing his work. **35** Don't you have a saying, 'Four more months and then it's time for harvest'? Look, I tell you: open your eyes and notice that the fields are already ripe for the harvest. **36** Those who harvest are receiving their pay and gathering fruit for eternal life so that those who sow and those who harvest can celebrate together. **37** This is a true saying, that one sows and another harvests. **38** I have sent you to harvest what you didn't work hard for; others worked hard, and you will share in their hard work." (CEB)

Did you notice the disciples' reaction to what they found upon their return from shopping for groceries? This was obviously a cultural reaction, not a Christ-like reaction!

After Jesus and the woman's heady discussion about the place and purpose of true worship, she left that life-changing conversation to become the **first evangelist to a whole community—a non-Jewish community—in the gospel record**. Now, if Jesus knew about her five husbands, I am sure he knew what she was going to do upon her return to her village. Yet, he did not stop her from being that evangelist. He did not send the male disciples running after her to stop her. Instead, he pointed out to them that the harvest they were about to reap (of people, not grain) was a result of *her* work. **This was the *first* time a whole community believed in Jesus—and they were not Jews!**

The Woman's Testimony Leads People to Jesus
John 4:39-43

39 Many Samaritans in that city believed in Jesus because of the woman's
word when she testified, "He told me everything I've ever done."
40 So when the Samaritans came to Jesus, they asked him to stay with
them, and he stayed there two days. **41** Many more believed because of
his word, **42** and they said to the woman, "We no longer believe because
of what you said, for we have heard for ourselves and know that this one
is truly the savior of the world."
43 After two days Jesus left for Galilee. (CEB)

In John's gospel, the Samaritans were the only people to call Jesus "the savior of the world." Jesus took time to be with the Samaritans for two more days. I'm sure the disciples got a crash course in culture shock and the inclusiveness of the gospel in those two days. Jesus had just broken all the social rules which his Jewish male disciples had grown up learning!

This story alone provides an example of extensive, inclusive, enthusiastic evangelism! The Samaritan Woman used her voice to testify to her neighbors about Jesus and, evidently, included a confession of her past. Her townspeople were willing to listen to someone who was so open and honest. The Samaritan woman was essential in helping Jesus accomplish his mission in that place at that time.

The Message in the Samaritan's Woman's Voice

While most people can tell you the Woman at the Well was transformed by the conversation she had with Jesus, they usually don't acknowledge her legacy as the first evangelist to a whole community of non-Jews! We must be about telling these stories to inspire the *whole* church—not just the women! A hurting world is depending on us as informed believers to demonstrate the equality, justice, and freedom proclaimed by Christ. Let the Samaritan Woman's voice remind you that just as her voice was essential in helping Jesus accomplish his mission in that place at that time, God has chosen your voice for the strategic time and location in which God has placed you.

Biblical Truths Taught through the Story of the Samaritan Woman

1. God communicates directly to and through women.
2. God chooses to have long conversations with women with spiritual questions.
3. God chooses women to evangelize whole communities.
4. God chooses women with misunderstood or questionable pasts to be God's spokespersons.
5. God affirms the value of individual women, regardless of their past circumstances, and chooses to use their voices to speak God's truth.
6. God chooses women who may seem marginalized to bring hope to others.

Why the Voice of the Samaritan Woman Matters . . .

To women: because the Samaritan Woman's story provides evidence of the high value God places on women's intellect since this is the longest recorded theological discussion Jesus had with anyone.

To non-Jews: because the Samaritan Woman's story illustrates the deep desire of a Jewish Messiah to have a relationship with all those outside the Jewish faith, even those who harbor hostile attitudes toward the Jews.

To proclaimers of the gospel: because the Samaritan Woman's story shows that the only real requirement for evangelizing others is an honest, life-changing encounter with the Savior.

To anyone with a tarnished reputation: because the Samaritan Woman's story presents a picture of the power of a transforming encounter with Jesus and the ripple effect of an authentic testimony.

To the spiritually curious: because it shows how much Jesus wants to share with you.

Questions Raised by the Story of the Samaritan Woman

What groups are you overlooking because of your negative attitudes toward them when they could be the ones most ready to accept Jesus?

Who has God placed in your path with whom you could take time to sit and be intentional about having a spiritual conversation?

What theological questions do you have that would benefit from a long one-on-one conversation with God or with a trusted wise friend?

Who are the women and girls in your church and community that God wants to become evangelists? What is your church doing to encourage and prepare them?

How can this story about this "unlikely evangelist" inspire girls and women today whom Jesus is calling to serve, to be evangelists and preachers, and to lead others to him?

The Samaritan Woman's Keys to Resilient Confidence

The Samaritan Woman would say, I believe, that **her keys to resilient confidence were genuine curiosity about deeply spiritual things and a willingness to be vulnerable regarding the truth.** She had no idea she would have a life-changing conversation that day which would give her a new purpose in life. Have you ever had a conversation like that? I have! Sometimes those conversations may be with another human being. Other times, God may speak directly and undeniably to you in your heart. The conversation between Jesus and the Samaritan Woman reveals characteristics of the kind of conversations we can initiate to point people to Jesus.

How to point people to Jesus

1. Recognize the abilities of *others*.
Jesus initiated the conversation with an acknowledgement of something the Samaritan Woman could do for him. Besides breaking the social customs of the day, this showed a humility on Jesus' part. He really didn't need help to get a drink of water! How can we be more observant of the people in front of us who need to know Jesus? How can we engage them by acknowledging one of their talents or abilities?

2. Recognize *their* need.
Jesus offered the Samaritan Woman something he knew she needed. We may not have his supernatural knowledge, but we can ask questions to ascertain someone's deepest desires or felt needs.

3. Listen to *their* questions.
Jesus had a *conversation* with the Samaritan Woman. He did not lecture her. He did not do all the talking.

4. Make *honest* statements, not condemning statements.
Jesus described the Samaritan Woman's situation, but did not voice a condemnation. Her confession was acknowledged and validated by Jesus in a time when women's voices were usually dismissed.

5. Allow the other person to redirect the conversation to *keep them in* the conversation.
When the Samaritan Woman asked a seemingly unrelated question, Jesus answered it and kept her engaged in the conversation. The last thing we want to do is shut down a conversation about Jesus.

6. After you've *earned* the opportunity, share whom you know to be the Truth.

Jesus revealed his true identity as the Messiah *first* to the Samaritan Woman, a non-Jewish woman. Sometimes, the people we assume would be the least likely to want to hear the good news may be the precise ones who are waiting to hear it. However, we must be patient and sensitive to when they are ready and willing to hear about the one we know is Truth.

7. Be willing to be vulnerable.

Authenticity is vital in sharing the truth of the gospel. When the Samaritan Woman shared her testimony with her townspeople, her honesty got their attention. Showing your weaknesses or confessing your past sins may help someone else see the genuineness in what you're sharing. Others do not need to know *all* your dark secrets, but if you can share an appropriate example of how Jesus transformed you in some way, an admission on your part, then that may give people a reason to listen.

A genuine curiosity about spiritual things and a willingness to be vulnerable are characteristics Jesus rewards with resilient confidence. Understanding who you really are, flaws and all, will help you develop a humility that can be empowering when controlled by the Spirit.

"The woman said, 'I know that the Messiah is coming, the one who is called the Christ. When he comes, he will teach everything to us.'"
—John 4:25 (CEB)

18

Martha's Story

ca. 25 - 30 CE

God chose Martha's voice to be the first . . .

- To be corrected by Jesus about her behavior in a woman's traditional gender role
- To give a public Messianic confession

Martha gently lifted Lazarus' head while Mary tried to get him to sip some soup. He was just too weak. He was burning up with a fever and they had tried all the remedies recommended by the best physicians in their village. Martha slipped her hands from under Lazarus' head and neck and stood up to pace the floor. She looked out the window at the setting sun. At that moment, their servant boy entered the room with yet another herb the sisters had sent him to purchase from the physician in Jerusalem. He was out of breath from running up and down through the steep and rocky valley that separated Bethany from Jerusalem. "Oh, Thaddeus, thank you," a grateful Martha whispered as she looked down and noticed his scraped and bleeding feet. She called out quietly to her servant girl, "Junia, quick, bring Thaddeus a basin of water and some ointment for his feet."

"Is Master Lazarus going to get well?" a concerned young Thaddeus asked Martha and Mary. He had never seen Lazarus so sick.

Junia appeared with a basin of fresh water and the ointment for Thaddeus.

Martha said with a desperate tone in her voice, "Junia, would you please make a tea with the herbs Thaddeus brought from town?"

"Yes, Mistress Martha. I have the water boiling on the fire already." She went quickly to her task.

Martha's attention returned to her brother's grimacing face. He wasn't talking now, and he seemed to be in pain. *Oh, where is Jesus?!* she wondered to herself. She stood next to her sister Mary sitting on the edge of Lazarus' bed. She could hold in her frustration no longer. She was unaware she was actually voicing a groaning noise until she heard Thaddeus drop the basin of water he was so carefully carrying back outside. Everyone was startled and a very apologetic Thaddeus scrambled to find some towels. She put her face in her hands and Mary stood to comfort her. "I can't believe he's not here yet, Mary! What could be taking so long?"

Mary hugged her sister and shook her head. She had no words. Junia handed a bowl of tea to Mary for Lazarus.

"He knows we wouldn't ask him to leave his preaching trip unless it was absolutely necessary," her anger was escalating. Her thoughts were racing. She was thinking of all the times Jesus and his band of followers had just dropped in on their way to or from Jerusalem. She had always welcomed them and provided for their needs in her spacious home. Her cooking skills were greatly admired by that collection of rough fishermen. And Jesus' traveling companions brought such joy to the neighborhood when they came. So, now, she was confused as to why he would ignore her plea for comfort and help at this time. She silently mouthed words to Mary, "Surely he won't let Lazarus die, will he?"

Mary's tears flowed freely now. Junia entered the room with the herbal tea and set it next to the bed to let it cool.

Exasperated, Martha left the room. She walked outside in the wintry night air hoping to find some solace for her heart's deep ache. Besides being worried about Lazarus, she was angry and hurt. She watched the stars become more visible in the darkening night sky. After a few moments and the awakening sensation of the brisk breeze, she returned to Lazarus' room.

Mary was unrolling the mat on the floor which she and Martha would share next to Lazarus so they could tend him throughout the night. These lengthening days of his illness were beginning to take a toll on them. They tried to no avail to get Lazarus to drink the tea. His facial expression had relaxed somewhat and they saw the glimmer of a grateful smile. They covered him with a fresh blanket that Junia had wrapped with fragrant spikenard that day; and he drifted off to sleep. Mary and Martha blew out the oil lamp, huddled under their blanket, and tried to get a little sleep themselves. They knew Lazarus' first stirring would awaken them.

~

"Mistress Martha, Mistress Mary, wake up, wake up!" whispered Junia who had crept silently into the room and was patting their arms.

Martha and Mary were surprised to see the sunbeams through the cracks in the shutters and that they had slept through the night. They looked at Lazarus and he lay still and quiet. Martha went over and put a hand on his face to see if his fever had gone. She gasped as she pulled it back quickly. "Mary, he's gone," she choked out the words. Mary put an arm around her sister and ran her fingers through Lazarus' hair. He was cold and lifeless. They sat there on the edge of his bed crying softly. Junia wasn't sure what to do, so she just came and knelt by the bed and put a hand on Martha's and Mary's backs.

When Junia heard Thaddeus in the other part of the house, she knew what to do. She quietly left the room and gave Thaddeus instructions for gathering the burial spices and for telling the neighbors and alerting the mourners. She then warmed the water for the wash basin the sisters would need to prepare Lazarus' body for burial. The necessary preparations were underway.

Martha and Mary had known this day would come someday, but had not thought their brother would be taken from them with an illness such as this. Martha went through the motions of being a responsible sister. She was quieter than usual. Even Mary noticed she was not giving out as many instructions as was her routine. They went about their separate tasks without much conversation. The silence was interrupted throughout the day by waves of sadness and tears. The men from the synagogue came later in the afternoon to wrap Lazarus' body and take it to the burial cave just outside the village gate. The sisters followed with bags of spices and the mourners walked behind them chanting their funeral dirge. It was sad and exhausting for them.

When they returned home, Junia and Thaddeus had prepared a simple meal for the sisters and had lit the oil lamps in Lazarus' room. Martha and Mary were grateful for the help of these servants who were also grieving the loss of Lazarus. Before retiring to their own rooms that night,

Martha and Mary spent some time in Lazarus' room. They tried to voice some happy memories, but their physical exhaustion took over and they just held each other and cried. After awhile, they went to bed, knowing that the mourners would return again in the morning for the ritual activities of remembering the dead.

As Martha lay in her bed, her thoughts turned to Jesus again. Her heart ached so deeply she could not even voice her hurt and anger anymore. She began to wonder if she had done something to make Jesus disappointed in her and that was his reason for not coming. She rehearsed his last visit over and over in her mind trying to make sense of his absence. *Is it my fault he didn't want to come to help? Is there some sin I have committed that he couldn't tolerate? Is Lazarus' death a result of my lack of faith in what Jesus could do?* Her troubled mind was finally overcome by sheer exhaustion and she fell asleep.

~

The next few days were filled with visiting friends and family, amidst the mourners who were being paid for their singing, chanting, and weeping. Martha and Mary went through the motions of greeting and being hospitable, as if by rote. They graciously received the gifts of food and the many condolences offered by those who came. The evenings were quiet as Martha and Mary spent time catching up on some mending and cleaning tasks that had been neglected during Lazarus' long illness.

"Should we take Lazarus' old clothes to the leper colony, Martha?" Mary asked trying to find something productive to do that would help others.

"That is a good idea," Martha responded. "Why don't we go together in a few days. I think some of his tunics need some repairs. I'll look at those tomorrow and then we'll go the next day. It will be good to get out of the house by then. Let's take a picnic lunch with us and stop on the hilltop Lazarus loved, the one where you can look over into the city."

"Oh, he would want us to do that, Martha. I'll have Junia pack our lunch with some of his favorites for us to enjoy. Oh, how I miss him!"

The tears welled up again. Martha's face and eyes were tender from all the wiping of salty tears. She nodded. Mary walked over to Martha's chair and knelt down and placed her head in Martha's lap. Such a time just needed a tender presence, no words. At dusk, they had a bowl of herbal tea and then went to bed. They would greet the mourners again tomorrow. The routine was oddly comforting.

~

The next morning's sun greeted the day in a perfectly blue sky. The crisp air brought a freshness into the house. Junia had made a sweet-smelling arrangement out of some dried herbs she found in the cupboard; and its aroma wafted through the house. As the mourners arrived to continue their ritual duties, Martha sent Thaddeus on some errands around the village. Mary got busy washing some of Lazarus' old clothes and hung them out to dry. Martha inspected each piece for tears or places that needed patches. Junia prepared the meals for the mourners just as Martha had instructed her. Busy-ness helped the grief seem a bit more tolerable.

Not long after Thaddeus had left the house to go to the market and return some dishes to the neighbors, he came running back in the front gate almost out of breath. With dishes still in hand and no purchases made, he loudly exclaimed, "Mistress Martha, he's here, he's here! Come! I'll show you."

Martha and Mary looked at each other puzzled. "Who's here, Thaddeus? What are you so excited about?" Martha tried to slow Thaddeus down and help him catch his breath.

"Jesus! I saw Jesus as I was headed to the market. In the valley on the other side of the Mount of Olives." Thaddeus was breathing hard. "And a big group was following him. I ran back here as fast as I could. Come! I'll take you to him!"

Martha looked back at her sister, and Mary encouraged her to go on ahead. Mary said that she would stay home and get things ready for their arrival. Martha pulled up her long skirt so she could walk faster with young Thaddeus. She knew she would be glad to see Jesus, but she was determined to speak her mind to him as well. She started composing her statement to him in her mind as they walked swiftly toward the edge of the village.

As they crested the Mount of Olives, they could see Jesus and his followers and the growing crowd filling the roadway coming up the side of the hill. Thaddeus yelled and waved, "Jesus! Jesus! Up here!"

Jesus looked up and could see a young boy and a woman with him. He waved. Thaddeus ran down the hill and Martha waited at the top of the hill. Jesus embraced Thaddeus when they met. Martha could see Thaddeus pointing her direction. Jesus looked up and waved. She held up a hand but couldn't muster a very energetic wave.

Jesus and Thaddeus, followed by a good number of villagers, the 12 disciples, and the women from Galilee, met Martha at the top of the hill. She looked Jesus squarely in the face. His penetrating, life-giving eyes melted her heart once more. She embraced him and whispered in his ear, "Lord, if you had been here, my brother would not have died."

Jesus just held her in silence as if allowing her the freedom to voice her hurt and disappointment. She took in a deep breath. She could smell the earthiness of his clothes and could feel the softness of the fabric, cloth like only his mother, Mary, could weave. She leaned back from his embrace. She looked into his face and resolutely said, "But even now I know that God will give you whatever you ask of him."

Jesus leaned down to be eye level with Martha and said smiling, "Your brother will rise again."

"I know," Martha responded rather matter-of-factly. Knowing her brother was already in the tomb, she still fully believed Jesus' teachings about eternal life for those who trust in him. Jesus kept his face near hers as if waiting for her to complete a thought. She realized he was expecting her to say more. She stated the truths she had accepted, "He will rise again . . . in the resurrection . . . on the last day."

Jesus stood up, and with one arm around Martha, he turned to face the crowd following him. He proclaimed to them, "I am the resurrection and the life. Those who believe in me, even though they die, will live, and everyone who lives and believes in me will never die."

His followers standing closest to him stood there in silence, waiting for more explanation. The group of villagers toward the back started murmuring, wondering if they had heard him right.

Then Jesus turned again to Martha, and asked her specifically, "Do you believe this?"

Seeing the crowd in front of them, including some of the Jewish religious leaders from the village, and yet feeling the strength and peace of Jesus' presence beside her, she took a deep breath and said quietly to Jesus, "Yes, Lord." Jesus squeezed her shoulder in affirmation. Then, with the boldness for which she was known, she turned to face the crowd, and said, with great confidence, "I believe." Looking again at Jesus, but with a voice loud enough for the dozens of gathered people to hear her, "I believe that you are the Messiah, the Son of God."

The murmurs in the back of the crowd grew louder.

Martha continued in spite of the menacing looks from some trouble-making faces in the crowd, "I believe you are the One coming into the world." Jesus smiled and quieted the crowd. Sensing the rising disturbance, Jesus reminded his close followers that they were there on God's mission and would see God's glory soon. He then asked Martha to run home and bring Mary out to meet him. He would wait for her.

Young Thaddeus stayed with Jesus and the crowd; and Martha ran quickly back to the house. She found Mary in the kitchen giving instructions to Junia to prepare for the large gathering they were about to host. "Mary, Mary, the Teacher is here."

"Here—at the house—already?" a flustered Mary asked, remembering why Martha was usually the one in charge.

"No, no, not at the house. He's waiting for you. He's asking for you to come out to him. Come, I'll take you. I'm sure Junia has things under control."

Junia nodded thinking she could get help from the visiting friends who were still at the house. But as soon as Mary left, all the friends and paid mourners followed Mary outside assuming she was going to the tomb to mourn there. Junia was left on her own.

Mary and Martha went as quickly as they could back to where Martha had left Jesus and the others waiting. Their friends were following close behind. When Mary saw Jesus, she ran and knelt at his feet. Looking up to him with tears in her eyes, she said, "Lord, if you had been here, my brother would not have died." Jesus raised her up and embraced her. He reached out to draw Martha into the embrace and just tightened his grip on them. His face was showing signs of deep grief. After a moment, he asked them, "Where have you laid him?"

"Lord, come and see," the sisters said, as they led him toward the cave just outside the village gate. Along the way, he stopped on the path and leaned down with his hands on his knees as if tired from a long run. The mourners decided to begin to recite one of their funeral psalms. As Jesus stood bent over, he began to weep. Mary and Martha reached out to console him.

The friends of Martha and Mary were overheard saying, "See how he loved him!"

Then a boisterous, irreverent voice from the back of the villagers said, "Could not he who opened the eyes of the blind man have kept this man from dying?" Peter, one of Jesus' disciples, turned in anger toward the voice, but Andrew, his brother, grabbed him by the arm and prevented him from making the situation worse.

Jesus composed himself; and, then they proceeded to the entrance of the tomb. A large, heavy stone sealed the doorway. He leaned a hand on the stone wall and bowed his head as if gathering his thoughts. Then, with a comforting confidence, he said to several of his stronger followers, "Take away the stone."

Martha stepped up and pleadingly looked at Jesus and said, "But, Lord, the smell. He's been in there four days."

And then, with that look only Jesus could give, he smiled as if he knew a secret. With eyebrows raised, Jesus reminded her, "Did I not tell you that if you believed, you would see the glory of God?" He stepped to the tomb's entrance and looked to the heavens and said, "Father, thank you for hearing me. I know you always hear me. I say this for the benefit of the crowd standing here so that they will believe that you sent me." Then he leaned down into the low doorway and shouted, "Lazarus, come out!"

Since Martha and Mary were standing closest to Jesus, they saw the moving figure in the tomb first. They both fell to their knees in worship of Jesus and in awe of what they were seeing. As Lazarus shuffled toward the light, it was obvious he was struggling to move with so many bandages wrapped around him.

Jesus said, "Untie him and let him go."

Martha and Mary quickly helped their brother. One of Jesus' disciples standing nearby offered Lazarus his coat. As soon as his arms and legs were free, Lazarus knelt at Jesus' feet. Mary and Martha knelt on either side of him. They worshipped Jesus by kissing his feet. Jesus helped bring Lazarus to his feet. With tears of gratitude, Lazarus embraced Jesus in great joy, and with his weak legs, fell into Jesus' arms. Jesus smiled and savored this sacred moment knowing his Father had allowed him to bring such renewed hope to this beloved family. He helped Lazarus to stand upright again and get his balance. Lazarus squinted against the bright light. He embraced his sisters and saw them with a new appreciation. They were so filled with stunned joy, they were unable to speak. Jesus watched the reunion with a look of deep compassion.

Lazarus was the first to break the silence. "Thank you, Jesus, oh, thank you!" he exclaimed to a happy Jesus. He stuttered his words, "How did . . . When did . . . I mean, where did . . .?" as he tried to make sense of what had happened to him.

Jesus smiled and simply lifted his eyes toward heaven. "We have the Father to thank!"

As the sisters helped to steady Lazarus, the cheers and murmurs of the assembled crowd became louder. A dazed Lazarus looked around and saw the faces of his friends. Several of Jesus' disciples approached him with outstretched arms and expressions of delight and disbelief. People toward the back of the crowd were pushing their way through to get a glimpse of this miracle. The disciples were able to form a wall of protection from the gawkers allowing the three and Jesus to start on the path toward home.

The grateful sisters escorted an unsteady Lazarus back to the house. Following close behind was a growing and curious crowd. The three siblings could barely speak as they walked arm in arm trying to grasp the reality of the situation.

The questions rippled through the skeptical onlookers, such as, "Who is this man who can raise people from the dead?" and "Is this man really from God?" The disciples continued to be amazed at Jesus' power, yet had stopped questioning it. Their acceptance—not understanding—of the miraculous was happening more frequently.

As the three siblings entered the courtyard of their home, they found a busy Junia filling a basket of dishcloths as she retrieved them from the laundry line. When she saw Lazarus walking and breathing, she dropped the basket and collapsed to the ground. Lazarus rushed to her side and helped her see he was not a ghost, but flesh and blood—and hungry. Martha's heart rejoiced as she heard a laughing Jesus and his followers enter the courtyard. She was looking forward to an evening of fellowship with Jesus and her brother Lazarus. She decided on the spot that she would stay out of the kitchen this evening and allow others to prepare and serve the meal—*this* time.

Note: The above story is based on John 11 and some of the phrasing of quotations comes from the CEB translation.

The Bible Speaks

Martha's story is found in Luke 10:38-42; John 11:1-16, 17-44; 12:2

The story we all know by heart is the one where Martha complained to Jesus that Mary was not helping her in the kitchen with all the food preparations for their guests (see Luke 10:38-42). It appears that Jesus chastised Martha for her busy-ness and praised Mary for her willingness to stop and take time to learn from Jesus. **This was the first time in Scripture where Jesus corrected a woman about a traditional gender role.** The lesson we learn from that story is that sometimes the priority should be sitting and listening to Jesus—and women are encouraged to do that—even when other responsibilities await their attention. While that story gives one picture of Martha, I really believe Martha has been remembered for the wrong thing! There is another side to Martha that is seldom ever presented, which I think results in our misrepresenting this important woman in Scripture. The other story of Martha and Mary is well-known, but because of their brother, not the sisters.

The gospel of John gives us the touching story of Jesus raising his friend Lazarus from the dead. While the miracle takes center stage in the story—as it should—there is a detail of that story that is not often highlighted. John 11 is the location of the story in Scripture. The small town of Bethany about two miles east of Jerusalem was the location of this miracle which occurred toward the end of Jesus' earthly ministry. Jesus had left Galilee and was being followed by his disciples and many women (see Matt. 27:55) on this final journey toward Jerusalem where he knew he would be crucified. The time is right for him to make himself fully known.

Jesus Learns of His Friend Lazarus' Sickness
John 11:1-16

1 A certain man, Lazarus, was ill. He was from Bethany, the village of
Mary and her sister Martha. (**2** This was the Mary who anointed the Lord
with fragrant oil and wiped his feet with her hair. Her brother Lazarus
was ill.) **3** So the sisters sent word to Jesus, saying, "Lord, the one whom
you love is ill."

4 When he heard this, Jesus said, "This illness isn't fatal. It's for the
glory of God so that God's Son can be glorified through it." **5** Jesus loved
Martha, her sister, and Lazarus. **6** When he heard that Lazarus was ill, he
stayed where he was. After two days, **7** he said to his disciples, "Let's
return to Judea again."

8 The disciples replied, "Rabbi, the Jewish opposition wants to stone
you, but you want to go back?"

9 Jesus answered, "Aren't there twelve hours in the day? Whoever
walks in the day doesn't stumble because they see the light of the
world. **10** But whoever walks in the night does stumble because the light
isn't in them." **11** He continued, "Our friend Lazarus is sleeping, but I am
going in order to wake him up."

12 The disciples said, "Lord, if he's sleeping, he will get well." **13** They
thought Jesus meant that Lazarus was in a deep sleep, but Jesus had
spoken about Lazarus' death.

14 Jesus told them plainly, "Lazarus has died. **15** For your sakes, I'm
glad I wasn't there so that you can believe. Let's go to him."

16 Then Thomas (the one called Didymus) said to the other disciples, "Let us go too so that we may die with Jesus." (CEB)

When Jesus arrived several days after Lazarus had died, Martha met him outside and Mary remained indoors. Jesus was accompanied by his disciples and many women, and his group had probably gathered others along the 4-day journey from Galilee, through Jerusalem, and into Bethany. Since the religious leaders were already trying to plot to kill him, I'm sure rumors spread quickly that Jesus was back in town.

The First Public Messianic Confession Allowed by Jesus
John 11:17-26

17 When Jesus arrived, he found that Lazarus had already been in the tomb for four days. 18 Bethany was a little less than two miles from Jerusalem. 19 Many Jews had come to comfort Martha and Mary after their brother's death. 20 When Martha heard that Jesus was coming, she went to meet him, while Mary remained in the house. 21 Martha said to Jesus, "Lord, if you had been here, my brother wouldn't have died. 22 Even now I know that whatever you ask God, God will give you."

23 Jesus told her, "Your brother will rise again."

24 Martha replied, "I know that he will rise in the resurrection on the last day."

25 Jesus said to her, "I am the resurrection and the life. Whoever believes in me will live, even though they die. **26** Everyone who lives and believes in me will never die. Do you believe this?" (CEB)

I heard a memorable sermon once, years ago, by Dr. Linda McKinnish Bridges entitled "Martha Comes Out of the Kitchen," which pointed out that there should be a big pause right here after verse 26 in the Scripture reading, because what Martha says next, as recorded in verse 27, is revolutionary.

John 11:27

27 She replied, "Yes, Lord, I believe that you are the Christ, God's Son, the one who is coming into the world." (CEB)

This conversation between Martha and Jesus places her in a unique position in Scripture: **Martha spoke the first public Messianic confession allowed by Jesus! She—nor anyone else in the group—could have made a bolder statement!** When Jesus asked his disciples earlier in a private conversation (see Matthew 16:13-20) who they thought he was, Peter's confession that Jesus was the Christ resulted in Jesus ordering the disciples *not* to tell anyone! Now that Jesus was on his way to Jerusalem, knowing he would be killed, the timing was right to allow this confession to be made public—and Jesus made a way for a *woman* to be the *first* to make such an announcement. (Note: This is slightly different than the story of Anna, whose actual words are missing in Luke 1, and the story of the Samaritan Woman, whose messianic confession is only implied in John 4.) Martha had to have been aware that saying such a thing could result in being stoned to death for blasphemy if the religious leaders wanted to accuse her. Apparently, she was willing to risk her own life to speak the truth. What a role model for the whole church today!

The next passage is the telling of the actual miracle. In this passage we also read the only spoken words by Mary of Bethany in Scripture and they were a complaint about Jesus' absence as well as a statement of belief in Jesus' power. This is one of the tender pictures in Scripture of Jesus' empathy with the human condition and his ability to show his own emotions. Note the mixed reactions to the raising of Lazarus in verses 45 and 46.

Jesus Raises Lazarus from the Dead
John 11:28-46

28 After she said this, she went and spoke privately to her sister Mary, "The teacher is here and he's calling for you." **29** When Mary heard this, she got up quickly and went to Jesus. **30** He hadn't entered the village but was still in the place where Martha had met him. **31** When the Jews who were comforting Mary in the house saw her get up quickly and leave, they followed her. They assumed she was going to mourn at the tomb.

32 When Mary arrived where Jesus was and saw him, she fell at his feet and said, "Lord, if you had been here, my brother wouldn't have died."

33 When Jesus saw her crying and the Jews who had come with her crying also, he was deeply disturbed and troubled. **34** He asked, "Where have you laid him?"

They replied, "Lord, come and see."

35 Jesus began to cry. **36** The Jews said, "See how much he loved him!" **37** But some of them said, "He healed the eyes of the man born blind. Couldn't he have kept Lazarus from dying?"

38 Jesus was deeply disturbed again when he came to the tomb. It was a cave, and a stone covered the entrance. **39** Jesus said, "Remove the stone."

Martha, the sister of the dead man, said, "Lord, the smell will be awful! He's been dead four days."

40 Jesus replied, "Didn't I tell you that if you believe, you will see God's glory?" **41** So they removed the stone. Jesus looked up and said, "Father, thank you for hearing me. **42** I know you always hear me. I say this for the benefit of the crowd standing here so that they will believe that you sent me." **43** Having said this, Jesus shouted with a loud voice, "Lazarus, come out!" **44** The dead man came out, his feet bound and his hands tied, and his face covered with a cloth. Jesus said to them, "Untie him and let him go."

45 Therefore, many of the Jews who came with Mary and saw what Jesus did believed in him. **46** But some of them went to the Pharisees and told them what Jesus had done. (CEB)

Martha and her sister Mary were able to have a front row seat to the ministry and miracles of Jesus. Yet, they also had the chance to see the truly human side of Jesus when he was tired, hungry, and needed a place to stay. They had been his refuge on numerous occasions. Martha's willingness to open her home to him and his followers must have been a rare gift for Jesus. Martha's story is one of several biblical women who have been remembered, by most, for the wrong reason, in my opinion. Her robust hospitality was matched by her willingness to speak the truth boldly. What an example for all of us!

The Message in Martha's Voice

Martha demonstrated qualities of being able to multi-task as a hospitable hostess, speak her mind, and express her needs. I'm sure all those qualities came into play when she stepped out and made the first public Messianic confession in the presence of those who could have accused her of blasphemy. Let Martha's voice remind you that God still chooses women's outspokenness to speak about the one who is the Truth, the one who will change people's lives.

Biblical Truths Taught through the Story of Martha

1. God chooses women with strong opinions to make bold statements of truth.
2. God sometimes chooses women instead of men to speak the truth in risky, public settings.
3. God communicates directly to and through women.
4. God affirms women who want to step out of cultural expectations to pursue a serious and studious relationship with God, which today could mean an opportunity to go to seminary or to pursue religious studies in other academic institutions.

Why the Voice of Martha Matters . . .

To busy women: because Martha's story illustrates that even when your skills may be necessary to accomplish the task at hand, God may choose you for a much bolder role with a bigger purpose. Sometimes, it will require you to stop and listen.

To people with siblings: because Martha's story shows that God can empower all different approaches to life, even that sibling's approach which you can't understand.

To women who speak out: because Martha's story lets us know that bold women's voices are needed in the world; yet, you need the silence to listen to the Spirit.

To those who think God only speaks through men: because Martha's story shows how Jesus set the stage for her to declare his identity even to his male disciples, and that you can follow Jesus' example by giving women an opportunity to speak their spiritual truths.

To timid women: because Martha's story exemplifies how Jesus gave women a voice during his earthly ministry, and lets you know he can still give you a voice to speak truth, even in the midst of a crowd of doubters.

Questions Raised by the Story of Martha

Why do so many people assume a woman's place is in the kitchen at home, and yet, if you talk about a professional chef, a man's picture comes to mind?

If you would prefer a behind-the-scenes task, is there a more prominent role God is asking of you?

Who is someone in your sphere of influence that needs to hear what you have to say—about Jesus or faith or grief or joy or some other life experience?

Why do you think Jesus allowed Martha to give the first public Messianic confession, and not Peter, James, or John?

What are the rituals of grieving in your family? Are there plans you need to make to help your family be prepared for your passing?

How do you talk about the hope of resurrection with others?

Martha's Keys to Resilient Confidence

Martha is remembered for being outspoken as a complainer when actually she should be revered for her bold proclamation of the Messiah. **I believe Martha would identify her keys to resilient confidence as learning to balance busy-ness with stillness and speaking the truth even in risky situations.** Jesus reminded Martha that the expected role of being in the kitchen is not always the best use of a woman's time. Her example in Scripture implies several strategies we could employ when we discover we need to escape an expected role.

How to escape an expected role:

1. Learn from the example of others

Martha's knowledge of Jesus being the Messiah must be a result of her choosing to spend time listening to Jesus' teaching (maybe she learned something from her sister Mary's example). If you want to change your role, you have to choose to learn from the example of others by observing them, reading their writings, and listening to them. Who are some people, speakers, or authors who have influenced you to become a better you and helped you to respond to God's voice?

2. Tell someone assertively what role you would rather have

Martha made a decision to make a bold statement in the midst of a doubting crowd. Martha chose to go outside her expected role of staying quietly in the background without recognition. If you want to change your role, you may have to tell someone assertively what role you would rather have. Who could you approach to talk about a role you believe God has in mind for you?

3. Focus on making Jesus happy

Martha's statement was spoken directly to Jesus in response to Jesus' direct question to her—even though she knew that others who were listening would disagree with her. She was focused on the Truth—Jesus Himself—and responded without fear. If you are a leader, you will never make everyone happy. When you know your position is based in Jesus' Truth, you do not have to fear the naysayers. Your responsibility as a leader is to make Jesus happy. Who are some of the naysayers you fear? How can you demonstrate your faith in the power of Jesus by speaking in spite of the doubters?

For women, this act on Jesus' part should encourage us to know that **Jesus gave women a voice then and Jesus gives women a voice now.** Whether you are the quiet, shy type who speaks more often by her example or the talkative, assertive type who never hesitates to speak, God has a purpose for your voice! Use your unique woman's voice—even if you'll be remembered for the wrong thing as Martha was. God wants *someone* to hear what YOU have to say. Someone needs *your* unique gifts. Finding the balance between busy-ness and stillness and speaking out when you have a truth to share will be evidence that you have resilient confidence.

"She replied, 'Yes, Lord, I believe that you are the Christ, God's Son, the one who is coming into the world.'"
—John 11:27 (CEB)

19

Mary Magdalene's Story

ca. 25 - 30 CE

God chose Mary Magdalene's voice to be the first . . .

- To converse with the risen Christ

- To tell the Resurrection News to the male disciples at the request of Christ Himself

Mary Magdalene watched in anguished amazement as Peter and John just walked away. They had seen the empty tomb with their own eyes and then simply headed back to the house where most of the disciples were huddled in fear. Peter acted as if he was in a daze, shaking his head in silence. At least John believed what Mary had told him, that the tomb's stone had been rolled away and Jesus' body was no longer where they had buried him Friday afternoon, just before Sabbath. Yet, neither he nor Peter seemed to feel the urgency to notify anyone about this apparent grave robbery.

Mary felt almost numb with confusion. As she leaned against the outside wall of the tomb weary with sadness, she looked down and saw her spilled bag of burial spices. She must have dropped them earlier when she first discovered that Jesus' body was gone and had run to tell the disciples. Still weeping, she knelt down to gather the cinnamon and myrrh, when suddenly there was a glowing light coming from within the tomb. She had to shield her eyes to look inside. As her eyes adjusted, she began to see the shape of two men sitting where Jesus' body had once lain.

"Why are you crying?"* they asked her.

Startled, wondering if she were imagining what she was seeing, she blurted out, "They have taken away my Lord."* Her tears were making it hard to get the words out.

The two men were smiling and waited patiently for her to continue.

"And . . . and I don't know," she fumbled for more words. In frustration, she finally said, "I don't know where they've put him."* She just couldn't make sense of what was happening. *Who are these men? Are they angels? Why are they here? How did they get inside the tomb? Why didn't Peter and John see them?* She decided she must be seeing things. She put her face in her hands and fell back against the cool stone doorway, crying.

Then she heard someone approaching. Still on her knees, she looked up, wiping her eyes and realized it was the gardener. He looked concerned and asked, "My dear woman, why are you crying? Who are you looking for?"*

Mary thought, *Finally, here is someone who might be able to help me!* "Oh, sir," pointing and looking into the now empty tomb, she said pleadingly, "If you were the one who carried him away, please tell me where you have put him and I will get him."* She couldn't take her eyes off the empty slab where Jesus' body had been.

"Mary."*

She knew that voice! Mary's heart was suddenly warmed with joyful relief and amazement. Turning around, her eyes were once again struck with a truth she had not expected: Jesus was standing in front of her, alive and whole and . . . talking to her. "Teacher!"* she said as she wrapped her arms around his knees.

Jesus helped her to her feet. She took his hands and saw the scars from the cruel spikes. She touched the piercings tenderly and then looked deep into his eyes and saw the same gaze of acceptance and love she had seen when he had first healed her several years ago. As she was about to start asking a myriad of questions, Jesus gently put a finger to her lips. He let go of her hands and placed his hands on her shoulders. With a reassuring tone, he said, "Don't hold on to me, for I haven't yet gone up to my Father."

Mary bowed her head in reverence.

Jesus lifted her chin and said very decisively, "I need you to go to my brothers and sisters and tell them, 'I'm going up to my Father and your Father, to my God and your God.'"*

Mary nodded in obedience, gave him a quick embrace and excitedly hurried off to share the good news. A ways down the path she realized she had left her burial spices at the tomb's entrance—again. *Well, I guess I won't be needing those today!* She smiled to herself and caught herself running through the narrow, shadowy streets of Jerusalem, as she made her way past the vegetable market, the fishmonger's, and the spice shop. Oh what news she had to share! She had seen the Lord—ALIVE!

*Certain phrases based on the text of John 20 (CEB)

The Bible Speaks

Mary Magdalene's story is found in Matthew 27-28; Mark 15-16; Luke 8 and 24; John 19-20

The gospel of Luke introduces Mary Magdalene in Luke 8:1-3. We discover that she and several other women were cured by Jesus and then became traveling companions and financial supporters of Jesus and his other male disciples. (Picture that for a moment—Jesus and the male disciples traveling with a group of wealthy women, who had become Jesus' disciples.) We seldom hear this part of the story of Mary Magdalene, yet Luke 8 states that she and other women had their own financial means with which to support Jesus' ministry. Since we are never told about a husband, one possibility is that she was single and a successful businesswoman.

Mary Magdalene Becomes a Follower and Financial Supporter of Jesus

Luke 8:1-3

1 After this, Jesus traveled about from one town and village to another,
proclaiming the good news of the kingdom of God. The Twelve were
with him, **2** and also some women who had been cured of evil spirits and
diseases: Mary (called Magdalene) from whom seven demons had come
out; **3** Joanna the wife of Chuza, the manager of Herod's household;
Susanna; and many others. These women were helping to support them
out of their own means. (NIV)

In those verses we're told that Mary was cured of seven demons. Often, when demon-possession is mentioned in the Bible, it is really a reference to what we know today as mental illness. So, we're not sure what Mary's condition was or exactly what she suffered. What we do know about mental illness in biblical times is how people who lived with it were feared, shunned, and even worse, discarded. I'm sure whatever her condition was, Mary Magdalene lived on the outskirts of society before Jesus healed her. If it was mental illness, she would have been mistrusted, overlooked, avoided, shamed, and possibly treated cruelly by those who didn't understand. If it was some other condition, she would have been viewed negatively by most.

Numbers had specific meanings in the ancient world that we don't often equate with them today. The use of the number seven usually meant "complete," or "whole." In this context, "seven demons" could imply the worst possible condition of corruption. Once again, we can't be sure what the exact problem was. We do not know if it was of her own making, as in suffering consequences of bad decisions, or if she was a victim of mental illness, as mentioned earlier. It is possible she was someone who had been so mistreated that her life was in shambles. It is important to note there is no evidence that Mary Magdalene was a prostitute, which seems to be the interpretation that has followed her through the centuries—talk about being misunderstood! It was a pope's sermon in the 6th century CE that confused the issue by saying that Mary Magdalene was the same person as the "sinful woman" who anointed Jesus' feet. This was not the case; Mary Magdalene and the "sinful woman" are two separate, historic, biblical women. Unfortunately, much Western art has still portrayed her, in error, as a prostitute. And even though the Catholic church officially changed her designation in 1969 and claimed she was not a prostitute, the misnomer lingers. The prostitute label is wrong, yet we do know she was healed of "seven demons" by Jesus who completely transformed her life.

Mary Magdalene's name is probably based on the name of her hometown since there are numerous women with the name of Mary in the New Testament. Magdalene refers to the fishing center on the western shore of the Sea of Galilee. The town has been identified by different scholars as Magdala, Tarichaea, or Magadan, yet it is not possible to know with certainty if this was the origin of her name or if one of these locations was, indeed, her hometown.

While all these facts are noteworthy, the important reason to remember Mary Magdalene is her relationship with Jesus. She was healed by Jesus and then became a faithful follower who traveled with him as a disciple and a financial supporter. We don't have many details about her background or experience, yet the few statements we do have about her time spent with Jesus indicate an unsurpassed loyalty on her part to him and a level of deep respect and trust on Jesus' part of her.

The first time we see Mary Magdalene in the gospel accounts of Matthew, Mark, and John, she is at the cross watching the horrific view of the crucifixion of the man who had changed her life. We cannot bring ourselves to feel that kind of pain. Along with Mary, Jesus' mother, Mary Magdalene was one of the women who stayed and witnessed the gruesome crucifixion scene, as did the other women who had followed Jesus from Galilee to Jerusalem. John is the only male disciple named in Scripture at the crucifixion. Mary Magdalene also helped to bury Jesus.

There are several versions of the resurrection story in the gospel accounts offering different details about which women came to the tomb on that first morning of the week. However, the fact that Mary Magdalene is mentioned in all four gospels as being at the tomb on the morning of the resurrection means her presence was unforgettable, verifiable, and integral to the Easter story. Since John was one of the disciples to whom she first reported the missing body, I'd say that his gospel account carries the closest thing to a firsthand account, so it is the one presented here.

Mary Magdalene Meets the Risen Christ
John 20:1-16

1 Early on the first day of the week, while it was still dark, Mary Magdalene went to the tomb and saw that the stone had been removed from the entrance. **2** So she came running to Simon Peter and the other disciple, the one Jesus loved, and said, "They have taken the Lord out of the tomb, and we don't know where they have put him!"

3 So Peter and the other disciple started for the tomb. **4** Both were running, but the other disciple outran Peter and reached the tomb first. **5** He bent over and looked in at the strips of linen lying there but did not go in. **6** Then Simon Peter came along behind him and went straight into the tomb. He saw the strips of linen lying there, **7** as well as the cloth that had been wrapped around Jesus' head. The cloth was still lying in its place, separate from the linen. **8** Finally the other disciple, who had reached the tomb first, also went inside. He saw and believed. **9** (They still did not understand from Scripture that Jesus had to rise from the dead.) **10** Then the disciples went back to where they were staying.

11 Now Mary stood outside the tomb crying. As she wept, she bent over to look into the tomb **12** and saw two angels in white, seated where Jesus' body had been, one at the head and the other at the foot.

13 They asked her, "Woman, why are you crying?"

"They have taken my Lord away," she said, "and I don't know where they have put him." **14** At this, she turned around and saw Jesus standing there, but she did not realize that it was Jesus.

15 He asked her, "Woman, why are you crying? Who is it you are looking for?"

Thinking he was the gardener, she said, "Sir, if you have carried him away, tell me where you have put him, and I will get him."

16 Jesus said to her, "Mary."

She turned toward him and cried out in Aramaic, "Rabboni!" (which means "Teacher"). (NIV)

The moment when Jesus said her name reminds me of the story of Hagar when the angel of the LORD (who may have been the pre-incarnate Christ) called Hagar by name in Genesis 16:8. Here, when Mary heard her name, she finally realized it was Jesus with whom she was talking. **This is the first encounter and first conversation recorded in Scripture between the Risen Christ and another person—and he chose that person to be Mary Magdalene.**

Jesus Commissions Mary Magdalene
John 20:17-18

17 Jesus said, "Do not hold on to me, for I have not yet ascended to the Father. Go instead to my brothers and tell them, 'I am ascending to my Father and your Father, to my God and your God.'"

18 Mary Magdalene went to the disciples with the news: "I have seen the Lord!" And she told them that he had said these things to her. (NIV)

Jesus telling Mary to announce his resurrection news to his disciples is one of the clearest instructions we find in Scripture. Jesus asked a particular person to deliver a specific message to a certain group of people. Comparable commissions include God's call of Moses at the Burning Bush, God's direction of Samuel to anoint David as the next king of Israel, and Gabriel's announcement to Mary that she would become the mother of the Christ child. **Jesus decidedly requested Mary Magdalene to be the FIRST person to share his Resurrection declaration: the greatest, most important, most life-changing news *ever* to be delivered—Christ is RISEN!!** This is significant since even though she was one of his faithful *women* followers and participants in his ministry, her gender would make her testimony invalid in that culture. Jesus' choice gave Mary Magdalene a unique calling and historic responsibility!

Decades after the resurrection, the Apostle Paul would remind his readers that if the resurrection of Christ is not true, then our faith is futile (See 1 Cor. 15:12-20). Without Christ's resurrection, there is no Christianity. Without the Easter story, there is no need for Christmas! Without the resurrection, there is no hope for any of us! The resurrection changed everything—for eternity, for everyone! The importance of the message usually implies the importance of the messenger and the method of communication. Logically, in our minds, Jesus should have chosen his best friend, John, or the outspoken Peter to be the first herald of this news. And yet, the Risen Jesus did not appear first to either of them nor to his own mother! **The woman, Mary Magdalene, was the first who saw the Risen Christ and the first to speak the truth of the resurrection!**

What makes Jesus' choice even more mind-boggling is that in their culture and time a woman's testimony was not to be trusted unless it had male corroboration. Yet, Jesus *still* asked Mary Magdalene to be the one to tell his *brothers* that he had risen from the dead. A little later in the story, when we read about the Walk to Emmaus in Luke chapter 24, we see Jesus scolding the two friends for not believing the women's testimony.

Followers Chastised for Not Believing the Women
Luke 24:17-27

17 He [Jesus] asked them, "What are you discussing together as you walk along?"

They stood still, their faces downcast.

18 One of them, named Cleopas, asked him, "Are you the only one visiting Jerusalem who does not know the things that have happened there in these days?"

19 "What things?" he asked.

"About Jesus of Nazareth," they replied. "He was a prophet, powerful
in word and deed before God and all the people. **20** The chief priests and
our rulers handed him over to be sentenced to death, and they crucified
him; **21** but we had hoped that he was the one who was going to redeem
Israel. And what is more, it is the third day since all this took place. **22** In
addition, some of our women amazed us. They went to the tomb early
this morning **23** but didn't find his body. They came and told us that they
had seen a vision of angels, who said he was alive. **24** Then some of our
companions went to the tomb and found it just as the women had said,
but they did not see Jesus."

25 He said to them, "How foolish you are, and how slow to believe all
that the prophets have spoken! **26** Did not the Messiah have to suffer
these things and then enter his glory?" **27** And beginning with Moses and
all the Prophets, he explained to them what was said in all the Scriptures
concerning himself. (NIV)

I would love to hear a Bible study led by Jesus, wouldn't you? Did you notice in verse 25 how he reminded these friends that what the women had told them was the same truths the prophets had spoken? Jesus obviously trusted a woman's ability to speak his truth. And because Mary Magdalene was faithful in fulfilling the calling Christ gave her, the message of Christ's resurrection power began to spread!

Mary Magdalene's story speaks to anyone who has ever felt less-than, misunderstood, or overlooked. With all the other choices Jesus had for communicating his resurrection news, he chose Mary Magdalene, a woman with a misunderstood past, to be the first person to share the news that would change the human experience for all eternity.

The Message in Mary Magdalene's Voice

After Mary Magdalene's healing, she became one of numerous women disciples who traveled with Jesus and the 12 male disciples. A few additional facts give her role in the gospel story even more significance:

First, in Jesus' day, a woman's testimony was not valid in a court of law; it always had to be corroborated by male witnesses.

Second, the gospel writers made it pretty clear that the inner circle of Jesus' disciples was Peter, James, and John.

Third, the news of the Resurrection is the most important truth in all of history. Even the Apostle Paul said that without the truth of the resurrection, our faith is futile (See 1 Cor. 15:14-19).

In light of those facts, it is astounding that **the Risen Christ chose and commissioned the voice of Mary Magdalene, a woman with a misunderstood or questionable past, over his best friends and over his own mother, to be the *first* to converse with the Risen Christ and the first to tell the *men*: CHRIST IS RISEN!** Let Mary Magdalene's voice remind you that *you* may be the first person to share with someone the hope of the resurrection!

Biblical Truths Taught through the Story of Mary Magdalene

1. God chooses women to announce truths about God to women and men.

2. God chooses women to be the first to experience God in new ways.
3. God chooses women with misunderstood and questionable pasts to be God's spokespersons.
4. Jesus can transform anyone into a vessel to preach the gospel, regardless of gender or personal background.
5. Jesus chose a woman's voice to be the first to announce the Resurrection—the most important news in history.
6. Jesus believed a woman had the ability to communicate truth—including to men—in spite of others' opposition or disbelief—and commissioned her to do just that.
7. Jesus' relationship with Mary Magdalene was so special that after his resurrection he chose to appear to her even before he appeared to his mother, or to his inner circle of Peter, James, and John.

Why the Voice of Mary Magdalene Matters . . .

To women: because Mary Magdalene's story shows that Jesus chooses to commission women, even women with misunderstood or questionable pasts, to deliver announcements of life-changing, miraculous events. Jesus entrusted the voice of Mary Magdalene to be the first to speak the truth of the miracle of his resurrection—the absolute foundation of the gospel—in spite of the obstacles in her culture against hearing or believing a woman's testimony.

To men: because Mary Magdalene's story reminds men to follow Jesus' example of giving women opportunities to discover and fulfill their callings, to give women a reason to use their voices for sharing gospel truth, and to introduce women to ways they can use their financial resources for ministry purposes. Jesus' female disciples supported him financially and they traveled with him throughout Judea during his ministry. The women disciples are identified in the gospels as examples of enduring loyalty and devotion during Jesus' ministry and crucifixion, and by being the first at the empty tomb.

To people with misunderstood or questionable pasts: because Mary Magdalene's story is a beacon of hope for the transformation available through Christ and evidence that active participation in the work of the ministry is possible, regardless of your background.

Questions Raised by the Story of Mary Magdalene

If you have something in your background that you think is preventing you from being useful to God, how can Mary's story change your perspective?

Which ministries are you supporting financially?

What truth is Christ asking you to share in spite of the way others will receive it?

Since Jesus commissioned Mary Magdalene to be the original herald of the world's best news, what implications should that act on Jesus' part have on our view of women's abilities and responsibilities in the church and other ministries today?

What more can you do to serve Jesus?

What is a way you could spend more time with Jesus—through prayer, meditation, Scripture reading, and/or fasting?

How could you rearrange your schedule or your finances to serve others?

How can you refocus to see a situation through Jesus' eyes and with a sense of eternity?

When you know of a woman being discouraged from sharing her truth or fulfilling her calling, what can you do to help her voice be heard?

Mary Magdalene's Keys to Resilient Confidence

Mary Magdalene faced those who misunderstood her, doubted her, and mistrusted her. Any leader today should expect those same occupational hazards. Such occurrences can make you feel debilitatingly paralyzed from wanting to continue with your responsibilities. For encouragement and strength, the story of Mary Magdalene shows a woman who demonstrated amazing fortitude. **Here is what I think Mary Magdalene would say were her keys to resilient confidence:**

1. A personal encounter with Jesus.

Mary first encountered Jesus when he healed her of "seven demons." Through prayer, you can take any problem you have to Jesus today. Allow him to heal you of the pain it is causing you. His healing is undeniable. If you don't have the words to express your deep concern or hurt, read the Psalms of David and hear his agony of heart and see his transformation in attitude in the final words of those psalms.

2. A deeper devotion to Jesus.

Even after Peter and John witnessed the empty tomb, Mary was the only one who lingered there. That devotion was rewarded by Christ's presence. The same will happen to us when we linger in God's Word, in prayer, and in our desire to know Jesus more deeply. Jesus always rewards our gift of time spent with him.

3. A determination to obey anything Jesus asks you to do, regardless of the risks or obstacles.

Jesus asked Mary to be the first to tell his resurrection news, knowing she would face disbelief from her audiences. Yet, she did it anyway! Once you have a personal encounter with Jesus and he asks you to do something, your decision to follow through on that calling, with the Spirit's help, gives you the freedom, the courage, and the empowerment to lead.

Mary Magdalene's discipleship was enduring in spite of the risks. The New Testament is filled with stories of how the power of the risen Christ transformed other people from worst to first. And he still does it today! A personal encounter with the Risen Christ, a deeper devotion to Christ, a calling from Christ, and a determination to fulfill that calling were Mary Magdalene's keys to resilient confidence. They can be yours, and mine, too!

"Jesus said to her, 'Don't hold on to me, for I haven't yet gone up to my Father. Go to my brothers and sisters and tell them, "I'm going up to my Father and your Father, to my God and your God." '
"Mary Magdalene left and announced to the disciples, 'I've seen the Lord.' Then she told them what he said to her."
—John 20:17-18 (CEB)

PART EIGHT

God Chose Lydia

THE TIME OF THE EARLY CHURCH

ca. 30 - 60 CE

Events that Shaped the World of Lydia

THE TIME OF THE EARLY CHURCH
ca. 30 - 60 CE

After Christ ascended around 30 CE, his followers began the task of trying to fulfill the Great Commission of going into all the world to make disciples. The book of Acts, attributed to Luke, tells the stories of the events that helped the church to grow in Palestine and beyond. In that book we read the stories of miracles experienced by Peter and we're introduced to Saul who was dramatically converted and renamed Paul sometime around 33-35 CE. During the 30s CE, Christ communities are known to have spread from Palestine to Syria among the Jewish Diaspora.

The emperor of the Roman Empire at the time when Christ ascended was Tiberius, who had succeeded Augustus (Octavian), his father and the first emperor of Rome, in 14 CE. Palestine was still a territory ruled by Rome and the local Roman ruler over Judea was Pontius Pilate while the local Roman ruler over Galilee was Herod Antipas, the youngest son of Herod the Great. The Roman Empire was still growing and stretched from Spain and North Africa, across southern and eastern Europe all the way to the Caspian Sea and Tigris River, and down to the Red Sea and Egypt. The Roman Empire was governing about 20% of the world's entire known population at its height.

Between 25 and 60 CE, while Palestine was just a small territory in the vast Roman Empire, there were several leadership changes:

- First, Emperor Tiberius, who had ruled since 14 CE, died in 37 CE and was succeeded by Emperor Caligula, who was considered a cruel tyrant by historians and was assassinated by his own body guards in 41 CE, just four years after becoming emperor. Caligula ordered the erection of a statue of himself in the Jerusalem Temple. This sparked Jewish resistance. Herod Antipas (son of

Herod the Great) ruled in Galilee and Perea until 39 CE under Caligula's reign.

- Second, Emperor Claudius succeeded Caligula and ruled the Roman Empire from 41-54 CE. Herod Agrippa I (grandson of Herod the Great) ruled from 41-44 CE during Claudius' time. Herod Agrippa I was mentioned in Acts 12:1 and reigned as king over Judea, Galilee, Batanaea, and Perea. He persecuted Christians and had James, John's brother, killed and Peter imprisoned. He was the last of the Herodian family to rule in Judea, yet his son Herod Agrippa II became the tetrarch and king of Chalcis, which was in Greece, making him the last Herodian ruler. Under Claudius, the Romans invaded Britain in 43 CE, and Colchester was named the capital of Roman Britain in 49 CE.

While the Romans were taking over Britain, Paul set out on his first missionary journey around 46-48 CE. In 50 CE, a 12-year-old Nero (the future emperor who would later burn Rome and have Peter and Paul executed) was being tutored by Seneca, a Roman Stoic philosopher, statesman, and dramatist. Also in 50 CE, the Romans continued their invasion of other European areas and made Cologne (in modern-day Germany) into a Roman colony.

Happenings in the Rest of the World

Here are a few highlights of what was happening in the rest of the world between 25 and 50 CE:

- Buddhism, which had begun in India, was introduced to China around the same time as Christ's death and resurrection. China was still under the rule of the Han Dynasty.
- In Central America, the Olmec culture was still flourishing, creating some of the most perplexing stone carvings in the ancient world, most of which were of the human figure.
- The city of Petra (in modern-day Jordan) was the thriving trading center and capital of Nabataea.

- In Africa, the Bantu peoples continued to migrate across sub-Saharan Africa to find new farmlands and to spread their farming skills wherever they went.
- In South America, the Moche peoples began to be ruled by warrior-priests.
- In North Africa, tradition provides us with the stories of the martyrdom of Photini (the Greek Orthodox name for the Samaritan woman from John 4) and her sons in Carthage.
- In Northern Europe, some traditions have legends from this era telling of the biblical Martha of Bethany, who traveled to France and helped rescue a city from a great dragon, and of a woman named Veronica (the extra-biblical story of the woman who shared a handkerchief with Christ on his way to the cross), who also went to France, and became a recluse.

Focusing on the Bible's Story

The year 50 CE (an estimate) marked the beginning of Paul's second missionary journey which lasted 2-3 years. During the decade of the 50s, some scholars believe Paul wrote some of his first letters (1 Thessalonians, Galatians, 1 Corinthians, Philemon, Philippians, 2 Corinthians, and Romans—all of which are now in our New Testament) to the churches he had started or hoped to visit, which means his writings may have preceded the writing of Mark, the first gospel. This second missionary journey was historic in that it was Paul's first venture onto the European continent. In the biblical record, this second missionary journey would also result in the first convert to Christianity in Europe when Paul visited the bustling commercial center of Philippi, home to Lydia, the seller of purple.

Let's listen to the voice of Lydia, when God chose her to be first. . . .

21

Lydia's Story

ca. 50 CE

God chose Lydia's voice to be the first . . .

- To respond to Paul's preaching of the gospel on the European continent

- To lead a house church on the European continent

Lydia and her friends were spreading out the beautiful reddish-purple cloth on the grass near the rushing river and began to unpack their lunch baskets. She was grateful this group of women friends had been meeting together ever since she moved to Philippi several years earlier. They had grown close and watched their group increase in number to about 15.

The group had been in existence long before Lydia arrived. A few Jewish women started this prayer group years ago and had welcomed any woman who wanted to join them. Lydia remembered when she discovered them meeting by the river on her first Sabbath day as a new resident in Philippi. She had gone to the riverside that day just to take a break from giving orders to her servants trying to set up her new fabric shop. As she rested on a rock, she listened to the prayers she heard from a small group of women gathered by the river. She was so glad to hear others praying to the one true God instead of to Apollo, as people did in the city. She had no desire to intrude on the women's group when she first found them; but one of the women, Euodia, spotted her behind the trees and invited her to join them. As a new businesswoman in town, she embraced the kind gesture and she and Euodia had been good friends ever since.

One of the things these women prayed about regularly was asking God to bring ten men together to form a synagogue. Philippi was a busy commercial center not far from the port city of Neapolis. While there were a number of Jews living in Philippi, there never seemed to be enough men committed to the task of forming a regular group to worship God and study Torah; so no synagogue existed.

Yet these women were committed. They met weekly without fail. They were so organized that if the weather prevented their meeting at the river, they had a rotating schedule of whose home would host them on which Sabbath of each month. They actually enjoyed having each other in their homes. The joy of their fellowship was a welcome respite to their daily lives in a busy city ruled by Rome and with little God-fearing influence. Lydia especially enjoyed transforming her home and business every few months into their meeting place.

This day was just a regular riverside day. One of the women talked about a new recipe for lentil soup she wanted them all to try. Another mentioned her disappointment that her yogurt had not turned out like she had hoped. And one brought her daughter's first attempt at date cakes and invited the others to share them. After the lunch was laid out, they gathered around the bountiful food and each one of them expressed their thanks to God. As they were praying they noticed a small group of four men approaching the river. The men stood off at a distance until they concluded their prayer.

Euodia whispered to Lydia, "Should we invite them to join us?"

"Well, they look harmless," Lydia whispered back. "And they did wait patiently for us to finish our prayer. I think it will be all right. There are more of us than there are of them."

Euodia leaned in to the circle of women and said softly, "Let's invite the men to join us. We have plenty of food."

Lydia started the approving nod and the others agreed.

In her usual hospitable way, Euodia stood and motioned to the four men, "Sirs, we have plenty of food and we would be happy to share with you on this beautiful Sabbath day."

The men looked at one another grinning. "It's a sign," Paul said eagerly.

Luke responded to Euodia, "Why, thank you. We are hungry travelers and would be grateful." The four of them walked over to the seated group who made room for them.

Paul began by introducing himself and his three companions, Luke, Timothy, and Silas, as traveling preachers of The Way. "We went looking for the synagogue when we arrived in town a few days ago, and we were disappointed not to find one, so we thought there might be a group meeting at the riverside today. We were so glad to find you and to hear you praying to our one true God. Are you all Jewish women?"

Lydia spoke up. "We are all God-fearers, yet a few of us do not have Jewish ancestry. This prayer group has been meeting for about seven years."

"That's impressive," remarked Luke.

The youngest of the four, Timothy, wanted to impress his mentor Paul and jumped in with a question, "Have you heard of Jesus of Nazareth who taught us The Way?"

Paul gently squeezed Timothy's shoulder and said, "My young friend here is very zealous for the message we preach; but we don't want to impose on your meal with our preaching."

"Is this a new Jewish message?" Lydia asked with great curiosity. "I have not heard about it." Looking at her companions, she asked, "Have any of you women heard about this Way?" She only saw questioning faces. "Well, sirs, apparently you have a captive audience. We consider ourselves well-informed citizens of this bustling town, so we would like to hear more. Who is this Jesus you mentioned—a man from Nazareth? That's in Galilee, in northern Palestine, right?"

The four men nodded.

Another woman in the group with deep Jewish roots piped in, "From Nazareth? I used to hear my father say that nothing good ever comes from Nazareth! This could be interesting!"

The other Jewish women nodded with a familiar understanding, while the Gentile women in the group did not relate to the reference.

"We are honored to share with you what we have been blessed to learn," Paul began.

Euodia asked, "So, Paul, how did you meet this Jesus?"

"Well, that is actually a good place to start because when I met him I was following the Jewish law to the letter; and he helped me realize I had totally misunderstood the purpose of the law. Are all of you familiar with God's Law, at least the Ten Commandments?"

The five Gentile women in the group kind of chuckled. Lydia spoke up, "Oh yes, our Jewish friends here have been good teachers. They have even persuaded us to obey the food laws."

Euodia and Syntyche, two of the most faithful Jewish women in the group, smiled with pride. Syntyche said, "And we have had good students, too. Although we do still hear complaints about their missing the shellfish their families love to eat."

Everyone laughed. They all knew the challenge of having to sacrifice something for the sake of their devotion to God.

Paul continued with his story about how Jesus had come to him in a vision of blinding light when he was on his way to arrest people who were Jesus' followers. He was very dramatic in his storytelling and the women were a great audience. His short, yet effective, description got the women's attention and he began to share how he learned that the purpose of the Law was to show people how they had not lived up to God's ideal. And since God is perfect, there is no way we could ever obey every law to God's standard of perfection.

The women understood and were visibly moved. "Can we ever truly please God?" asked a sincere Lydia.

"Only through faith in God's Son, Jesus." Paul continued the dialogue with the women about how their sins had already been forgiven through Jesus' death on the cross and how Jesus had defeated the power of sin and death through his resurrection. If they would accept that forgiveness by repenting of their sins and following Jesus, they could be baptized into this new Way of living.

Syntyche looked serious and reminded Paul, "But the Jews are God's Chosen people. You must be Jewish to find God's favor."

"Syntyche, you are right that the Jews are God's Chosen people. God chose them to bring the Source of everyone's salvation into the world—God's Son, Jesus Christ."

Syntyche wasn't convinced; and the other Jewish women in the group seemed a little miffed at Paul's message.

Lydia, in her eagerness, spoke up, "Are you saying, that even though I am Gentile, I can accept this Jesus and God will forgive my sins, too?" Lydia was trying not to offend her Jewish friends.

"Yes, Lydia, yes, that is exactly what I am saying!" Paul and his three companions were nodding with great expectation.

"Oh, ladies, do you hear this?" Lydia looked at her Gentile friends with a fresh hope in her eyes. "We—even we Gentiles—can become part of God's great promise!" Lydia's heart was bursting with excitement, yet she was met with disinterested stares from most of the women in the group. "Paul, what must I do to begin to be a follower of Jesus' Way? I want this kind of forgiveness. I want to know I belong to God forever."

Paul looked directly into her eyes. "Lydia, if you call on the Name of Jesus and claim him as your Savior and Lord, you will be saved. You will receive eternal life and the Holy Spirit will come to live within you."

With tears streaming down her cheeks, Lydia was overcome with joy. "Oh, Paul, I do believe what you said, every word of it. I want Jesus to be my Savior and Lord."

"Do you repent of all your past sins?" Paul asked.

"Oh yes!" Lydia responded. "I want to live my life in a way that is pleasing to him. I am so grateful he died for my sins."

"Can you voice a prayer thanking God for this gift of salvation?"

"Oh, yes, yes I can!" Lydia lifted her tear-filled eyes toward heaven with her hands outstretched as if trying to reach up to God. "Lord Jesus, thank you for sending your messengers to us today. Thank you for dying on the cross for my sins. Thank you for this gift of knowing I am forgiven and I belong to you. Help me to be the woman you want me to be. Amen."

There was a sacred hush among the group after Lydia prayed. As she wiped her eyes with her cloak, she looked at Paul and the other three men and thanked them again for coming. Paul asked, "Lydia, since we're already at the river, would you like to be baptized now?"

"Oh, may I?" a smiling Lydia responded. "I would be honored to be baptized by you and for these dear friends to witness it." She turned to the group of women and asked, "Would you stay awhile longer and be part of this with me?"

The women all nodded because they loved Lydia and wanted to support her decision, even though most of the group gathered were skeptical. Several of them were savvy businesswomen or married to men who were politically connected, so it was understandable they wanted to be cautious about their associations with people who could damage their reputations.

Paul led Lydia into the river. The water was chilly, but Lydia hardly noticed. Paul asked her once again to confirm her commitment to Jesus and then plunged her quickly beneath the clear, flowing water. As Lydia came up out of the water, she was beaming. She raised her hands and voice in praise to God for this new feeling of freedom and forgiveness. The women gathered around her with the beautiful reddish-purple cloth to warm Lydia in her wet clothes. Paul and his companions also gathered around her and prayed for her. Lydia's joy was radiant.

As they began to pack up their lunches, some of the other women talked to Silas, Timothy, and Luke, asking them more questions. This was such new information for them. Having watched Lydia's baptism and hearing her praise God, they wondered if it were really possible to have such joy. Committing to this Way could be dangerous since so many gods were worshipped in Philippi; and, of course, the emperor expected to be worshipped. They wondered how Lydia would be able to remain true and keep her business going.

"So, Paul, how long are you and your friends staying in Philippi?" asked a still dripping Lydia.

"We don't have a set schedule. We are able to stay as long as God wants us here."

"Well, I have an invitation for you. I have a large home where I run my fabric business and I have plenty of room for you all to stay at my home. I also want you to preach your same message to all my workers and servants."

"Oh, Lydia, that is a generous offer, but we don't want to be an imposition."

Lydia looked at her friends. "Ladies, would you please help Paul and these gentlemen know that I have plenty of room for them."

All the ladies started talking at once describing the different occasions they had visited Lydia's home. The men were overwhelmed and just stood there nodding, not being able to take it all in.

Paul finally interrupted, "I believe you have persuaded us, ladies. Thank you, Lydia. We would be happy to accept your offer of hospitality." With that, the group made their way back into town and Lydia showed the men where she lived. She had no idea how her life was about to change.

The Bible Speaks

Lydia's story is found in Acts 16

The story of Lydia gives us a glimpse into some of the early intersections between commerce and church growth. We are all keenly aware of the need for those with successful businesses and financial resources to help support today's church and the many ministries and missionaries across the world. Yet, do we ever stop to think where that started? Who were the people in the early church who provided the financial means to help the church grow? It may surprise you to discover that it was wealthy women who supported Jesus and the disciples (see Luke 8:1-3) and also supported early missionaries and church leaders such as Paul (see Phil. 4:3, 15-16). And more specifically, it was the wealthy businesswoman Lydia who led the first church on the European continent.

We are introduced to Lydia in Acts 16 when Paul is on his second missionary journey. His traveling companions and fellow missionaries on that journey were Luke, Silas, and Timothy. Notice in verses 6 and 7 the reason they were not able to preach in a certain parts of Asia or in Bithynia. The Holy Spirit, today, is still in charge of what God's servants can, and cannot do, for God's kingdom.

Paul Called to Macedonia in a Vision
Acts 16:6-10

6 Paul and his companions traveled throughout the regions of Phrygia and Galatia because the Holy Spirit kept them from speaking the word in

the province of Asia. **7** When they approached the province of Mysia, they tried to enter the province of Bithynia, but the Spirit of Jesus wouldn't let them. **8** Passing by Mysia, they went down to Troas instead. **9** A vision of a man from Macedonia came to Paul during the night. He stood urging Paul, "Come over to Macedonia and help us!" **10** Immediately after he saw the vision, we prepared to leave for the province of Macedonia, concluding that God had called us to proclaim the good news to them. (CEB)

Verse 10 shows us the reason Paul felt compelled to go to Macedonia, which is what we know as Greece today. **This is the first time in the Scriptures where we know the gospel spread to the European continent.**

Paul Arrives in Philippi
Acts 16:11-12

11 We sailed from Troas straight for Samothrace and came to Neapolis the following day. **12** From there we went to Philippi, a city of Macedonia's first district and a Roman colony. We stayed in that city several days. (CEB)

Philippi was ten miles off the coast of Macedonia (today's Greece) and on a prominent trade route. It was named after Phillip II, the father of Alexander the Great. At the time when Lydia lived there, the city was experiencing great privilege. As a Roman colony, it's citizens were considered citizens of Rome itself. The growing population included many retired miliatry men who had been given land in the vicinity.

Paul Finds a Women's Prayer Group
Acts 16:13

13 On the Sabbath we went outside the city gate to the riverbank, where we thought there might be a place for prayer. We sat down and began to talk with the women who had gathered. (CEB)

Paul's usual practice was to go first to a city's synagogue on the Sabbath. Since he and his fellow missionaries went outside the city to the riverbank, there must not have been the minimum number of ten Jewish men in Philippi to form a synagogue. I'm sure they were happy to find that prayer group down by the river. Was it awkward, I wonder, for a group of men to approach an all-women prayer group?

Lydia is Converted through Paul's Message
Acts 16:14

14 One of those women was Lydia, a Gentile God-worshipper from the city of Thyatira, a dealer in purple cloth. As she listened, the Lord enabled her to embrace Paul's message. (CEB)

Lydia, a Gentile woman who worshiped the true God, was a member of this prayer group. Lydia was originally from Thyatira, a city about 200 miles away in Asia (today's Turkey). The city was known for its many craft guilds and its industry of manufacturing beautiful reddish-purple cloth dyed with a plant native to that particular region or from a certain type of marine mollusk. This cloth was expensive and could only be afforded by the wealthy and was often worn by royalty. Paul met Lydia on his first trip to spread the gospel on the European continent.

We don't know why Lydia moved from Thyatira to Philippi, yet we can make some educated guesses based on what we know about these cities. Thyatira's craft guilds made that city a center for commerce in the region. In the ancient world, each craft guild had its own patron god. Since the Scriptures tell us Lydia was a God-fearer, it is possible that she chose to leave the city so she would not have to worship the god of her craft guild. Philippi was a good choice because it was also on a prominent trade route and near the coast. She could continue to cater to the wealthy in a busy city away from her craft guild.

With no mention of a husband or a father or a son, we can assume Lydia was single and/or had no more living male relatives. She could have been a widow or divorced. She was a Gentile living in the Roman world, so divorce would not have carried the shame or stigma it would have among the Jews. She was called a God-fearer in the Scripture, meaning she believed in the one true God. But, Lydia was not of Jewish ancestry, so she would have been viewed as an outsider by devout Jews. And yet, Acts 16:14, makes it clear that "the Lord opened her heart to listen eagerly to what was said by Paul" (NRSV). Obviously, the Lord was at work in the hearts of outsiders or no one (sinners and/or non-Jews) would ever be able to accept him.

According to Scripture, Paul's call to Macedonia resulted in Lydia becoming the *first* convert on the European continent, host of the first house church, and probably the leader of that first church in Europe!

Lydia Exercises Her Gift of Hospitality
Acts 16:15

15 Once she and her household were baptized, she urged, "Now that you have decided that I am a believer in the Lord, come and stay in my house." And she persuaded us. (CEB)

Apparently, Lydia had a thriving business large enough to support a household, which probably included the workers in her business. She was already a leader and manager of people and apparently had the gift of hospitality, indicated by her willingness to open her home to Paul and his companions for their work while they were in Philippi. It was a risky offer. Soon after meeting Lydia, Paul and Silas got into trouble as you'll read in the next passage.

Paul and Silas Imprisoned in Philippi; Upon Release, Visit Lydia's House Church
Acts 16:16-40

16 One day, when we were on the way to the place for prayer, we met a
slave woman. She had a spirit that enabled her to predict the future. She
made a lot of money for her owners through fortune-telling. **17** She began
following Paul and us, shouting, "These people are servants of the Most
High God! They are proclaiming a way of salvation to you!" **18** She did
this for many days.

This annoyed Paul so much that he finally turned and said to the spirit, "In the name of Jesus Christ, I command you to leave her!" It left her at that very moment.

19 Her owners realized that their hope for making money was gone. They grabbed Paul and Silas and dragged them before the officials in the city center. **20** When her owners approached the legal authorities, they said, "These people are causing an uproar in our city. They are Jews **21** who promote customs that we Romans can't accept or practice." **22** The crowd joined in the attacks against Paul and Silas, so the authorities ordered that they be stripped of their clothes and beaten with a rod. **23** When Paul and Silas had been severely beaten, the authorities threw them into prison and ordered the jailer to secure them with great care. **24** When he received these instructions, he threw them into the innermost cell and secured their feet in stocks.

25 Around midnight Paul and Silas were praying and singing hymns to God, and the other prisoners were listening to them. **26** All at once there was such a violent earthquake that it shook the prison's foundations. The doors flew open and everyone's chains came loose. **27** When the jailer awoke and saw the open doors of the prison, he thought the prisoners had escaped, so he drew his sword and was about to kill himself. **28** But Paul shouted loudly, "Don't harm yourself! We're all here!"

29 The jailer called for some lights, rushed in, and fell trembling before Paul and Silas. **30** He led them outside and asked, "Honorable masters, what must I do to be rescued?"

31 They replied, "Believe in the Lord Jesus, and you will be saved—you and your entire household." **32** They spoke the Lord's word to him and everyone else in his house. **33** Right then, in the middle of the night, the jailer welcomed them and washed their wounds. He and everyone in his household were immediately baptized. **34** He brought them into his home and gave them a meal. He was overjoyed because he and everyone in his household had come to believe in God.

35 The next morning the legal authorities sent the police to the jailer with the order "Release those people."

36 So the jailer reported this to Paul, informing him, "The authorities sent word that you both are to be released. You can leave now. Go in peace."

37 Paul told the police, "Even though we are Roman citizens, they beat us publicly without first finding us guilty of a crime, and they threw us into prison. And now they want to send us away secretly? No way! They themselves will have to come and escort us out." **38** The police reported this to the legal authorities, who were alarmed to learn that Paul and Silas were Roman citizens. **39** They came and consoled Paul and Silas, escorting them out of prison and begging them to leave the city.

40 Paul and Silas left the prison and made their way to Lydia's house where they encouraged the brothers and sisters. Then they left Philippi. (CEB)

After a dramatic jail release including an earthquake and the conversion of the jailer, Paul and Silas returned to Lydia's home to meet with the "brothers and sisters," indicating this was the gathering place of the new church in Philippi (see Acts 16:16-40). Lydia and the jailer, and their households, were Gentiles. Paul's ministry to the non-Jewish population was growing.

Lydia's story gives us a glimpse of some of the surprises God uses in people's lives to bring about God's ultimate purposes. The Holy Spirit had to *prevent* Paul from going to some of the places he had planned to go in order to get him directed to Macedonia (modern-day Greece) where he would meet a very open Gentile woman named Lydia. Her conversion was a confirmation of Paul's call to the non-Jewish world and the open door for the church to start on the European continent.

The Message in Lydia's Voice

When you read the book of Philippians, you can get a sense of the closeness Paul felt for the members of this church which began in Lydia's home. The book of Philippians tells us that they were the only group who supported Paul financially at one point in his ministry. What joy that kind of generous support must have given that itinerant missionary!

Lydia's story shows us that today's church leaders need to seek out the leadership gifts, prayerfulness, and hospitality gifts of the women among them. Today's church still needs the support of wealthy businesspeople, the hospitality of people who offer their homes for ministry, and of women business leaders who can also be great church leaders. Let Lydia's voice remind you to be a good steward of all the blessings God has given you by making them available for ministry.

Biblical Truths Taught through the Story of Lydia

1. God chooses women to lead Christian church movements.
2. God chooses women to provide financial support of God's kingdom.
3. God chooses successful businesswomen to start and/or support churches and ministries.
4. God chooses women to begin to change a culture.
5. God chooses wealthy women to illustrate that the gospel transcends all class distinctions.
6. God chooses single women to be church leaders.
7. God chooses women to advise God's servants, ministers, and missionaries.

Why the Voice of Lydia Matters . . .

To European history: because Lydia, according to the Bible, is the first convert to Christianity in Europe, introducing Christianity to the Western World.

To Church history: because Lydia probably led the first house church in Europe, thus beginning the church's history in the West.

To the wealthy: because Lydia's story illustrates how a financially successful businesswoman, who chose to follow Jesus, is evidence that the gospel transcends class distinctions.

To those with the gift of hospitality: because Lydia's story demonstrates how the ministry of hospitality was extended by a single woman to Paul and his companions in their time of need, for both a center for ministry and a place of refuge.

To male church leaders: because Lydia's story reveals how Paul acknowledged the gifts and devotion of Christian women leaders, accepted their financial resources, and acted upon their advice.

To singles: because this story seems to imply that Lydia was single and that did not stop her from becoming a church leader or from offering hospitality for ministry purposes.

Questions Raised by the Story of Lydia

Who are the single women, businesswomen, and community leaders in your church who could be filling church leadership roles?

Who are the "outsiders" in your pews waiting to be invited to be included?

How are the wealthy business people in your church being challenged to share their business skills and resources with your church?

How often do home fellowships happen among your church members? How could you encourage more home fellowships?

Lydia's Keys to Resilient Confidence

Lydia's story shows how courageous conviction, an open heart, and an open home can be the keys to resilient confidence. Lydia accepted Paul's message of salvation and immediately made all her resources available for God's work. On the surface, we may think that must have been easy, since she was wealthy. However, let's consider her surroundings.

Courageous conviction

Lydia lived in Philippi where there were not even enough Jewish men to form a synagogue, let alone many others who worshiped the true God. Her community would not have encouraged her new beliefs and practices. Soon after she became a believer, Paul, the man who had led her to the Lord, was arrested, beaten, and thrown in prison in Philippi because he made some people mad by healing a girl—from an evil spirit —who was a fortune-telling moneymaker for her owners. Can you imagine what Lydia's association with Paul could have done to her business in Philippi? **She must have had a courageous conviction about her newfound beliefs which gave her the resilient confidence to follow through on her beliefs regardless of the consequences.**

An open heart

As a single woman running a business that catered to the wealthy in Philippi, she probably knew or had connections to many of the "movers and shakers" in town. Acts 16:14 says, "The Lord opened her heart." She was receptive to what Paul was inviting her to believe. I am sure when her changed religious practices became known, it affected the way people viewed her. Some were probably intrigued and some were probably skeptical. We don't really know. However, we do know that she first wanted her whole household to become believers. **She made a way for others to receive the same salvation she had. Her open heart was a key to her confidence that others would believe.**

An open home

As soon as she became a believer, she offered the use of her home to Paul and his traveling companions. She must have had a large home that probably housed her business as well. The Scripture says she "persuaded" or "convinced" or "constrained" Paul and his companions to come stay at her house (see Acts 16:15). Paul listened to the advice of a single, wealthy businesswoman and acted upon it. Later, when Paul and Silas were released from prison in Philippi, the first place they went was to Lydia's where they met with the new believers meeting in her home. **Lydia's hospitality of opening her home for a group of new believers resulted in the birth of the first church in the West, on the European continent. As the owner of that home, she was most likely the leader of that church. Opening one's home for God's use is a key to resilient confidence.**

Resilient confidence develops when we make available to God all the gifts, talents, and resources we already possess. As we begin to let go of our ownership of these blessings, we get to see God at work right in front of us.

"Once she and her household were baptized, she urged,
'Now that you have decided that I am a believer in the Lord,
come and stay in my house.' And she persuaded us."
—Acts 16:15 (CEB)

CONCLUSION

So What?

Over the centuries, women have been told—more often, than not—all the things they cannot or should not do in regard to their leadership, their work, their abilities, their education, their opportunities, and the list goes on. Unfortunately, both in society and in many church settings, the Bible has been the misused, misquoted, and misinterpreted source of much of that instruction. Enough is enough! God's original design of equal responsibility, shared leadership, and equal partnership and respect between the human genders is something we can all aspire to achieve as God's image-bearers.

The biblical women we've studied in this book are great examples of the many times God chose a woman—instead of a man—to be the first or to be the leader. This does not imply God always wants women to be first. This means that women are as qualified as men to be first or to lead. I believe the stories we've examined in this book bear out the fact that, **according to Scripture, the most foundational truths of our faith were first proclaimed by women** (other than those proclaimed by Jesus himself), including authenticating a written prophecy as God's Word, prophesying the coming birth of the Messiah, identifying the Messiah publicly, and heralding the Resurrection—the hallmark of our faith.

Another observation worth repeating is that these women represent people from a variety of cultures, ethnic, and religious groups who spoke languages different from the one you're reading. That fact encourages me to seek to learn from all kinds of people. I must be more intentional about listening to people different from me, who may have had an experience with God or learned a truth about God about which I need to hear.

This book has taken you on a journey through the lives of 13 women whom the Bible records as people chosen by God to be the *first person* to experience God in a new way, to express a new truth about God, or to proclaim a new message from God. God can choose *anyone* to fulfill God's purposes as illustrated by the variety of ages, classes, and circumstances represented by these women, which include young adult, teenaged, widowed, married, infertile, childless, mother, elderly, poor, wealthy, enslaved, overlooked, abused, mistreated, misunderstood, Jewish, non-Jewish, outsider, and insider.

Here is a summary of the ways Scripture records these women's voices as chosen by God to be the first, a reminder of the keys to resilient confidence their examples portrayed, and a few ways their stories empower our thinking about how God continues to choose women today to build God's kingdom.

God chose Eve's voice to be the first . . .

- To speak as a woman
- To speak with equal responsibility for dominion of the earth with her husband
- To have the first theological debate
- To speak with both Satan and God
- To acknowledge God's role in the birth of her child

Eve's key to resilient confidence was learning to think carefully about the extent of one's influence in the world.

Be empowered with the knowledge that women are created in God's image as much as men are, which is the essence of being human. This means women deserve the same respect as men simply by being human. God never intended a hierarchy among humans. Humans ruling over other humans is a consequence of our sinful condition, and we can choose instead to live the way God intended. Such a choice, like all choices, will influence the people around us. Just as Eve acknowledged God's role in the birth of her child, you can have a positive influence by telling others about the ways God has blessed you and been a vital part of your life.

God chose Hagar's voice to be the first . . .

- Human voice to encounter the angel of the LORD

- With whom God would discuss the gender and name of an unborn child
- To give God a name
- To communicate her son's name to his father, Abram

Hagar's keys to resilient confidence were an empowering encounter with God and a purpose grounded in a relationship with God.

Be empowered by the fact that God's unique purpose for you has nothing to do with your background or family and everything to do with God choosing to initiate a relationship with you. God chose to see and hear Hagar's pain and brought her hope and security even as a single mother. Just as Hagar gave God a name, you can name the ways God has been present with you in your pain and boldly acknowledge how God has sustained you through difficult times.

God chose Miriam's voice to be the first . . .

- Praise and worship leader among the Israelites
- Woman prophet among the Israelites

Miriam's key to resilient confidence was praising God in song, in prayer, and in daily conversation.

Be empowered knowing that the act of praising God will bring you literally into the presence of the Almighty God who loves you, values you, equips you, and wants to deliver you. Just as Miriam led others to sing God's praises, you can lead others to recognize God's activity in their lives and to praise God for deliverance and direction.

God chose Deborah's voice to be the first . . .

- Prophet's voice to judge Israel
- And *only* woman's voice to judge Israel

Deborah's key to resilient confidence was her adept skill of collaboration, finding ways to share leadership.

Be empowered with the knowledge that a woman's approach to difficult situations, including working collaboratively with others and sharing victories with those collaborators, is a process God has used for centuries to bring peace to nations, families, and other groups. Just as Deborah sought God's strategy for her nation, you can pursue God's desire for your nation, family, business, church, or any other group and choose to lead others to understand God's plan.

God chose Hannah's voice to be the first . . .

- To use the term "messiah" in a prophetic way

Hannah's key to resilient confidence was an expectant hope based on the knowledge that God is the source of our confidence and we can entrust to God's care the results of our prayers and of our acts of service.

Be empowered with the fact that God has chosen women's voices to speak hope, truth, and mercy since the beginning of human history. Just as Hannah's prayer prophesied the fulfillment of God's promises and influenced future generations, you can pray bold prayers filled with hope for the younger generations and make yourself available to invest in the youth around you.

God chose Huldah's voice to be the first . . .

- To authenticate and interpret a written document as the prophetic word of God, thus beginning the centuries-long process of scripture canonization

Huldah's keys to resilient confidence were the diligent study of God's Word and communicating with bold and righteous intent.

Be empowered with the fact that God chose a woman's skills of discernment and worked through her biblical knowledge to help a man in power understand God's will for his people. Huldah's reputation as a trustworthy prophet caused the king to request her wisdom specifically. Just as Huldah could recognize a written document as an authentic copy of God's Word, you can become so familiar with biblical truth as to be able to discern the path God has set before you and others, and then proclaim that knowledge with humility and courage.

God chose Elizabeth's voice to be the first . . .

- To break the 400 years of silence with a new prophetic word from God
- Human to confirm to Mary that she was pregnant with the Messiah

Elizabeth's keys to resilient confidence were expectant faithfulness and open-hearted hospitality as a mentor for the next generation.

Be empowered with the hope illustrated by God's choice of a woman's voice to break 400 years of prophetic silence with a renewed promise of the coming birth of our Savior. Just as Elizabeth confirmed God's activity in the life of a younger woman, you can encourage those who are coming behind you with God's promises and with your helpful presence.

God chose Mary's voice to be the first . . .

- To discuss with the angel Gabriel the news that the Messiah was about to be born and that his name would be Jesus
- To rejoice with Elizabeth about both their pregnancies
- To sing a song of prophetic praise after 400 years of prophetic silence from God
- To request a miracle from Jesus

Mary's key to resilient confidence was strength in surrender.

Be empowered with the truth that our Creator God—who made all things from nothing—chose to work through a woman's body to bring the Savior into the world, forever ordaining the uniqueness of a woman's role in the birth process from conception to birth to a baby's first meals. Just as Mary surrendered her whole self—mind, heart, and body—to God's service, you can be strengthened for God's service through complete surrender to the Savior she birthed and then share him with others.

God chose Anna's voice to be the first . . .

- Eye-witness proclamation by a prophet that the Messiah had been born

Anna's keys to resilient confidence were faithful participation in a worshipping community and purposefully communicating truths experienced in the presence of God.

Be empowered by the fact that God chose a woman prophet's voice to announce the fulfillment of God's promises to a waiting world. Just as Anna went out to proclaim the birth of the Savior, you can use your voice to tell others how God has changed their world through the Savior.

God chose the Samaritan Woman's voice to be the first . . .

- To have the longest recorded theological conversation with Jesus
- To evangelize a non-Jewish community

The Samaritan Woman's keys to resilient confidence were genuine curiosity about deeply spiritual things and a willingness to be vulnerable regarding the truth.

Be empowered with the knowledge that Jesus wants to tell you deep spiritual truths. Just as the Samaritan Woman's life was changed when she had a personal encounter with Jesus and she went immediately to tell others about him, you can expect to learn life-changing truths from conversations with Jesus and then, with honest vulnerability, express those truths to others longing to hear them.

God chose Martha's voice to be the first . . .

- To be corrected by Jesus about her behavior in a woman's traditional gender role
- To give a public Messianic confession

Martha's keys to resilient confidence were learning to balance busyness with stillness and speaking the truth even in risky situations.

Be empowered by remembering that Jesus encouraged a woman to step out of a culturally acceptable role to find her voice and then allowed her to use it publicly to reveal his identity as the Messiah to a skeptical crowd. Just as Martha voiced a life-giving truth in the midst of her grief, you can have the courage to share messianic truths with people yet unwilling to understand, maybe even as a missionary to a people hostile to Christians.

God chose Mary Magdalene's voice to be the first . . .

- To converse with the Risen Christ
- To tell the Resurrection news at the request of Christ Himself

Mary Magdalene's keys to resilient confidence were a personal encounter with the Risen Jesus, a deeper devotion to Jesus, and a determination to obey anything Jesus asked of her, regardless of the risks or obstacles.

Be empowered by knowing that the most important news in history—Christ is RISEN!—was first delivered by a woman because Jesus asked her to go tell his other followers about his resurrection . Just as Mary Magdalene was faithful to fulfill Jesus' request in spite of being dismissed and disbelieved by her audience, you can speak God's truths to closed minds and ears and await their opening by Jesus himself, trusting that your obedience is your only responsibility.

God chose Lydia's voice to be the first . . .

- To respond to Paul's preaching of the gospel on the European continent
- To lead a house church on the European continent

Lydia's keys to resilient confidence were courageous conviction, an open heart, and an open home.

Be empowered by trusting that regardless of your ethnicity or social status —whether high or low—God's economy requires the same humility and repentance from everyone. Just as the wealthy, Gentile, businesswoman Lydia yielded her whole life and livelihood to the service of God's people, you can make available all that God has given you—whether much or little—to help bring God's kingdom on earth.

~

Each of these stories taught us something about the infinite love and value God bestows on women. These biblical women exemplified God-given resilient confidence and their stories have been preserved through the ages to empower women today. Our God, who is the same yesterday, today, and forever, has demonstrated through these stories that women's voices, abilities, and bodies have God-ordained purposes to fulfill. I hope you have gained new knowledge or been reminded of biblical truths that will encourage you to be ready to hear God's call and to act on it. The opportunity before all of us is to take this knowledge and apply it in our own lives, churches, communities, and in other parts of the world. Women need to know that God equips them, calls them, and entrusts them with messages of truth, hope, justice, and mercy. God's Spirit will embolden them to lead—even in difficult places. *This is why the voices of biblical women matter to the whole **world**!* These keys to resilient confidence taught through the voices of biblical women is what God has chosen my voice to proclaim.

What has God chosen *your* voice to proclaim?

If this book has been helpful to you, please leave a review on the book's page on Amazon.com and/or on my website at WomensMinistryCoach.com Thank you!

GROUP DISCUSSION GUIDE

The questions at the end of each woman's section can be used by individuals or groups to dig a little deeper into the concepts and stories presented. Some of the questions provided are unanswerable, actually. Yet, those questions can cause you to ponder your current situation or women's status where you are. The questions may prompt you to research women's status in other parts of the world. The questions should generate some lively discussion about the roles of women as they were, as they are, and as they could be. Here are some suggested formats for a group discussion.

For a one-hour gathering:

- In advance of your gathering, choose questions you'd like the group to discuss and consider how much time each question might require for 2 or 3 people to contribute an answer. Have enough questions to fill 30 minutes.
- Also in advance, ask one person to give a 5-minute overview of the book's purpose and format and to mention 2-3 concepts that really made an impression on them.

At the gathering,

- Provide name tags and about 15 minutes of get-acquainted time.
- Ask for the 5-minute overview.
- Then have your 30-minute discussion with someone facilitating.
- Use the last 10 minutes to consider more in-depth study of some of the women in the book or another topic.
- Take a moment to photograph your group and send it to the author so she can post it on the Women's Ministry Coach Facebook page. Be sure to include a note about something you enjoyed in the book or about your gathering. Email her at Laura@WomensMinistryCoach.com.

For a two-hour gathering:

In advance of your gathering, invite different people to be involved in the gathering in one of several ways:

- Some to bring refreshments
- One person to prepare a 5-minute overview of the book's purpose and format and the most interesting concepts they gleaned
- Some to set up the room and others to clean up the eating area
- Consider asking 1 or 2 women to read one of the women's stories aloud or to act it out as a first-person account, 5-10 minutes each
- One person to provide name tags and/or to be the greeter
- Someone to facilitate the meeting by asking the questions. That same person could choose which questions should be asked in advance. Trying to have a group discussion covering the whole book in one gathering would be very challenging, so pick and choose which chapters you want to include. Plan how long it might take for 2 or 3 people to answer each question in a discussion and then try to have no more than 45 minutes worth of discussion. You could possibly cover a few highlighted questions for 4 of the women in the book if you only give each woman a 10-minute focus.

For the event, here's a suggested schedule:

- 20 minutes get-acquainted and refreshment time
- 5-minute overview of the book
- 10-20 minutes of dramatic reading or presentation
- 45 minutes of discussion including a moment to take a photo to send the author along with something you especially enjoyed about the book to Laura@WomensMinistryCoach.com so she can post it on the Women's Ministry Coach Facebook page.
- 15-20 minutes to discuss a follow-up discussion about another woman in the book or another topic.
- 5-10 minutes to clean up

For use in an ongoing group, such as a Bible study or weekly discussion group:

1. Choose to study one woman each session for a 13-session study.
2. Choose to study 2-3 women each session for a 5- or 6-session study.

3. Select a few of the women from the Hebrew Scriptures/Old Testament and a few of the women from the New Testament to hit the highlights of the book overall.

Other suggestions

1. Invite the author to visit your group to do a reading and/or presentation with a book signing.
2. Invite the author to speak at your church, book club, community group, or school/university/seminary classroom.
3. Invite the author to lead your group in a weekend retreat based on the book.

Contact Dr. Laura Savage-Rains directly via her website at www.WomensMinistryCoach.com and go to her Speaking page to submit a request, or email her at Laura@WomensMinistryCoach.com.

ACKNOWLEDGMENTS

When you write a book, you quickly discover that it takes a village. I could never list everyone who has in some way been a part of the development of this book. I hold within my heart anyone who has said an encouraging word to spur me on to complete this task. Here are the few I want to name specifically:

Above all, I am grateful to Jesus Christ, my Savior and Lord, for his creative power, sinless life, sacrificial death, hope-giving resurrection, and embodied Truth. To him be the glory for being the one who is "able to accomplish abundantly far more than all we can ask or imagine" (Eph. 3:20 NRSV). I am humbled by the 50+ years of adventures I've had with Jesus and by the abundant life he has provided.

My husband, Rev. Mark Savage-Rains, has been my biggest supporter and encourager throughout this project, reading every word multiple times and providing wise direction. I'll never be able to thank him enough for the many ways he loves me as his equal partner in all things. He is God's gift to me beyond anything I could ask or imagine!

My late parents poured their lives into me and I will be forever grateful: Rev. Edgar L. Savage, Jr., who mentored me as a child for my future ministry career and believed I could do anything, and Charlcie Joyce Spelce Savage, who birthed in me a desire for academic excellence and a love for teaching.

My WomensMinistryCoach.com business advisory team: Beverly Moreland; Carol Gardner, PhD; and Jane Wilson, who are also women's ministry leaders at The Lakeway Church, have each showered me with love, gracious advice, and tangible expressions of encouragement.

My editors were some of the brilliant, accomplished women with whom God has blessed me as special sisters in Christ. I am indebted to their attention to detail, their love of God's Word, and their interest in helping me achieve this goal. Thank you, Sue Bridges, PhD; Sheryl Churchill Buckner, MRE; Cindy Lewis Dake, MAComm; and Alice Draving, PhD.

Two artists took the book cover from idea to reality: He Qi, who generously gave me permission to use his painting *The Empty Tomb* (please visit HeQiArt.com to view more of his biblically inspired artwork), and Jane Wilson, who gave of her time, talent, and computer skills to design the cover.

My writing coach, Jodi Detrick, DMin, cheered me on with an unwavering belief in me and this project.

My "big sisters" and former co-workers, Andrea Mullins, DMin; Sheryl Churchill Buckner, MRE; and Rev. Brenda Warren provided extended stays in their homes for my writing retreats.

The women's Sunday morning Bible study class members at The Lakeway Church patiently listen to my teaching, encourage my latest ideas for book projects, and prayed me through this project.

The women's ministry steering team members at The Lakeway Church have encouraged me beyond measure by inviting me on numerous occasions to speak and lead in various capacities.

The many reviewers listed on the back cover and in the opening pages of this book were generous with their time and comments, and I am grateful.

I have been blessed in different seasons of my ministry experience by these church families who have loved me and acknowledged my gifts of teaching and leadership in different ways: Williams Trace Baptist Church (now Sugar Land Baptist Church), Sugar Land, TX; Wedgwood Baptist Church, Fort Worth, TX; Riverchase Baptist Church, Birmingham, AL; First Christian Church (Disciples of Christ), Beaumont, TX; and The Lakeway Church, Lakeway, TX.

My graduate school professors at Southwestern Baptist Theological Seminary (1984-1986) and The University of Alabama (1998-2003) were my inspirations to read broadly, keep learning, and teach well.

God has brought many brilliant, faithful, gifted women friends into my life. They have helped me see and understand the biblical women I study and have been a big part of my becoming the woman I am.

Going back to the days of my early discipleship training as a future ministry leader, I must acknowledge the late Tappy Johnson, who was my youth Sunday School teacher at First Baptist Church, Port Neches, TX, and the woman who taught me how to have a personal, daily quiet time. She helped me discover how to read God's Word for myself and apply it in such a way that it shaped my life. The church family at Calvary Baptist Church, Nederland, TX, nurtured me as a high school student for leadership as an adult. My college experiences at Houston Baptist University (1979-1983) let me prove to myself that I have teaching and leadership gifts. HBU's professors and staff set me on the road to future success, especially Rev. Dr. Kenneth Corr, my campus minister at the time, who later became my pastor and spiritual mentor.

And lastly, I want to thank my readers, who give purpose to this book.

FOR FURTHER READING

Women's History and World History Resources

Bingham, Jane, Fiona Chandler, and Sam Taplin. 2002. *The Usborne Internet-Linked Encyclopedia of World History.* London: Usborne Publishing Ltd.

Bingham, Jane, Fiona Chandler, Jane Chisholm, Gill Harvey, Lisa Miles, Struan Reid, and Sam Taplin. 2005. *The Usborne Internet-Linked Encyclopedia of the Ancient World.* London: Usborne Publishing Ltd.

Greenspan, Karen. 1994. *The Timetables of Women's History: A Chronology of the Most Important People and Events in Women's History.* New York, NY: Simon & Schuster Inc. 1994.

McEvedy, Colin. 1984. *The World History Factfinder.* New York, NY: W.H. Smith Publishers, Inc.

Millard, Anne, and Patricia Vanags. 2008. *The Usborne Book of World History.* London: Usborne Publishing Ltd.

Biblical Women Resources

The CEB Women's Bible. 2016. Nashville, TN: Common English Bible.

Cohick, Lynn H. 2009. *Women in the World of the Earliest Christians: Illuminating Ancient Ways of Life.* Grand Rapids, MI: Baker Academic.

Freeman, Lindsay Hardin. 2015. *Bible Women: All Their Words and Why They Matter.* Cincinnati, OH: Forward Movement.

Lockyer, Herbert. n.d. *All the Women of the Bible.* Grand Rapids, MI: Zondervan.

Meyers, Carol, ed. 2001. *Women in Scripture: A Dictionary of Named and Unnamed Women in the Hebrew Bible, the Apocryphal/Deuterocanonical*

Books, and the New Testament. Grand Rapids, MI: Wm. B. Eerdmans Publishing Co.

Richards, Sue Poorman, and Lawrence O. Richards. 2003. *Women of the Bible: The Life and Times of Every Woman in the Bible.* Nashville, TN: Thomas Nelson.

Smith, Carol, Rachael Phillips, and Ellyn Sanna. 2011. *Women of the Bible: A Visual Guide to Their Lives, Loves, and Legacy.* Uhrichsville, OH: Barbour Publishing.

Tidball, Derek, and Dianna Tidball. 2012. *The Message of Women: Creation, Grace and Gender.* Downers Grove, IL: InterVarsity Press.

Vamosh, Miriam Feinberg. 2008. *Women at the Time of the Bible*. Nashville, TN: Abingdon.

Jewish Life and History Resources

Garrard, Alec. 2000. *The Splendor of the Temple: A Pictorial Guide to Herod's Temple and Its Ceremonies*. Grand Rapids, MI: Kregel Publications.

Jeremias, Joachim, trans. 2014. *Jerusalem at the Time of Jesus*. Peabody, MA: Hendrickson Publishers Marketing, LLC. (Previous copyright 1969 by SCM Press Ltd.)

Richardson, Peter. 1996. *Herod: King of the Jews and Friend of the Romans.* Columbia, SC: University of South Carolina Press.

Telushkin, Joseph. 1991. *Jewish Literacy: The Most Important Things to Know about the Jewish Religion, Its People, and Its History.* New York, NY: William Morrow and Company, Inc.

Trepp, Leo. 2001. *A History of the Jewish Experience*. Springfield, NJ: Behrman House, Inc.

Vamosh, Miriam Feinberg. 2004. *Food at the Time of the Bible: From Adam's Apple to the Last Supper.* Nashville, TN: Abingdon.

Vamosh, Miriam Feinberg. n.d. *Daily Life at the Time of Jesus.* San Francisco, CA: Purple Pomegranate Productions.

General Bible Resources

The Amplified Bible Mass Market Edition. 1987. Grand Rapids, MI: Zondervan.

Barker, Kenneth, gen. ed. 1985. *The NIV Study Bible.* Grand Rapids, MI: Zondervan Bible Publishers.

Berlin, Adele, and Marc Zvi Brettler, eds. 2004. *The Jewish Study Bible.* New York: Oxford University Press.

Berrett, LaMar C. 1979. *Discovering the World of the Bible.* Nashville, TN: Thomas Nelson. (Previous copyright 1973 by Young House.)

The Complete Jewish Study Bible. 2016. Peabody, MA: Hendrickson Publishers Marketing, LLC.

Coogan, Michael D., ed. 2001. *The New Oxford Annotated Bible with the Apocryphal/Deuterocanonical Books,* 3rd Edition. New York, NY: Oxford University Press.

Green, Joel, B., ed. 2013. *The CEB Study Bible with Apocrypha.* Nashville, TN: Common English Bible.

Kroeger, Catherine Clark, and Mary J. Evans, eds. 2002. *The IVP Women's Bible Commentary.* Downers Grove, IL: InterVarsity Press.

Newsom, Carol A., Sharon H. Ringe, and Jacqueline E. Lapsley, eds. 2012. *Women's Bible Commentary,* 3rd Edition, Twentieth-Anniversary Edition. Louisville, KY: Westminster John Knox Press.

Sakenfeld, Katharine Doob., gen. ed. 2006.*The New Interpreter's Dictionary of the Bible, Volumes 1-5.* Nashville, TN: Abingdon Press.

WORKS CITED

The Amplified Bible Mass Market Edition. 1987. Grand Rapids, MI: Zondervan.

Camp, Claudia V. 2001. "Huldah." In *Women in Scripture: A Dictionary of Named and Unnamed Women in the Hebrew Bible, the Apocryphal/ Deuterocanonical Books, and the New Testament,* edited by Carol Meyers, 96-97. Grand Rapids, MI: Wm. B. Eerdmans Publishing Co.

Carr, David M. 2001. "Genesis." In *The New Oxford Annotated Bible Third Edition,* edited by Michael D. Coogan, 9-81. New York: Oxford University Press.

The CEB Women's Bible. 2016. Nashville, TN: Common English Bible.

Cohick, Lynn H. 2009. *Women in the World of the Earliest Christians: Illuminating Ancient Ways of Life.* Grand Rapids, MI: Baker Academic.

Davidson, Maxwell John. 2006. "Angel." In *The New Interpreter's Dictionary of the Bible, Volume 1,* edited by Katharine Doob Sakenfeld, 148-155. Nashville, TN: Abingdon Press.

Freeman, Lindsay Hardin. 2015. *Bible Women: All Their Words and Why They Matter.* Cincinnati, OH: Forward Movement.

Hiebert, Theodore. 2013. "Genesis Commentary." In *The CEB Study Bible with Apocrypha,* edited by Joel B. Green, 1-79. Nashville, TN: Common English Bible.

Peterson, Eugene H. 2002. *THE MESSAGE: The Bible in Contemporary Language.* Colorado Springs, CO: NavPress.

Pew Research Center. 2016. "The Gender Gap in Religion Around the World." Pew Research Center (website), accessed April 25, 2019, https://www.pewforum.org/2016/03/22/the-gender-gap-in-religion-around-the-world/.

Scholz, Susanne. 2012. "Judges." In *Women's Bible Commentary,* 3rd Edition, Twentieth-Anniversary Edition, edited by Carol A. Newsom, Sharon H. Ringe, and Jacqueline E. Lapsley, 113-137. Louisville, KY: Westminster John Knox Press.

"St. Photini, the Samaritan Woman," Antiochian Orthodox Christian Archdiocese of North America (website), accessed April 18, 2019, http://ww1.antiochian.org/st-photini-samaritan-woman.

Trible, Phyllis. 2001. "Miriam 1." In *Women in Scripture: A Dictionary of Named and Unnamed Women in the Hebrew Bible, the Apocryphal/Deuterocanonical Books, and the New Testament,* edited by Carol Meyers, 127-129. Grand Rapids, MI: Wm. B. Eerdmans Publishing Co.

Youngblood, Ronald. 1985. "Genesis." In *The NIV Study Bible,* edited by Kenneth Barker, 1-4, 6-83. Grand Rapids, MI: Zondervan.

APPENDIX

Just in Case You're Wondering How to Have a Relationship with God

If you are curious about how to have a relationship with God, such as was experienced by the women in this book, I would like to offer some more food for thought. Here is the way I began my Christ-following journey.

I was born into a Christian family, but that did not make me a Christ-follower. Becoming a Christ-follower requires conscious thought and decision, for anyone capable of making such a decision for themselves. (God's grace is extended to those who are unable to make such a personal choice due to mental challenges.) I grew up going to church, but that did not make me a Christ-follower any more than spending time in a garage would make me a mechanic.

One summer day when I was seven years old, I was playing at the church building while my minister father worked in his office. I took time to sit down in the sanctuary and listen to the organist and soloist practice for the Sunday service. Sitting on the front pew in the stillness of the moment, I "heard" in my heart an invitation, "Laura, I want you to become a Christian." I was startled and wondered if I had said that to myself. I knew I hadn't. I immediately responded to that "voice" with a conscious decision to become a Christ-follower. I told my mom about it and she invited our pastor to come to our house to talk to me about my decision. I remember Dr. Lambert sitting on the couch beside me and talking to me, but I couldn't tell you a thing he said. What I do remember is that a few months later, at my baptism, I felt deep within my heart that God had a special purpose for me and that my job from that point on was to make Jesus happy—not my parents or even myself—but Jesus.

I was a naive child at the time, yet I understood enough to know that Jesus loved me and Jesus had died for me to pay for my sins. I knew that by believing in what Jesus had done for me, asking for forgiveness for all the things I had ever done wrong, and by asking Jesus to be my Savior, I would receive eternal life and would go to heaven when I died. I have lived with that simple belief ever since—for more than 50 years now! As I learned more about my faith, I realized that the "voice" I heard in my heart as a child was the Holy Spirit prompting me to say, "Yes" to Jesus.

Since that time I have grown in my knowledge and understanding of Scripture, learned more about God the Father/Son/Holy Spirit, and I have striven to let Jesus be the Lord of my life, consciously trying to allow Jesus to direct every decision I have ever made. Have I lived a perfect life or always made the right decision? No! Have I had the assurance that Jesus was by my side through everything I have experienced? Yes! Have I had the chance to fulfill a meaningful purpose with my life? Absolutely!

As someone who wants everyone to have that same peace and assurance through a relationship with Jesus, I want to offer an explanation of God's plan of salvation in a more direct way. I'll use an outline of A, B, C, D.

I. Admit your sinful condition.

The Bible says,*"All have sinned and fall short of God's glory" (Romans 3:23 CEB).*

"The wages that sin pays are death, but God's gift is eternal life in Christ Jesus our Lord" (Romans 6:23 CEB).

"If we claim, 'We don't have any sin,' we deceive ourselves and the truth is not in us. But if we confess our sins, he is faithful and just to forgive us our sins and cleanse us from everything we've done wrong. If we claim, 'We have never sinned,' we make him a liar and his word is not in us" (1 John 1:8-10 CEB).

We have all done something against God's law. We are all guilty in some way. We are all sinners.

God's standard is perfect holiness because God is holy and cannot look upon sin. God gave us freewill and when we choose to use it against God's law, then we're doomed. Yet, God has a solution to the problem of sin and death: a Savior, Jesus Christ!

2. Believe in the sacrificial death of Jesus as the payment for your sins and in his resurrection as the proof of his power to conquer death.

The Bible says, *"God so loved the world that he gave his only Son, so that everyone who believes in him won't perish but will have eternal life"* (John 3:16 CEB).

"God caused the one who didn't know sin to be sin for our sake so that through him we could become the righteousness of God" (2 Corinthians 5:21 CEB).

"When [Jesus] found himself in the form of a human, he humbled himself by becoming obedient to the point of death, even death on a cross" (Philippians 2:7b-8 CEB).

Jesus said to his disciples, *"I am the way, the truth, and the life. No one comes to the Father except through me"* (John 14:6 CEB).

"If Christ hasn't been raised, then your faith is worthless; you are still in your sins, . . . but in fact Christ has been raised from the dead. He's the first crop of the harvest of those who have died" (1 Corinthians 15:17, 20 CEB).

No one else, in any other religion in history, has died to pay the penalty for sin for us.

The Bible says, *"You are saved by God's grace because of your faith. This salvation is God's gift. It's not something you possessed. It's not something you did that you can be proud of"* (Ephesians 2:8-9 CEB).

We cannot do anything to *earn* God's grace or mercy. God gives it freely and we are given the opportunity to choose to accept it.

3. Call on the name of the Lord as you turn from your own willful life and give control of your life to Jesus, beginning a personal relationship with Jesus.

The Bible says, *"If you confess with your mouth 'Jesus is Lord' and in your heart you have faith that God raised him from the dead, you will be saved. Trusting with the heart leads to righteousness, and confessing with the mouth leads to salvation. The scripture says, All who have faith in him won't be put to shame. There is no distinction between Jew and Greek, because the same Lord is Lord of all, who gives richly to all who call on him. All who call on the Lord's name will be saved"* (Romans 10:9-13 CEB)

There is no special formula for calling on Jesus' name. One way to say it could be, "Jesus, I need your forgiveness. I accept you as the one God sent into the world as the Savior. I want you to be my Savior and Lord."

4. Determine to live a life of gratitude through the power of the Holy Spirit, starting with baptism as a symbol of your inward transformation.

The Bible says, *"Repent and be baptized, every one of you, in the name of Jesus Christ for the forgiveness of your sins. And you will receive the gift of the Holy Spirit" (Acts 2:38 CEB).*

"We are God's accomplishment, created in Christ Jesus to do good things. God planned for these good things to be the way that we live our lives" (Ephesians 2:10 CEB).

"[Jesus] came so that they could have life—indeed, so that they could live life to the fullest" (John 10:10b CEB).

God has a unique purpose only **you** can fulfill. Enjoy this new journey —a new life with Jesus!

The Bible offers so much more wisdom, truth, and hope. If you are not currently involved in a Bible-teaching church, I encourage you to find one and begin your journey there. If you have more questions about Jesus, the Bible, how to become a Christ-follower, or how to grow in your faith, I'd love to hear from you. Let me know how this book has helped you. You can email me at Laura@WomensMinistryCoach.com. It is not in my power to convince you of what I believe to be true. It is simply my privilege to share what I have learned as I try to fulfill my responsibility toward Jesus' final command to his followers to *"go and make disciples of all nations, baptizing them in the name of the Father and of the Son and of the Holy Spirit, teaching them to obey everything that I've commanded you" (Matthew 28:19-20a CEB).*

The Witness of Women

Eve and **Hagar** had a turning point in their lives when they encountered God one-on-one and they began a relationship with God.

Miriam and **Deborah** sang songs of praise for God's deliverance.

Hannah's faithful prayers to God influenced future generations.

Huldah's commitment to studying and teaching God's Word brought change to a whole nation.

Elizabeth's lifetime of obedience to God encouraged a younger woman in need of her love and wisdom.

Mary's willing surrender to God resulted in the birth of Jesus, who can still be born in each of our hearts today!

Anna's long period of waiting for God's promise to be fulfilled was rewarded with a life-changing message to share.

The Samaritan Woman's conversation with Jesus gave her the courage to share an honest testimony and brought new hope to her whole hometown.

Martha's bold personality combined with her relationship with Jesus gave her the courage to reveal Jesus' identity even in a risky situation.

Mary Magdalene's commitment to following Jesus, regardless of her background, was rewarded by Jesus asking her to herald the greatest news ever told: Christ is RISEN!

Lydia's new-found faith in Christ transformed her life, her home, and her business.

Jesus offers all those things to YOU today!

"Glory to God, who is able to do far beyond all that we could ask or imagine
by his power at work within us;
glory to him in the church and in Christ Jesus for all generations,
forever and always. Amen"
—Ephesians 3:20-21 (CEB)

SCRIPTURE INDEX

H

I

J

N

P

R

SUBJECT INDEX

C

(list cont'd next page)

F

G

H

I

J

N

O

P

Q

(list continued next page)

U

V

W

(list cont'd next page)

Y

Z

ABOUT THE AUTHOR

Laura Savage-Rains, EdD, is an extroverted author who finds it challenging to sit still long enough to write a book. She'd much rather be coaching her clients in how to be better leaders in ministry and the marketplace or be speaking to groups about the life-changing lessons gleaned from the stories of biblical women. However, she feels called to share her 30 years of ministry and leadership experience through writing.

Laura is a native Texan who grew up in a minister's home as the only child. (Her testimony is in the Appendix.) While single, she held a variety of professional ministry and leadership roles: denominational level work, local church pastoral and administrative staff positions, and as a full-time academic missionary in Romania. She is now a minister's wife with her own business of coaching and training leaders, especially women.

She earned a bachelor's in education from Houston Baptist University and a master's in communication from Southwestern Baptist Theological Seminary. After more than 10 years of professional ministry experience, she earned a master's in women's studies, and a doctorate in education, both from The University of Alabama. Laura has used her award-winning teaching skills with all ages, from preschoolers to senior adults, and has had the privilege of speaking and training in countless churches across the US, and in seminaries and universities in four countries.

She has developed and taught several ministry courses for different seminaries over the years. Her blog at WomensMinistryCoach.com provides practical help for women involved in ministry. She spends her time writing, coaching leaders, training ministry leaders, and speaking to church and community groups of all sizes. She is also a certified spiritual intelligence coach who offers spiritual tools for the secular marketplace.

At age 45, Laura finally met the man of her dreams on eHarmony.com. Her husband, Rev. Mark Savage-Rains, serves as the director of music ministries at The Lakeway Church (near Austin, TX). Laura and Mark love to attend musical events, travel, and spend time with family and friends. Laura is Grammy to three growing girls, relishes girlfriend time, savors women's biographies, and enjoys re-watching favorite old movies.

HOW TO WORK WITH ME

***Speaker** for your next church event or retreat, business or community event, or women's conference on topics such as: Leadership, Biblical Women, How to Read the Bible Like a Woman, Women's History, and Spiritual Intelligence*

***Coach** in areas such as:*
Leadership skills for ministry and the marketplace
Success skills for new church staff members and missionaries
Personal life goals, projects, and transitions
Speaking, teaching, and group facilitating skills
Spiritual Intelligence for schools and the secular marketplace

***Consultant and Trainer** for churches and ministry groups in areas such as:*
Age-level teacher training and professional development
Women's ministry and women in ministry
Church staff and organizational development

Dr. Laura Savage-Rains, The Women's Ministry Coach, is ready to put her 30+ years of leadership and ministry experience to work for you. She is available to you as a one-on-one coach, speaker, retreat leader, trainer, or consultant. Contact her to start the conversation at no risk. You'll be able to tell in just a few minutes whether her skills can help your unique situation. She's ready to encourage you to new levels of achievement for your goals, projects, or ministry.

Contact Dr. Savage-Rains at Laura@WomensMinistryCoach.com
*or visit her website at **WomensMinistryCoach.com***
Subscribe to her blog and receive a free downloadable book on biblical leadership exclusively for subscribers.
*Follow her on Facebook **@The Women's Ministry Coach***

Made in the USA
Columbia, SC
20 September 2019